POSTCOLONIAL HOSPITALITY

MIREILLE ROSELLO

Postcolonial Hospitality

THE IMMIGRANT AS GUEST

STANFORD UNIVERSITY PRESS

STANFORD, CALIFORNIA

2001

Stanford University Press
Stanford, California

© 2001 by the Board of Trustees of the
Leland Stanford Junior University

Printed in the United States of America
On acid-free, archival-quality paper
Library of Congress Cataloging-in-Publication Data

Rosello, Mireille.
    Postcolonial hospitality: the immigrant as
guest / Mireille Rosello.
        p. cm.
    Includes bibliographical references and index.
    ISBN 0-8047-4232-4 (alk. paper) —
    ISBN 0-8047-4267-7 (pbk. : alk. paper)
        1. Immigrants—France.   2. Immigrants—
Europe.   3. Hospitality—France.   4. Hospitality—
Europe.   I. Title.
    JV7925.R67   2001
    325'.1—dc21   2001032020

Original Printing 2001

Last figure below indicates year of this printing:
10   09   08   07   06   05   04   03   02   01

Designed by Janet Wood
Typeset by TypeWorks in 10/14 Janson Text

Contents

Preface

How is immigration historically and theoretically linked to hospitality? How does the memory of colonization and decolonization alter the definition of hospitality between individuals and states whose cultures may construct the host and the guest in radically incompatible ways? Why are immigrants often imagined as the "guests" of other nations, and how can we conceptualize a postcolonial guest? Is it someone who has been invited by a postcolonial host? Is a postcolonial host always defined as a citizen of a host nation?

My initial intuition was that the changing shape of international relations was bound to modify our definition of hospitality in general: ideally, the proliferation of new types of journey should correspond to different types of hospitality: migrants, the members of diasporas, jet-setters, business travelers, refugees, asylum seekers, commuters, tourists, delocalized workers, powerful and powerless travelers, all need to receive or grant hospitality. Yet there is no sign that our supposedly global village has started thinking about a global yet diverse law of hospitality, and this book seeks to reflect upon this paradoxical absence.

It is illusory to posit the existence of a good old time when sedentary tribes could rest assured that their timeless routine would never be challenged by the arrival of a stranger. And I suspect that people who perceive their own cherished homeland as threatened by herds of dangerous foreigners could be contradicted by statistics. But what is the power of statistics against fear or mutual mistrust? Symbols, images, slogans, and stories may be much more representative of the anxieties, pains, or joys experienced by individuals and communities grappling with what it means to offer or deny hospitality. Such narratives include vastly different types of discourses, including the texts of new European immigration laws, for example, but also the stories of ordinary people who choose to practice hospitality, including migrants receiving migrants from their own villages.

My theoretical point of departure is that hospitality is a form of gift, and that, like most forms of gift-giving, the practices that transform two individuals or two communities into, respectively, the host and the guest, are meticulously prescribed by sets of laws that differ from culture to culture, and vary depending on historical contexts. Such laws are a type of power, and, as Michel Foucault has taught us, they are bound to generate or contain their own forms of resistance, which the dominant ideology of the community will define as bad or illegitimate: hospitality as prescribed by the "law of hospitality" can be revisited and replaced by other practices that cover the whole range of the ethical spectrum. And, as is often the case, subversive or dissident forms of hospitality are not necessarily better than the currently accepted norm: depending on the dominant definition of hospitality, forms of dissidence will range from examples of blatant inhospitality to the offering of sanctuary that power will condemn as an excess of hospitality.

This book concentrates on those problematic moments when hospitality and benevolence create perverse dynamics: when the host does not give what the rule expects him or her to give, when the guest is mistreated rather than protected, or when the guest abuses the host rather than being grateful. Debating such issues requires that I consider the relationship between ownership and hospitality, that I ask myself what connections exist between nationalism and hospitality, and how the issue of immigration is linked to national definitions of hospitality. I therefore propose to study how hospitality and its perverse variations are defined, practiced, and represented in contemporary Europe, and, more specifically, in France, where fiction and official discourses talk about the encounter between the French and immigrants, often of African origin. Because the intersection between the national and the private often exposes the fragility or arbitrariness of hospitable conventions, I focus on texts, films, or current affairs that explore those moments of crisis when several sets of laws of hospitality clash and reveal not only profound differences between two communities, but also internal contradictions within each definition of hospitality.

Acknowledgments

Many friends and colleagues shared their knowledge, read drafts, invited me to contribute articles or to read presentations, in a word, inspired me. I could, of course, make each of their contributions explicit, but why would academic gifts be easier to measure than friendship and affection? Not all happy encounters can be explained, and I am also resigned to being unfair and ungrateful: after all, this book is about imperfect hospitalities. Suffice it to say that all those whose names appear below were all, in some capacity, my hosts and my guests, *mes hôtes*, as the French put it. I visualize them sitting around virtual tables where they will continue the conversation while I circulate among them. I thank them all.

Jean Mainil	Alain Montandon	Françoise Lionnet
Ross Chambers	Jean-Xavier Ridon	Colin Davis
Alec Hargreaves	Nancy Wood	Elisabeth Boyi-Mudimbe
Mary Jean Green	Kach Tölölyan	Dominic Thomas
Abiola Irele	Carrie Tarr	
Amanda Mac Donald	Thomas Spear	Helen Tartar
Doris Ruhe	Rosemarie Scullion	Peter Dreyer
Jane Warren	Jim Ferolo	Joe Golsan
Pit Ruhe	Nick Hewitt	Jordan Stump
Kate Warne	Christopher Miller	
Anne Freedman	Lynn Higgins	Larry Goldsmith
Russell King	Dalton Krauss	Cindy Marker
Martine Antle	Steve Ungar	Peter Bloom
Dominique Fisher	Seth Lerer	Van Kelly

POSTCOLONIAL HOSPITALITY

Introduction: Immigration and Hospitality

In Europe in general and in France in particular, the 1990s were marked by a whole series of heated debates about immigration. Controversial new laws were discussed, amended, passed, and enforced, while the media regularly focused on their consequences on individuals and communities. Grassroots movements emerged among immigrant communities, and many internationally known intellectuals mobilized to try and exert an influence on the ideological directions taken by governmental decisions. In 1993, the so-called Pasqua laws became the most obvious manifestation of the French government's anti-immigration attitude.[1] They reflected an increasingly repressive and restrictive philosophy, turning the *clandestin* (illegal immigrant) into an enemy of the state, the most easily identifiable national scapegoat. Although measures then adopted by the National Assembly were supposed to be the democratic expression of an increasingly xenophobic public opinion, whose overt desire was to be less hospitable to immigrants, they eventually met with forms of resistance that went largely beyond the scope of militant associations for the defense of immigrants.

1

But even dominant ideologies do not remain unchallenged for long, and the government's anti-immigrant policies were eventually questioned and opposed, especially in the summer of 1996, when French people, perhaps for the first time, had the opportunity to hear the voice of the demonized *clandestins*. During what the media dubbed the "affaire des sans-papiers de Saint-Bernard" (the affair of the undocumented immigrants of the Church of Saint Bernard) approximately 300 African men and women occupied several public spaces in Paris until they arrived at the Church of Saint Bernard in Montmartre. There, they defied the government for months, ten of the *sans-papiers* starting a long hunger strike under the scrutiny of national television cameras.[2] Their goal was to propose an alternative interpretation of their presence in France and to inform the public about the perverse consequences of the Pasqua laws: according to their critics, the new texts were less effective in preventing new immigrants from entering the country illegally than in turning long-term immigrants into undocumented aliens whose administrative status was an inextricable knot of contradictions.[3]

The high profile of the *sans-papiers* movement was due to intensive media coverage during the summer of 1996, and to the involvement of an interdisciplinary team of intellectuals, the *collège des médiateurs* (committee of mediators), whose search for a long-term solution was eventually thwarted when the government ordered the brutal evacuation of the church by the riot police on August 23, 1996.[4] The authoritarian intervention marked the limits of the most visible phase of the protest, but it did not put an end to the movement. For if the police had successfully removed the African families from the church, the term they had chosen to describe themselves, *sans-papiers*, proved much more difficult to dislodge from the French language: one of the most obvious symbolic victories of that summer was the replacement of *clandestin* with *sans-papiers*.[5] This linguistic watershed is a social and political event, and I would suggest that it is indistinguishable from another major cultural shift in which this book seeks to participate: the emergence of a widespread, diverse, and multicultural debate about hospitality.

To use the word "hospitality" to reflect on my encounter with the stranger is either a deliberate or sometimes unconscious choice of issues: focusing on the figures of the guest and of the host is neither the only nor the most obvious way of theorizing the relationship between a country and its immigrants. Today, the term "host nation" is perfectly understandable in the absence of any specific pro- or anti-immigrant agenda. And saying that "France has long been a land hospitable to migrants" (Wihtol de Wenden 1999b) is such an accepted reference that the link between immigration and hospitality seems to need no explanation. Yet I would argue that the vision of the immigrant as guest is a metaphor that has forgotten that it is a metaphor. It is surprising that the myth of French hospitality should have survived not only the darkest days of the twentieth century but even earlier foundational moments during the French Revolution, when contradictions were rife.

In *L'impossible citoyen: L'étranger dans le discours de la Révolution française* (The Impossible Citizen: The Stranger in the Discourse of the French Revolution), Sophie Wahnich argues convincingly that the original rhetorical gestures seeking to present the new French Republic as a generous and hospitable nation were marred by ominous ambiguities.

On the one hand, the conviction that the founding values of the new nation were universal led the best revolutionary orators to imagine France as a nation where the rights of each (hu)man must be guaranteed, regardless of where he (or less obviously she) came from. Rights were not perceived as the natural privilege of whoever was born within a national border but as a universal (supranational) principle. At first, that belief allowed revolutionary thinkers to foreground words such as "friendship" or "affection" between peoples rather than issues of nationality. The *Archives parlementaires* (Parliamentary Archive) that Wahnich scrutinizes seem to promise a generous, open-minded attitude to strangers, be they migrants or not. Saint-Just's 1793 *Essai de constitution* stated:

> The French people declares itself to be the friend of all peoples; it will religiously respect treaties and flags; it offers asylum in its harbors to ships from all over the world; it offers asylum to great men and virtuous unfortunates of all countries; its ships at sea will protect foreign ships against storms. Foreigners and their customs will be respected in its bosom.[6]

"First and foremost, citizens are men, and the purpose of national law is not to identify the frontier but to guarantee universal law, without limits," Wahnich concludes (1997b, 109). Other spectacular excerpts from the *Archives parlementaires* make similarly altruistic promises: even strangers who have been forced by their princes to fight against France will not be denied refuge (ibid., 108). Presumably, even soldiers invading French territory behind their officers can be interpreted as guests to be rescued from cruel princes. Rather than considering that each nation owes hospitality to its own nationals, France presents itself as the ultimate asylum-granting principle, a universal host.

But these grand declarations, Wahnich argues, do not pass the test of reality. Located in a chapter entitled "The Defeat of Hospitality" (ibid., 107–17), the quotations are framed by a carefully constructed argument that shatters the myth of a triumphantly hospitable Revolution. A pessimistic and demystifying essay, *L'impossible citoyen* offers no definitive answer to the "the enigma of a hospitality subverted by suspicion, of a friendship experienced in terms of treason, and of a fraternity that invents the most radical forms of exclusion" (ibid., 347). For no sooner was the principle of revolutionary hospitality established, than it was immediately betrayed, compromised, limited, and sometimes perversely turned into its opposite.

In 1793, a decree made it legal to expel individuals whose nations of origin were at war with France, although a few exceptions were made for those who could demonstrate their loyalty: "Those who will have been deemed worthy of staying will have to wear a tricolor ribbon bearing this word: Hospitality. They will also carry their certificate of hospitality."[7] The mention of this "tricolor ribbon" strikes the historian's imagination and triggers a whole series of potentially tragic associations: "The mere reading of this decree, at the beginning of my research, was troubling. I could not but associate the image of a tricolor ribbon with that of a black armband, as if mourning were involved. And another superimposition came to mind, the image of the yellow star, of sinister memory" (Wahnich 1997b, 24).

From one "superimposition" to the next, Wahnich invites us to think about more recent manifestations of what she calls an "enigma": that the profoundly ambiguous definition of hospitality by states that want to treat their migrants as if they were sacred guests, but fail to abide by their own laws of hospitality. The rapid deterioration of state hospitality at the time of the French Revolution is food for thought, and the fact that Sophie Wahnich published excerpts from an earlier version of her book in a collection of essays entitled *Les lois de l'inhospitalité: Les politiques de l'immigration à l'épreuve des sans-papiers* suggests that she intended her research to shed light on more recent events (Wahnich 1997a, 11–26).

Since the end of World War II, the social, racial, and gender characteristics of the typical immigrant have regularly changed, sometimes rapidly, sometimes gradually, each phase corresponding to various images and forms of representations negotiated by the press, popular culture, literature, or political discourse.

By the 1980s, the single male migrant worker of the 1950s and 1960s had been replaced by a whole generation of *beurs* (children of Maghrebian immigrants), whose relationship to France, to French culture, and to French laws needed to be rearticulated. Postwar migrants had struggled with miserable living standards, with cultural illiteracy, and with the effects of the war of Algeria (1954–62). Their children were spared some of these difficulties but encountered others: chronic unemployment started to plague French economy, and the children of immigrants were among the hardest hit. Cultural alienation did not disappear among the so-called second generation with education, although the 1980s was also the decade of *beur* novels, a time when children of Maghrebian immigrants told their autobiographies, stories of latent or blatant racism, of biculturalism or double disidentification (see Silverman 1992; Laronde 1993; Hargreaves 1995).

Each phase corresponds to different ways of formulating the encounter between French nationals and strangers (the "stranger" being a foreigner, a recently arrived immigrant, the naturalized child of immigrants, or even a French child born to non-European parents who continues to be treated as an other). In the 1950s and 1960s, the issue was better housing and less exploitative work conditions. The 1970s and 1980s privileged different key words: integration or anti-racism. "Touche pas à mon pote!" (Hands off my buddy!), the famous slogan of the S.O.S. Racisme organization, was a response to a policy of "closed borders," the control of immigration gradually becoming a high political priority, or at least one of the most effective electoral catchphrases.[8]

In the 1990s, the *sans-papiers* affair further displaced the debate toward new symbolic ground, which the following chapters explore. When television cameras and newspapers covered their struggle, the *sans-papiers* created a space of sociological, legal, and philosophical debate in the very heart of the French capital: they asked questions about the relationship between the city and the nation, between the refugee and the law, between rights and equity. The *sans-papiers* forced Parisians to admit that they lived right alongside the illegal immigrants that the government was trying to make them fear. New internal and intangible borders were suddenly revealed, within the city, inside a church. Constantly threatened with deportation, the *sans-papiers* had drawn around themselves a sort of magic circle that forced everyone to think about asylum, about refuge. Symbolically, churches have always been associated with sanctuary, and the images of men in uniform breaking through the heavy wooden doors of the Church of Saint Bernard with axes may have made people reconsider their own unwritten law of hospitality. And while the spectacular eviction coincided with the end of the most visible aspect of the affair, it fueled, rather than extinguished, the ideological debate about France's responsibility as a host nation, and about each individual's ethical choices.

Immigration issues are a symptom of how profoundly the citizens of a modern European state can disagree about the definitions of hospitality. And whether or not the word is explicitly used, hospitality is now at the center of this political, social, and economic controversy: immigrants, their families, friends, and relatives, immigration officers, political leaders, and the most anonymous of citizens are all affected by the ways in which the state legitimizes some forms of hospitality while declaring others irresponsible, unrealistic, dangerous, or even illegal. Immigration policies reflect and impose official laws of hospitality that are both distinct from and unavoidably linked to the daily practices of ordinary citizens who offer hospitality on a smaller scale but at a less abstract level. In a country whose idealized mythic identity has long been associated with willingness to welcome strangers, the evolution of the concept of hospitality is bound to generate conflicts and passionate arguments: the laws of hospitality form a symbolically significant part of any national identity, and France is no exception to the rule, especially since the Revolution. But because it is at the same time an ancient classical tradition, a philosophical value, an ethical imperative, a political issue, and also a polymorphous individual practice, hospitality cannot be reduced either to publicly formulated definitions or to social practices that either confirm or contradict such definitions. A nation's hospitality can hardly be quantified, because it is made up of the untotalizable sum of individual or collective social practices, as well as of the layer of statements that comment on and judge the practices in question. Hospitality is both proposed and imposed by normative and prescriptive discourses that seek to be obeyed as laws of hospitality: they try to police the limits of what is acceptable or forbidden, morally or politically desirable. Simultaneously, hospitality also exists through constantly reinvented practices of everyday life that individuals borrow from a variety of traditions—from what their parents have taught them, from what they identify as their own traditional background—and practices that are sometimes similar to, sometimes different from, a supposedly shared norm.

Since the beginning of the 1990s, a number of important books have put hospitality on a constantly expanding cross-disciplinary map.[9] Sociologists, political scientists, and historians, who have always scrutinized various facets of immigration, now look at the phenomenon through that theoretical lens. And other disciplines, including poetry and literary studies, cultural studies, and philosophy, are now adding their voices to the chorus on hospitality. In 1991, Edmond Jabès published his moving *Livre de l'hospitalité* (Book of Hospitality), a collection of aphorisms and prose poems, short stories that talk about the beauty of hospitality, its mysteries, its ineffable tenderness, without ever trying to pin it down or assign it a unique definition (Jabès 1991). Here "hospitality" is in the singular, but it is constantly reinscribed, reimagined, so that by the end of the book it has acquired the kaleidoscopic radiance of a forever-changing mosaic. A few discreet but poignant allusions to anti-Semitism and racism leave no doubt as to the presence of dark shadows behind the celebration of sometimes incomprehensible forms of gifts. And other writers are quite aware of the monsters lurking behind Jabès's poems. In 1993, the year when the Pasqua laws were discussed, René Schérer published a subtle and elegant study of the intricate manifestations of fictive hospitality in Homer's *Ulysses*, Aeschylus's *The Suppliants*, Diderot's *The Nun*, Pierre Klossowski's *The Laws of Hospitality*, and Pier Pasolini's *Teorema*. Insisting that his book is written in praise of hospitality, the author starts out by registering his concern that hospitality has become an impossible luxury, a form of excess, almost madness:

> Isn't hospitality the madness of our contemporary world? To praise hospitality just when, in France and almost everywhere else in the world, the main concern is to restrict it, from the right to asylum to the code of nationality!
>
> Disturbing, excessive, like madness, it resists all forms of reason, including *raison d'état*. (Schérer 1993, 7–8)

For Schérer, hospitality may be mad, but that madness is the desirable, or ethical, supplement to the unreasonable reason that seeks to eradicate it. I should mention that most of the recent publications on hospitality are meant as a counterdiscourse, individual and collective voices speaking up against states that want to shut their doors and close their borders. Titles often speak for themselves, or at least alert readers that authors have a specific agenda: Didier Fassin, Alain Morice, and Catherine Quiminal's collection of articles is provocatively entitled *Les lois de l'inhospitalité* (The Laws of Inhospitality), and Monique Chemillier-Gendreau, one of the members of the committee of mediators, called her book *L'injustifiable: Les politiques françaises de l'immigration* (The Unjustifiable: French Immigration Politics).[10] In other words, by choosing to concentrate on the notion of hospitality and on some of the representative studies that have recently been published, this book self-consciously defines and tackles an object of study that cannot hide its political positioning. I am not pretending to stage a dialogue between two sides identifiable as pro- or anti-immigration: the setting up of the opposition would be a theoretically bankrupt vision.

On the other hand, writing in praise of "hospitality" in general would imply that I already know what hospitality is, whereas it is the purpose of this book to ask that question rather than to start from a preset definition. I do not seek in the following pages to posit hospitality as a categorical imperative that has to be resurrected. Following Schérer's lead, I would rather not assume that hospitality is on the side of rationality, of evidence and clarity: if I sought simply to defend hospitality, I would have to presuppose that I can identify an ideal, universal law of hospitality. Instead, I recognize that hospitality is indeed in crisis, not simply because our contemporary (Western?) world may not have enough of it, but because it is in the process of being redefined. The following chapters seek to analyze different manifestations of hospitality, including the most ambivalent and potentially malevolent faces of the host and the guest. In the end, even the apparently self-evident opposition between the guest and the host is problematic.

Moreover, the parallels between the immigrant and the guest, and between the state and the host, are culturally significant, and they have consequences that will tend to remain unexplored as long as we do not question their invisibility and hegemonic transparency. Because the portrait of the immigrant as ill-mannered guest is such an odious caricature, it is of course tempting to concentrate on the negative effects of the image and to propose a countervision of the immigrant as good, polite, and industrious guest. But choosing to problematize the notion of the immigrant as guest may be more difficult. It is perhaps more important to state that depicting immigrants as guests obscures the fact that the reason why they were "invited" had nothing to do with hospitality.[11] After World War II, when the largest movements of non-European migrations started, so-called invitations had more to do with active recruitment. The unskilled migrant workers who helped build French suburbs, or *banlieues*, in the 1950s and 1960s were not regarded as guests in a house; they were hired.

It is, then, surprising that the metaphor of hospitality should seem so appropriate: does someone who works for a private corporation today feel as though he or she is a "guest" of the firm? It is interesting that the distinction between being hired and being invited, being a worker and being a guest, can be so easily blurred, especially after the class struggles of the nineteenth century in Europe, in which the identity of the worker was defined in opposition to that of the dominant classes. Doesn't the confusion sometimes lead to cynical redefinitions of servitude as gift?

Isn't a guest always implicitly an equal, who could, presumably, reciprocate at a later date, in a different space, at a different time? Confusing the guest and the employee risks depriving the so-called guest of the type of contract that exists in a businesslike relationship. If you are a tenant or a worker, you are not at the mercy of a benevolent host who has the power to invite or disinvite you, whose perfect right it is to let you stay or kick you out when he or she decides that you have overstayed your welcome. Abuses do take place in the workplace, but it is to be hoped that they can be challenged as breaches of contract. Mutual responsibilities protect both parties, in the sense that even if the manager is arbitrary, his or her duty is not interpretable as a form of generosity. Conversely, hospitality as metaphor blurs the distinction between a discourse of rights and a discourse of generosity, the language of social contracts and the language of excess and gift-giving. Sometimes the implicit valorization of excess and gift and generosity masks ruthless forms of non-rights that cultural critics may find sadly ironic.

For a long time, the state tolerated newly arrived immigrants who encountered housing conditions worse than what they had experienced at home, even if their rural areas were plagued by poverty. In the France of the

1950s and 1960s, huge *bidonvilles* (shantytowns) gave a strange twist to the idea that the nation was the equivalent of a house. Other immigrants, and not the state, provided housing, and even that practice was sometimes exploitative rather than generous. Today, the constant reference to state hospitality continues to hide the fact that literal acts of hospitality are constantly going on, but at the private level: in what is called "chain migration," earlier immigrants take their relatives into their homes (Courade 1997). Immigrants who start out living with other immigrants may feel grateful to their relatives but will have difficulty grasping in what sense the state is being hospitable. Being grateful to the so-called host nation is a baffling proposition if the only contact between the immigrant and that abstract entity is a bureaucratic labyrinth of impersonal and alienating administrative procedures. And the most problematic aspect of the metaphor of state hospitality may be that in times when the official policy advocates "inhospitality," the individual, whose hospitality was originally the model for state hospitality, is now expected to abide by the state's inhospitable norm.

The word "hospitality" can be used in many different contexts: when a refugee asks for political asylum, when a foreign head of state meets the French prime minister, when a film director invites a foreign colleague to work with him or her for a while, or when an African migrant pays for a relative's plane ticket and then puts that relative up in a small and crowded flat. But because we use the same word to refer to drastically different conceptions of hospitality, voices seeking to resist the inhospitable dictates of the state often find themselves caught in double binds and contradictions that are very difficult to translate into daily tactics.

Of course, it is probably illusory to try and distinguish once and for all between state and individual hospitality. State legislation defines what is public and what is private, which means that whatever law of hospitality is adopted by ordinary people will, at some point, encounter and perhaps clash with state laws. On the other hand, even the most generous form of private hospitality may resemble the type of sophisticated calculation of self-interest that state economies deploy when they encourage or discourage immigration. The difference between official hospitality and private hospitality is better inscribed on a continuum of values, mutual reciprocation, and unquantifiable generosities. For both private and state hospitality can ultimately fall into the category of ethically undecidable acts. Hospitality is thought of as a sacred law, but no certitude in this domain resists a careful examination of the law and of its applications.

One of the books that most lucidly addresses the potential ambivalence of hospitality is Jacques Derrida's *Adieu to Emmanuel Levinas*. Written in homage to the dead philosopher, *Adieu* is a reading of Levinas's *Totalité et infini*, which Derrida calls an "immense treatise *of hospitality*" (Derrida 1999a, 21). Derrida distinguishes between an ethics of (infinite) hospitality and a politics of (finite) hospitality. The issue, as he puts it, "would concern, on first view, the relationships between an *ethics* of hospitality (an *ethics as* hospitality) and a *law* or a *politics* of hospitality" (ibid., 19).

An ethics of hospitality would thus be infinite and beyond any human law. Paradoxically, the ethics of hospitality is the ultimate law that demands that each act of hospitality transcend it. This takes us back to the most mythical encounters between heroes who take care of absolute strangers without even asking who they are. A politics of hospitality, on the other hand, involves limits and borders: calculations and the management of finite resources, finite numbers of people, national borders and state sovereignty.

Derrida's analysis is slightly disconcerting at first, because the opposition he proposes seems to suspend the lessons of deconstruction: isn't the pair of concepts he offers us eminently deconstructible? Is a politics of hospitality simply a philosophy of the limits of hospitality and, in that case, aren't margins infinitely extendable? Does the distinction correspond to supposedly commonsensical comments about thresholds and acceptable percentages, about the control of migratory flows? Except that as soon as one tries to take Derrida's definitions to their logical extreme, it becomes clear that he is not proposing a choice between ethics and politics. On the one hand, it is not possible to separate politics and ethics (both come first, as it were), but, simultaneously, it is just as unthinkable to imagine the two concepts together. The apparently incompatible pair are doomed to cohabit, unhappily, chaotically, because that tension is what hospitality is precisely all about. It is neither possible to give up on one of the elements of the equation nor to pretend that they are not incompatible.

Politically, and ethically, the duplicity of ethical-political hospitality has terrible consequences. In a reformulation of the difference between unconditional hospitality and a politics of hospitality, Derrida writes: "Pure, unconditional or infinite hospitality cannot and must not be anything else but an acceptance of risk. If I am sure that the newcomer that I welcome is perfectly harmless, innocent, that (s)he will be beneficial to me . . . it is not hospitality. When I open my door, I must be ready to take the greatest of risks" (Derrida 1999b, 137).

Paradoxically, then, what may seem like the most extreme form of ethical hospitality, the most generous and altruistic invitation, is also a form of mistrust, or, at least, a completely open-minded expectation that does not exclude the hypothesis that the other might be evil. Here, no (supposedly) generous script depicts the other as a trustworthy visitor, as a noble savage. The guest is not necessarily a threat but does contain incalculable and unknown futures.

Concretely, then, if a nation invites immigrants because they are valuable assets, because it needs them for an economic or demographic purpose, that country is not being hospitable. At least not unconditionally, infinitely hospitable, for it is difficult to assume that not inviting immigrants at all would be a more hospitable option. Refusing to receive my friends for fear of symbolically or even economically profiting from doing so does not solve the problem. I may know that I derive pleasure from my guests' company; I may even be aware that the risk of ostentation is always lurking behind the desire to make them comfortable; I may be aware that I reinforce my identity as owner of the house when I invite someone in. Does this mean that I should close my doors so as better to preserve the purity of hospitality? Even if the ultimate logic of ethical hospitality means, in certain cases, that inhospitality is the most perfect form of hospitality, immigrants denied work permits because it has come to the (generous) administration's attention that they were invited for selfish reasons would probably not appreciate the joke. Versions of such inhospitable arguments have indeed been tried by cultural differentialists who would protect immigrants' authentic culture against their own will if they could. All in all, knowing that the hospitality granted to immigrants is tainted with considerations of national interests redefines hospitality rather than canceling it out.

Envisaging the guest as a completely unpredictable creature who can bring chaos into the house has two other consequences. First of all, the model seems to forget that the risk is shared by the guest: the host could be a murderer too, and the guest could be betrayed. Secondly, envisioning the host as stoically confronting such apprehensions and doubts about the guest implies an almost puritanical hero who chooses hospitality over his or her psychic comfort. After all, the risk is immense: "After all, my guest may be a rapist, a murderer, he may introduce havoc into the house: I cannot rule out any of those possibilities" (Derrida 1999c, 100).

Isn't willingness to invite even a potential murderer a form of selfish hubris, too? How can the host be sure that the only subject he endangers is him or herself? How can the risk of infinite hospitality ever be self-contained? The house whose doors I open to the potential rapist may be mine, but it may be shared by others, who might become victims without having been consulted about the desirability of infinite hospitality, which is when the politics of hospitality (as long as the polis also includes the home) has to ask ethical questions: "As for politics, it starts where I have no right to favor risky situations, to take risks for others" (Derrida 1999b, 137).

Suggesting that hosts are responsible if they endanger others is especially meaningful when we think about situations where they constitute themselves as the only legitimate authority, the subject who grants other subjects or non-subjects the right to be treated as sacred guests or dispensable elements in the transaction between guests and hosts. I have in mind those moments when the granting of hospitality to some has the most violent consequences for others: not because the host or the guest abuses the other's trust, but because a third party is made to take responsibility for the consequences of the host's decision. Two passages from the Bible have been read together as problematic examples of failed hospitality where the guest is finally protected, but only because someone else (a woman) is sacrificed for his safety or honor. In Genesis 19, when his angelic guests are threatened with molestation by "the men of Sodom, both young and old" (New English Bible), Lot vainly offers his daughters as substitutes. In Judges 19:22, a Levite and his concubine are taken in by an old man while on the road, only to have a mob of Benjamites demand that the man be handed over to them "for us to have intercourse with him" (ibid.), and after the host offers his daughter in vain, the concubine is pushed outside, where she is gang raped and found dead the next morning. In both cases, the apparently heroic protection of the sacred guest is achieved at the expense of a woman whose body is offered as a substitute. Recently, theologians and critics have come back to those two passages to try and explain why the first one has been so infamously canonized, and why it has led to the demonization of homosexuality. In *The*

Invention of Sodomy in Christian Theology, Mark Jordan writes: "Many contemporary exegetes agree that the Old Testament story about the destruction of Sodom cannot be read as a lesson about divine punishment of same sex copulation. If any lesson is wanted from the story, the lesson would be about hospitality" (Jordan 1997, 30).

But what lesson exactly would that be? Like John Boswell and Derrick Bailey before him, Jordan is interested in debunking the homophobic interpretation of the biblical passages, but once that analysis is done, the alternative lesson is not spelled out: the issue of what has to be foreclosed in order to describe hospitality as the protection of men by men remains unexplored (Boswell 1980; Bailey 1955). All commentators register indignation and express sympathy for the women's plight. As Boswell shows, the Jerusalem Bible seeks to justify the men's conduct by stating that the law of hospitality was more sacred than a woman's honor. And to explain why Lot is willing to offer his young daughters, he reminds us of the "very low status of female children at the time" (Boswell 1980, 95). In his introduction to *Mythes et représentations de l'hospitalité* (Myths and Representations of Hospitality), Alain Montandon proposes a different interpretation of Lot's sacrifice: he suggests that the daughters' sacrifice represents the ultimate gift made by a host who values hospitality beyond what is dearest to him. He equates Lot's sacrifice with the efforts made by the poorest hosts of legends and myths, such as Philemon and Baucis's goose, offered to the divine guests, and the supernatural pitcher of wine given to the leper by St. Julian the Hospitaller (Montandon 1999, 21).

The fact that commentators feel the need to explain is some consolation, because they presume Lot's gesture to be incomprehensible to the modern reader. But I find even more interesting what our critics choose not to explain: the fact, for example, that hospitality should be presented as a law that can be in contradiction with another law (a woman's honor) or that a woman's honor cannot be included in a definition of hospitality. I must admit that the conclusions that I am supposed to draw from the passages escape me. The model leaves me stranded as soon as I try to imagine what is, apparently, unimaginable: what happens if the guest is a woman? What happens if the host is a woman? And what would happen if the crowd was made up exclusively of women? And I dare not even ask what would happen if, by any chance, that crowd of women preferred women? The string of questions is hardly facetious because, although I know that they are not meant to be asked, they are completely foreclosed by a definition of hospitality that explains that the woman's body is the element of latitude that allows such transactions between the men and the city. The "low status of female children" may explain why Lot is willing to give them up. But then we may wonder why the substitution can even be proposed: how can female children stand in for precious and sacred (male) guests? And more important, does the crowd's refusal mean that women can never take the place of the guest, even in the most degraded aspects of the role? Is the ultimate lesson, then, that women can never be guests, that they can never be hosts?

That proposition seems to resurface regularly in different narratives and different contexts. Less violent and less explicit versions can be found in eighteenth-century utopian literature where a white European male travels to distant lands and encounters a type of hospitality that baffles his sense of sexual propriety. In Bougainville's *A Voyage Around the World*, the captain and his men set foot on the island of Tahiti. And the ways in which the natives welcome them is described as the realization of a daring sexual fantasy, as a dream come true.[12] Here, the offering of women is presented as a harmonious (if astonishing) moment of exotic beauty:

> They were invited to enter the houses, where the people gave them to eat; nor did the civility of their landlords stop at a slight collation, they offered them young girls. The hut was immediately filled with a curious crowd of men and women, who made a circle around the guest, and the young victim of hospitality. . . . Here Venus is the Goddess of Hospitality, her worship does not admit of any mysteries, and every tribute paid to her is a feast for the whole nation. (Bougainville [1796] 1951, 227–28, quoted in Hénaff 1997, 53–54)

Keeping in mind that such narratives are not always encoded as travel diaries, and that they are often presented as fictions or even philosophical dialogues that interrogate our ethical values as well as the other's, it is worth pondering the questions triggered by the supposedly unthinkable gesture, the offering of young girls. After all, as we have seen, proposing to exchange a woman's body is not new.[13] What is presented as in need of explanation, in this text, is the fact that sex is public and shameless, and that women's modesty is replaced by a supposedly healthier sense of the virtue of physical pleasure. It should be noted that, ultimately, the only reason women are offered to the male newcomers is that they are expected to produce children for the greater good of the community. The islanders' benevolence is in fact a careful calculation of their own demographic interest. But the discovery of the ultimately selfish agenda behind this hospitality is not what interests me here: after all, it is one of the innumerable rewritings of the generous script. What does surprise me is that this valorization of childbearing should appear as radically other to the voyagers simply because it supersedes sexual modesty as the first norm. Why should they be so taken aback by a model that, after all, takes their own (Western) logic a little further than they do themselves?

Meanwhile, what is foreclosed in this whole story is the astonishment that other Candides might indeed express at the idea that no gender reciprocity is possible: in Tahiti, men offer women to men, always. Venus may be the goddess of hospitality, but in this model, her law is rather conventional. For the hospitable gesture to be radically different, other possibilities would have to be included: perhaps the possibility of male bodies being offered to female travelers, or male bodies to male travelers, or female bodies to female travelers. Even then, one may wonder why we should even celebrate a form of hospitality that gives anyone, any host, the power to "offer young" bodies (of any sex) to anyone. Wouldn't respect for the guest also entail that each of the subjects that (s)he encounters, inside the foreign house (neighborhood, nation), be shown the same consideration as him- or herself? Can a slave owner be hospitable at all? And doesn't Bougainville's text seem to have an intuition of this paradox when it suggests that hospitality has "victims," as if the gift were an expiatory rite?

How can the host construct himself as the sole guardian of (Venus's) hospitality? In order for that type of hospitality to take place, the subject who welcomes the stranger must see himself as the primordial owner of the land, of the house, and of the other human beings who live in his shadow. Forgetting that the land is always the first host, that we are, in the sense, only the guardians of what Western documents tell us we "own," the host may well treat the relationship between his residence and his guests as evidence of his ownership and of his prerogatives as master of the house:

To dare say welcome is perhaps to insinuate that one is at home here, that one knows what it means to be at home, and that at home one receives, invites, or offers hospitality, thus appropriating a space for oneself, a space to *welcome* [*accueillir*] the other, or, worse, *welcoming* the other in order to appropriate for oneself a place and then speak the language of hospitality— of course, I have no more intention than anyone else of doing this, though I'm already concerned about the danger of such a usurpation. (Derrida 1999a, 15–16)

In this case, a politics of hospitality might seek to limit the arrogance of the postcolonial host who thinks of himself as capable of infinite hospitality. It might also give to those who are eternally constituted as powerless postcolonial guests some of the (obviously dangerous) prerogatives that the metropolitan host has monopolized. For just as unconditional hospitality puts both the host and the guest in danger, it is fair to say that the right to construct one's dwelling place as a home where I can welcome another as the host (even at the risk of "usurpation") is not always a given for immigrants. In *L'immigration, ou, Les paradoxes de l'altérité* (Immigration, or, The Paradoxes of Otherness), Abdelmayek Sayad presents us with the postcolonial guest's point of view: that of the subject who can never become the host. The author tells the story of a migrant worker who has lived in France for twenty-eight years and is on the verge of retiring (Sayad 1991, 107). For five years, he has lived in a *foyer*, one of those workers' residences designed specifically for immigrants, whose organization precisely excludes the possibility of dwelling there as if one were at home. When the worker meets his interviewer, he explains:

I would love to invite you to my room, to make you coffee, a pot of tea; we could have it together, but it's forbidden. You come visit me at my place—I gave you the address, I told you I live at that address—, you came but this is no home. You are not at home when someone comes to your door and you tell them: "Come on, let's go out, we'll talk, we'll have coffee, we'll eat." (ibid., 107)

Being at home is being where you can not only eat and drink but also invite someone to eat, to drink, to chat. Being at home is being where you can be the host, where you can offer hospitality. If Derrida's host is always capable of the perversion that consists of inviting someone in order to appropriate the land, the migrant worker shows that the right to offer hospitality would construct his dwelling place as a home that he could, finally, appropriate. If one cannot offer hospitality, one has an address, not a home: "You live here, but you are not at home" ("Ici, tu habites mais tu n'es pas chez toi" [ibid.]). As the sociologist aptly remarks, " 'at home' means the residence, of course, but it may also mean France as a whole" ("chez soi . . . cela désigne bien sûr le foyer mais, peut-être, aussi toute la France" [ibid.]). Does "integration" mean that the stranger, after accepting a nation's hospitality, can finally offer hospitality, that is, not reciprocate, but lengthen the chain of possibly incommensurable hospitable gestures? Is hospitality better served when the distinction between the guest and the host moves along a continuum that constantly displaces the necessary moments of usurpation and power that the welcoming gesture requires?

In the following chapters, I follow the constantly changing variations of that continuum between host and guest: just as the distinction between the colonizer and colonized had to be rewritten by critics interested in the postcolonial condition, it may be that the opposition between the guest and the host is worth revisiting as a continuous and problematic line between power and powerlessness, ownership and dispossession, stability and nomadism. Intuitions that tell us that the postcolonial guest tends to be protected, homeless, nomadic, and poor will have to be reconfigured, because hospitality is often in flux: power comes and goes, and so do protection and respect, servitude and care. At the best of times, the host is the master (the owner of the house) and the servant of the guest. At the worst of times, the guest is the servant of the master, who is also the guest in his own house. In his study of Levinas's work, Colin Davis writes:

> Levinas's work is commanded by a simple but far-reaching question: what would it mean if, rather than responding to the threat of the Other with violence, we endeavoured to accept our dispossession of the world, to listen to the voice of the Other rather than to suppress it? . . . Levinas offers an ethics without rules, imperatives, maxims or clear objectives other than a passionate moral conviction that the Other should be heard. (Davis 1996, 144)

For lack of an answer to Levinas's urgent question, and for fear that a sense of impatience and emergency might tempt me to find an undesirable shortcut instead of an "ethics without rules," I have chosen to concentrate on fictional, literary, journalistic, or legal narratives of hospitality that offer not one, but many different solutions to the philosopher's dilemma.

The first chapter starts from the pessimistic premise that state hospitality seeks to control and restrict individual hospitality while pretending to model itself after it, and examines the roles played by intellectuals as self-appointed mediators between the French government and individuals who are directly targeted by immigration policies. I compare the different types of discourses generated by the "undocumented immigrants of Saint Bernard" affair as well as by another highly publicized court case, known as "l'affaire Deltombe," involving a French citizen who was arrested, tried, and condemned for having allowed an illegal immigrant to stay with her. Located at the intersection between politics and philosophy, this layer of commentary is constituted by the intervention of internationally known scholars, scientists, historians, and artists such as Jacques Derrida, Jean Baudrillard, Ariane Mnouchkine, and Léon Schwarzenberg. When the Deltombe case started, fifty-nine film directors launched a national campaign, which had unforeseen political consequences, and this chapter teases out the contradictory repercussions of their public action.

The second chapter explores the interconnection between international policies and fiction and analyzes the perverse consequences of discourses that idealize hospitality as if one universal generic type existed. This study of Didier van Cauwelaert's Goncourt prize–winning 1994 *Un aller simple* (A One-Way Ticket) focuses on the thought-provoking fictionalization of the human consequences of new European immigration laws. To avoid separating the book from its cultural and political context, I first analyze the changing policies that redefine the parameters of a new Europe. I then move on to a close reading of a novel whose satirical message suggests that new traditions of hospitality must be invented in such a context. Aziz, an orphan raised by Gypsies as an immigrant (simply because a fake Moroccan passport is less expensive than a fake French one), will eventually be forced to "return" to his non-homeland, that is, to a village in Morocco that, in reality, does not even exist. *Un aller simple* invents forms of (perverse) hospitality and carefully distinguishes them from benevolence. Accompanied by a so-called "humanitarian attaché," who treats him as a native informant, and whose identity is even more fragile than his, Aziz exposes the contradiction of a system whose assumptions are based on obsolete definitions of hospitality. Rather than (cynically) idealizing the idea of hospitality while refusing to practice it, Cauwelaert suggests, it might be more ethical to recognize the existence of imperfect, flawed, and even hostile forms of hospitality that protect individuals from the perverse interpretations of purportedly benevolent scripts.

In a third chapter, I move from a nonidealization of hospitality to the difficulties of comparing different sets of laws dictated by different cultures that postcolonial conditions have put in contact. In this reading of three postcolonial narratives (Karim Dridi's film *Bye-bye*, François Maspero's *Roissy Express*, and Yamina Benguigui's *Mémoires d'immigrés* [Immigrants' Memoires]) I look at the tightly interwoven narratives of nationality, ethnicity, immigration, and gender to see what happens when these concepts intersect in difficult circumstances: whenever any type of exchange between people occurs (be it commercial exchange or a gift or a ritualized transaction), different laws of hospitality may clash, sometimes violently. Europeans can both idealize Berber hospitality, for example, and resent their next-door neighbor's forms of communication. The chapter focuses on a level of misunderstanding that persists even if cohabitation has more or less ensured that each individual knows that hospitality is not universally defined, and proposes to look at new models of cross-hospitality hidden in postcolonial stories.

The fourth chapter adds to the discussion of immigration and hospitality those issues that immigration laws tend to dismiss as irrelevant, or at best secondary: the questions of language, culture, and literary references. My exploration of the troublesome connection between the host and the teacher takes a film by the Algerian director Merzak Allouache as its pre-text, and Jean de La Fontaine's *Fables* as its omnipresent intertext. La Fontaine's *Fables* need no introduction, even if we have not memorized them as children, like most French people, but Merzak Allouache's work may not be as familiar. The Algerian director's most recent film is a double story of immigration that documents the evolving relations between France and Algeria. Alilo who has come to France for a few days on a (shady) business trip ends up staying in France as an undocumented immigrant, while his cousin, Mok, who thinks of himself as French, is deported at the end of the movie. Both state and individual forms of hospitality are explored, analyzed, and sometimes criticized by a humorous camera that insists on highlighting the limits of each of the characters' discourses and desires. Perhaps more important, this bitter comedy invites us to address several distinct issues related to international and intracommunal hospitality: the film suggests that the role of the "host" will remain structurally unattainable for immigrants as long as the state forces them to inherit their parents' precarious in-betweenness. Allouache criticizes the principle of interchangeability between immigrants by exploring different types of hospitality: the (in)hospitality of language and that of cultural references. Like Abdelkebir Khatibi's *Amour bilingue* (1983; trans. as *Love in Two Languages* [1990]) and Jacques Derrida's *Le monolinguisme de l'autre* (1996; trans. as *The Monolingualism of the Other* [1998]), the film explores the translatability of hospitality and questions what Hélène Cixous has called the "infinite hospitality of language" (Cixous 1998, 155).

The fifth chapter focuses on the more private and domestic aspects of hospitality, in the hope that this different filter or point of view will shed light on areas that a focus on immigration in general tends to leave in the shadow or even construct as negligible details: gender differences. Through a reading of narratives that present the woman of the house as a cruel hostess who either does not welcome guests or, worse, drives them to suicide, I turn to issues of parasitism and dependency, of colonialism and sexism. Jean Renoir's classic film *Boudu sauvé des eaux* (*Boudu Saved from Drowning* [1932]; remade as *Down and Out in Beverly Hills* [1986]), provides a comic example of what happens when the bourgeois owner establishes a distinction between welcoming and taking care of his guest: typically, this is achieved by a fragmentation of hospitality that follows gender lines (the spouse and the servant acting as hostile caretakers while the bourgeois takes credit for his hospitality). In a second part, I concentrate on the figure of the (female) servant to analyze the potentially tragic and violent consequences of this displacement of hospitable labor from man to woman, from social class to social class, and between racial groups. Jean Genet's play *The Maids* offers a good example of the potentially destructive forces lurking in the schizophrenic division between servitude and hospitality, but a short story by the Senegalese author and director Sembène Ousmane ("Black Girl") adds racism and colonial prejudice to the already complicated model. Here, a young maid who has been "invited" to follow her employers to France is driven to suicide by the ambivalent construction of hospitality as servitude. Finally, I move to *La promesse*, the internationally acclaimed portrait of a young immigrant from Burkina Faso forced to trust the son of the man who is responsible for her husband's death.

In the final chapter, I consider the ambiguity of the concept of "refuge" and its consequences for hospitality in general. One of the first initiatives of the International Parliament of Writers, founded in 1993, was to resurrect the concept of "cities of refuge" to help writers, filmmakers, and artists in general escape persecution. It negotiated with municipal authorities and helped create a whole network of self-designated "cities of refuge" where a few refugees can find temporary shelter. Was hospitality thus finally restored? But how is the identity of the refugee affected by the definition of refuge? What is the relationship between the city and the state that surrounds the "city of refuge," especially when the larger entity is supposed to be less hospitable than its parts? Was the initiative of the Writers' Parliament merely a symbolic gesture or the much-needed theoretical seed of a new hospitable model? Can the refugee ever reconcile him- or herself to the limits of a city, or will its boundaries start functioning like the bars of a new prison? To think about those issues, I6p propose to go back to Emmanuel Levinas's *L'au delà du verset* (1982; trans. as *Beyond the Verse* [1994]), an obvious point of reference for the Parlement des écrivains, and to test his hypotheses against Julien Duvivier's famous 1936 colonial film *Pépé le Moko*, where the Casbah in Algiers functions both as city of refuge and as prison.

CHAPTER ONE

Intellectuals, Politicians, and the Media:
Hospitality, Ethics, and the State

One of the assumptions of this essay is that Europe currently shares with the rest of the Western world a tendency to view foreigners with suspicion and resentment. But the statement may be a useless truism (and an ahistorical blanket statement) unless I add that the end of the twentieth century manifested its xenophobia in ways that reflected local and global contexts: in Europe, and especially in France, the issue of "immigration" has been politicized for more than three decades. Going back in time and wondering when hospitality disappeared is a self-defeating exercise, but we may somewhat arbitrarily remember symbolic dates, such as 1974, when President Valéry Giscard d'Estaing tried to "close the gates" of France to foreign workers. Even if the attempt failed in many ways, it was significant because it made it clear that previous laws of hospitality would no longer apply.

More recently, a new cultural phenomenon seems to have slightly altered the politicization of immigration issues: the involvement of cultural agents, intellectuals, artists, and social scientists who are taking strong and visible

positions, using the media's willingness to relay their voices as a way of in-
tervening in the debate. If the 1980s was the decade of associations (with the
rise of S.O.S. Racisme, for example), the 1990s saw the reappearance of intellectuals and artists who did not hesitate, especially during and after the
"affaire des sans-papiers de Saint-Bernard," to intervene at various levels
(sometimes to oppose the decisions made by the government, sometimes to
participate in the policy-making process, sometimes to mobilize and raise
consciousness through manifestos and public calls to disobey). In this chapter, I propose to observe the different forms of intervention chosen by different cultural actors and their influence on the larger context.

One of the most obvious signs of interest in hospitality and immigration
by respected and internationally recognized intellectual figures was the publication of a large number of books on the topic. I have studied some of the
most representative or striking examples in the Introduction, but it may not
be enough to focus on recent publications by writers whose work is more
easily disseminated because of their familiarity with academic disciplines
or access to the publishing industry. It is also worth mentioning that filmmakers, actors, and theater directors worked hand in hand, using their own
resources. New technologies also served to relay powerful messages of resistance on the Internet: petitions, newspapers articles, bills or laws, and up-
dates of all kind were offered the hospitality of new forums. When Léon
Schwarzenberg and Ariane Mnouchkine found themselves working together to help the "sans-papiers de Saint-Bernard," the world of cancer research and of avant-garde theater were unexpectedly united around the
same cause.[1] The "Collège des médiateurs" (committee of mediators) that I
mention in the Introduction was composed of specialists from many different disciplines. Although their intervention was deemed unsuccessful—it
could not prevent the violent evacuation of the Church of Saint Bernard—
it nonetheless spawned publications, public meetings, and declarations that
allowed the movement to continue.

It is also worth considering the efforts made by certain publishers to
reprint books on hospitality that had been written in different contexts. Like
all cultural practices, the politics of reprinting volumes that are suddenly
deemed relevant to what the French call *l'actualité* (current affairs) is not innocent. In this case, the idea of republishing studies by intellectuals or es-
sayists who had already written on hospitality and the right of asylum could

even be seen as self-referential: we can imagine it as the building of a library hospitable to the idea of hospitality. All the books on hospitality would then constitute a virtual study room where travelers, refugees, or concerned citizens of all countries could gather, and through their reading invent a community of "guests for the night."[2] On the other hand, it is difficult not to suspect less-than-generous motives when the publishing industry seems to be capitalizing on the plight of immigrants in whose names more essays are being reprinted. Or perhaps, it would be more accurate to say that such moments generate an unusually high level of duplicity, in which the most sincere authors find their own agendas complicated by commercial imperatives. For example, Gérard Noiriel's *La tyrannie du national: Le droit d'asile en Europe, 1783–1993* originally came out in 1991. In 1998, the book was republished practically unchanged, except for a new very brief preface, under a different title: *Réfugiés et sans-papiers: La République face au droit d'asile, XIXe–XXe siècle*. I am sure that I was not the only (absentminded or not-too-discerning) consumer to have bought the book thinking that this was a "new" Noiriel, and I must confess to feeling disappointed and slightly cheated when I discovered that this promising title hid or resurrected Noiriel's earlier study. On the other hand, the new preface has the advantage of clarifying the author's use of his own research and his vision of what his work as an intellectual and a social scientist can or cannot do. In a context where intellectuals, militants, or artists engaged in cultural critique are routinely dismissed as unrealistic troublemakers and "angelic" thinkers about to become fallen angels, Noiriel's analysis of his own position is welcome. Responding to reviews of the first edition that criticized the book for insisting too much on the suffering of immigrants and asylum seekers, the preface makes a forceful and useful statement about his complex positioning *between* policy making and pure research. To Patrick Weil, who suggests that "some of [his] statements reveal a bias that is incompatible with the manifest concern to remain above current controversies about immigration" ("certains de [ses] propos trahissent un parti pris peu compatible avec le souci affiché de garder une distance par rapport aux polémiques actuelles sur l'immigration" [Noiriel 1998, iv]), Noiriel explains:

> I don't mind admitting that I refused to reduce my thinking to a "here is what must be done," above all, to better expose the forms of domination

suffered by the victims of the "Etat de droit." Without seeking to speak
for them, this study aims to contribute to the reflections of asylum rights
activists rather than to those of experts. I think that one of the essential
functions of the social sciences is to highlight forms of social misery that
would otherwise remain invisible. (Noiriel 1998, iv)

Noiriel thus openly recognizes that there may be unavoidable discrepancies between the discourses of the "activist" and the "expert," and, remarkably, he takes sides. Making the asylum seeker visible as the guest who was
denied hospitality is a first step toward a politics of hospitality that does not
have to be radically distinguished from an ethics of hospitality.

In 1998, the Moroccan novelist Tahar Ben Jelloun likewise republished
his famous *Hospitalité française* (1984; trans. as *French Hospitality* [1999]),
with a long new preface.[3] The book was originally inspired by a series of violent attacks and murders, and the sadly ironic title was meant to denounce
French inhospitality to Arabs. Ben Jelloun pointed out that hospitality to
long-term immigrants was by no means granted unconditionally. In his
1998 preface, he focuses on the deterioration of the situation of new immigrants, who now find themselves confronted with an intolerable level of suspicion and administrative hostility, in a "France that goes on modifying the
hospitality it offers, making no distinction between those who had to travel
to get here and those who did not."[4]

The book is ostensibly addressed to a general public, and although the
author alludes to Derrida's studies of Levinas, Kant, and Heidegger (*Adieu
to Emmanuel Levinas*), he does not critically engage with the philosopher's
argument. Like Ben Jelloun's 1998 book *Le racisme expliqué à ma fille* (Racism Explained to My Daughter), *Hospitalité française* privileges a certain simplicity at the risk of generalizing some of the concepts. If Noiriel's agenda is
to underplay bureaucratic logic, Ben Jelloun seems determined to stay away
from philosophical or academic discourse. As a result (but this deliberate
rhetorical choice may not be a totally satisfactory explanation), the concept
of hospitality remains a somewhat monolithic and generalized one in Ben
Jelloun. Even when specific illustrations are given (the case of Morocco, for
example), the author still refers to hospitality in general rather than to forms
of hospitality in particular, and he does not distinguish very clearly between
what he describes and what he prescribes, what he observes as a dominant

norm and what he desires (sometimes a dissident type of hospitality). When he says, "Moroccan hospitality is a tradition, a part of the Moroccan character, the legacy of a culture combining Arab-Berber, Muslim and Jewish elements" (Ben Jelloun 1999, 2), I wonder if Ben Jelloun is not reproducing a type of ethnographic discourse that glosses over existing inner tensions with a view to idealizing a type of Moroccan hospitality that could replace the betrayed model of French hospitality. In the next two chapters, we shall see that novels such as Didier van Cauwelaert's *Un aller simple* and Yamina Benguigui's interviews propose other solutions. While there are tactical advantages to performatively reinventing a "Moroccan hospitality," it is obvious that this can only be a reactive proposal. Ben Jelloun often uses "hospitality" as the subject of his sentences, as if the ethical imperative were generated by the word itself, as if hospitality had the power of making us, magically, hospitable (in perfect ways): "Hospitality is akin to generosity" (Ben Jelloun 1999, 4, translating "L'hospitalité est de l'ordre de la prodigalité" [*Hospitalité française*, 1998, 13]). But, perhaps, certain forms of hostile, grudging, and limited hospitality may be better than nothing. "Hospitality can exist only where there is complete disinterestedness and a guest is seen as a gift" (Ben Jelloun 1999, 3). But such a perfect equation between gifts and hospitality may lead to the type of aporias that Derrida explored in *Donner le temps* (1991; trans. as *Given Time* [1992]), and we may argue that complex understandings of exchange might not preclude the possibility of evolving practices of hospitality.

Ben Jelloun's conceptualization of hospitality may be too general to include problematic cases of ambiguous forms of hospitality, but the end of his preface creates a new genre of discourse on hospitality that takes into account the specific context in which he is writing: Ben Jelloun concludes with what we could call a letter of noninvitation to his mother (even if the letter is not addressed to his mother but to the generic public that does not allow him to adopt a dignified position as host). That text is also reprinted from *Le Monde* (where it appeared in February 1997). The title of the article is "Ma mère ne viendra pas en France" (My Mother Won't Be Coming to France), and it lists the reasons why the writer does not want even to consider inviting his mother to come for a short visit.

"Obviously, a foreign woman who is seventy years old might easily disturb the peace or even take a job away from a Frenchwoman," Ben Jelloun observes (1999, 32,), making visible and tangible the human consequences of immigration laws that systematically suspect any foreigner of being a troublemaker or future illegal immigrant. He invents the figure of the non-host and the non-guest. Ben Jelloun refuses to invite: he analyses his own position as that of the non-host. He knows that he is placed in a situation where the state denies him the right to have a guest, even if that guest is the person who taught him generosity (ibid., 32). Similarly, the mother becomes, not even an undesirable guest, but a non-guest, whom the non-host must protect against state inhospitality. As if the Good Samaritan's perverse, perverted generosity now consisted of sparing others the humiliation of being denied a visa.

Monique Chemillier-Gendreau's *L'injustifiable: Les politiques françaises de l'immigration*, mentioned in the Introduction, was one of the books directly inspired by the odyssey of the "sans-papiers de Saint-Bernard." The author accuses the French government of jeopardizing the very existence of hospitality.

> Through the continuous and short-sighted enforcement of repressive anti-immigrant politics, one minister of the interior after the other has contributed to eliminating hospitality from the list of French virtues. They have allowed the coinage of the terrifying phrase "crime of hospitality" [*délit d'hospitalité*], and they have dared to put a value that should be preserved and encouraged into the category of reprehensible acts. (Chemillier-Gendreau 1998, 8)

In Chemillier-Gendreau's formulation, hospitality as a "French" virtue has already disappeared, but, at the same time, this disappearance seems to confirm that there had always been such a thing as "French hospitality." The statement thus performatively gives and takes: it tells the French that the nation both had and has just lost a typically French virtue, or, even worse, that hospitality has suddenly been erased from the list of options. Hospitality no longer belongs in the repertoire from which French citizens may presumably choose their ethical principles.

The accusation is extremely serious, and the indignant reference to what the ministers of the interior have "dared" and to the "terrifying" coinage confirms that the author is so shocked that she does not see the need to make an argument. All readers are expected to be appalled at a government's attempt to "eliminate hospitality from the list of French virtues," since the very national identity that xenophobes try to protect through anti-immigrant policies is, in reality, disfigured by those who betray what this identity has traditionally stood for.

What is interesting in the rhetorical position adopted by Chemillier-Gendreau in this passage is that she does not propose a revised definition of "hospitality": it is assumed that we all agree about what hospitality means and that the government's policy amounts to turning hospitality into a reprehensible act. The government's only possible response to this accusation would be to deny the charges, to insist that hospitality has not disappeared from the list of "French virtues," and that its policies are in no way incompatible with what it would call hospitality. Chemillier-Gendreau's tactic is thus to appeal to a shared definition of (French) hospitality at the very moment when several political and intellectual forces are vying for the right to redefine the concept according to their own agendas and principles.

Chemillier-Gendreau's position and rhetorical tactics are worth noting because they sharply contrast with other statements (or other strategies) that have been used in the battle fought at the intersection between the discourse on hospitality and the social practices that the word legitimizes. In *La transparence du mal* (1990; trans. as *The Transparency of Evil* [1993]), Jean Baudrillard's exploration of the notion of hospitality takes on a much more original (if predictably provocative) course. Rather than suggesting that the evil of our time is the cynical abandonment of the value of hospitality, Baudrillard's book seems to imply that it may be dangerous to fetishize the concept. Hospitality is not necessarily a "French" value, and, more surprisingly, it may not be a value at all: perhaps we should not idealize hospitality, because it is sometimes akin to a form of devouring. Comparing "us" (a monolithic French culture?) to Brazil and Japan, Baudrillard establishes a parallel between degrees of "hospitality" and degrees of "absorption":

> All other cultures are extraordinarily hospitable: their ability to absorb is phenomenal. Whereas we waver between the other as prey and the other as shadow, between predation pure and simple and an idealizing recognition, other cultures still retain the capacity to incorporate what comes to them from without, including what comes from our Western universe, into their own rules of the game. (Baudrillard 1993, 142)

Baudrillard apparently differentiates between the myth of French "integration" and an ability to "absorb" otherness that is not grounded in a universalistic discourse about the relationship between same and other. If the word "still" ("other cultures *still* retain . . .") is to be taken seriously, this narrative, like Chemillier-Gendreau's, talks about a loss that other cultures have not experienced. But the loss in question may not be a reprehensible setting aside of hospitable ideals: for Baudrillard, the Japanese are capable of a form of hospitality that does not request any "psychological internalization" (ibid., 143). In other words, the presence of otherness is completely separated from a rhetoric of effort, personal cost, and internal change. The net result of this redefinition of hospitality is that the host literally devours the guest: Japanese hospitality

> is thus a cannibalistic form—assimilating, absorbing, aping, devouring. Afro-Brazilian culture is also a rather good example of cannibalism in this sense: it too devours white modern culture, and it too is seductive in character. Cannibalism must indeed always be merely an extreme form of the relationship to the other, and this includes cannibalism in the relationship of love. Cannibalism is a radical form of hospitality. (Ibid., 144)

This paragraph is admittedly far from clear, and its ideological implications are problematic: Baudrillard moves from what sounds like a sweeping generalization about "Japanese culture" to an even more universalizing statement about "cannibalism" and "hospitality." And if the first comparatist declarations are obviously marred by a double and contradictory desire to be both specific (about Japan) and totalizing (about all of Japanese culture) that makes Baudrillard's conclusions about "Japanese" hospitality suspiciously stereotypical, the strength of the last formula ("Cannibalism is a radical form of hospitality") comes from its gnomic construction and its provocative association between words that the West immediately associates with opposites, with good (hospitality) and with evil (cannibalism).

My first reaction to Baudrillard's analysis of "Japanese" and "Afro-Brazilian" traditions was to suspect that his anthropological comments are a convenient way of othering two supposedly monolithic cultures while revealing facets of his own culture that he does not feel comfortable with. After all, isn't it commonly accepted that France "absorbed" and "devoured" its colonial others to a degree unparalleled by other imperial powers? Isn't Baudrillard's portrait of a vague and ahistorical Japan a useful if unconscious comment on the dark side of hospitality when practiced by a powerful (post)colonial nation?

Instead of assuming that only "Japanese" and "Afro-Brazilian" cultures can illustrate his point, we might consider the ethical consequences of Baudrillard's last statement without ruling out the possibility that it can precisely be applied to the France of the 1990s rather than those others that have not participated in what he calls the "orgy" of liberation of the 1960s. Then the counterintuitive proposal of Baudrillard's provocative formula is worth considering: for he goes so far as to suggest that hospitality can be bad, cruel, selfish, and egotistical.

The realization that some forms of hospitality resemble cannibalism is a welcome understanding of the element of power involved in a guest-host relationship, and Baudrillard's formulation could be interpreted, for example, as a critique of "our" own colonial and postcolonial assimilationist policies, which have transformed a supposedly welcoming gesture into a demand for dissolution. If the host strips the guest of his or her identity, then it can be said that cannibalism has occurred, precisely the form of "cannibalism" that Aimé Césaire denounced in his *Discours sur le colonialisme* (1950; trans. as *Discourse on Colonialism* [1972]).

I would argue that decolonization and independence have not brought about the disappearance of what Baudrillard calls "radical" hospitality (cannibalism), and his warning that hospitality is not, in and of itself, a cardinal virtue, is a salutary reminder to anyone who wants to act as host and practice hospitality. In a strange and roundabout way, Baudrillard allows his readers to formulate a critique of selfish forms of "cooperation" that, according to Chemillier-Gendreau, are synonymous with domination (Chemillier-Gendreau 1998, 221 ff.).

Clearly, Baudrillard's and Chemillier-Gendreau's rhetorics are poles apart, and I doubt that the author of *L'injustifiable* would be particularly eager to entertain the notion that there are many similarities between the postmodern fragments of *The Transparency of Evil* and her rigorously argued, thoroughly documented, passionate political essay. Besides, Chemillier-Gendreau and Baudrillard radically part company when they identify the most urgent form of "evil" that threatens not only the marginalized of European societies, but also the very ideal of democratic states. If the predecolonization period gave rise to innumerable instances of cannibalistic hospitalities, if the perversion of hospitality consisted of a hypocritical definition of devouring disguised as welcoming, our postcolonial times are scripting a new version of cynicism: rich Western states are purely and simply declaring that they can no longer afford to be hosts, that hospitality is a luxury beyond their means. Hospitable and powerful hosts that constantly threatened to swallow their guests have turned into supposedly weakened hosts that can no longer welcome the "huddled masses" gathering on our "uncertain shores."[5]

One of the effects of this historical shift is that it is difficult to formulate a definition of state and private hospitality that most citizens, regardless of their political orientations, could be expected to accept. When I remember what I know of ancient Greek hospitality, for example, I mostly assume that any self-respecting individual would have been willing to act according to the laws of hospitality, and I also take for granted that the law itself was unanimously revered as a "good" law, as a desirable and respectable code. Perhaps this vision of a wonderful consensus is an illusion: transgressions may have existed, and they may have constituted the exception that strengthens the rule, but it might also be the case that the ancient tradition of how to receive guests was not as monolithic as we sometimes like to think. Yet, a preexisting narrative gives us the impression that the law of hospitality was not perceived as a profoundly controversial issue.

Today, however, a whole range of hospitable practices are being scrutinized and the very definition of hospitality is up for grabs. Conflicting definitions no longer fall neatly along a right-wing/left-wing watershed. Those who are shocked by the gradual decline of the idea of state hospitality suspect moderate right-wingers of siding with the definitions of the vociferously inhospitable theses of the National Front and accuse the socialists of hiding behind inhospitable right-wing parties to pretend that no other policy can be implemented. Their opponents plead for more realism and common sense, and for definitions of hospitality that take into account what they claim is many people's wish to limit hospitality, to put an end to immigration. Both sides vie for a redefinition of hospitality and want theirs to prevail.

Keeping Baudrillard's cautionary suggestion at the back of my mind, I suspect that it may be worth scrutinizing the different meanings of the same word in different contexts: without acknowledging the possible ambivalent facets of the cultural manifestations of hospitality, it may be difficult to resist a contemporary current of thought that seems to accept the very real possibility of collective and private inhospitality as a norm. If it becomes culturally acceptable for some to openly advocate inhospitality, we may well find ourselves tempted by the logic of binary oppositions, which would urge us to insist simply that hospitality is much preferable to inhospitality. But the 1980s have also taught us that the most effective answer to "racism" is not necessarily the self-righteous and unambiguous discourse of anti-racism (Taguieff 1988). Rather than opposing hospitality and inhospitality as if they were two new manifestations of good and evil, it should be possible to analyze the different definitions of hospitality favored by various communities, by more or less empowered voices, in order to ascertain which more or less desirable forms of hospitality are proposed, recommended, rejected, or adopted.

In the private, individual sense, Western hospitality can be practiced without being strictly defined, and it involves the mixed sense of responsibility and pleasure that we expect to experience when a friend, a relative, or, more rarely, a stranger visits for a little while. Note that this is not very ambitious, and that my definition of hospitality is quite limited to a set of ordinary and unexamined practices. I suggest, however, that this rather unformulated model of individual hospitality is always implicitly presented as the model of hospitality in politics. Political discourses seem to invite us to treat immigrants as if "France," the country, functioned like a self-contained private house where the owner receives a relative.

For better or for worse, the representatives of the state, in their political speeches, speak as though France is the house and the immigrants, the Guest, with a capital G. From an ethical point of view, the ideological logic of the analogy can cut both ways, it can be generous or hostile, can welcome or reject: political leaders can either urge the French to be more hospitable and to greet the Guest, that is, the immigrants, with open arms, or construct images of the bad Guest who overstays his or her welcome, pockets the silver, or ransacks the fridge:

> The image used by the minister of the interior to talk about immigration during an electoral meeting on April 28, 1997 (he referred to France as "our house" and described foreigners as people who "walk into our homes, settle down, open the fridge, and help themselves") is significant of the turn taken

by the public debate on immigration during the past few decades. By presenting a historically inaccurate caricature of the foreigner as an incon-
siderate parasite, it is possible to justify increasingly repressive laws, while
pandering to the xenophobic tendencies of a portion of French society.
(Fassin et al. 1997, 263)

When the analogy between the guest and the immigrant means that the
individual is supposed to take it for granted that his or her own foreign
guests are undesirable parasites, then it becomes urgent to point out that referring to the nation or country as a "house" is a metaphor, and that the
choice of the metaphor is subordinated to political agendas. I wonder, for
instance, how different the rhetoric would be if I were to argue that the so-
called hospitality of nations may more closely resemble commercial hospitality: isn't it more accurate, for example, to imagine the state as a hotel,
rather than as a private house?

The commercial logic that governs hotels and inns, restaurants and coffee shops is a very specific form of hospitality: it may be said that that type of
hospitality mimics the "real" one, that it imitates the signs of generosity the
better to justify an exchange of goods that continues to seduce customers
precisely at the moment it makes them forget that they are paying for the attention they receive, for the comfort they are able to indulge in, sometimes
in the midst of poverty. Invoking the ideal of France as a *terre d'accueil* does
not square very well with the notion that strangers might have to buy their
way into a country, pay for the right to stay, and be responsible for a bill that
represents a certain level of services. For now at least, no democratic leader
would go so far as to officially replace the ideal of "hospitality" with a rhet
oric of commercial tourism, for example. The idea of the foreigner as paying customer is still linked to sordid and unanimously rejected practices that
are viewed as forms of human trafficking.

The figure of the foreigner as guest makes cultural sense, the stranger as
paying visitor does not. Symbolically, the latter metaphor would dissociate
state hospitality from generosity: it certainly sounds less altruistic to provide
services than to take care of the other as if he or she were a member of one's
family who has come to stay. Even that model of perfect hospitality and the
implication that family visits are idyllic is an illusion, and we all know how
perfect families sometimes treat their own others (their gay son or daughter

or their married-to-the-wrong-person child, for example), but as long as the state chooses that model over the principle of hotel-like systems, a tremendous level of hypocrisy has to be maintained. Recognizing that the foreigner is locked in a commercial logic with the so-called host nation would at least allow cultural commentators to articulate a description of the immigrant as "paying" guest that would be less cynical than the caricature used by the minister of the interior. Naturally, different metaphors are competing for the best place under the sun of common sense and obviousness. It is also true that the same metaphor can be recruited by radically opposed agendas. But it may be desirable that the images we use reveal rather than mask such agendas.[6]

I am not suggesting that changing metaphors would necessarily cause hostility to strangers to dissolve: xenophobic reflexes will always be able to accuse the foreigner of being a bad customer, probably a thief, but avoiding the vocabulary of exchange may be a cynical deception when the constant reference to state hospitality tends to hide the profoundly economic and financial logic of state-organized migrations while invariably blaming individual migrants who conceive their trajectories as "economic" projects.

After all, when Algerian workers came to France after World War II, they were not so much invited as recruited by companies. It is not clear why the needs of employers that locally translated into the hiring (and the subsequent firing) of workers must be interpreted, at the level of the state, as an "invitation" of Algerians.

One of the eminently problematic consequences of the analogy between what we think of as state hospitality and private hospitality is that each citizen is implicitly required to abide by the laws of (in)hospitality dictated by the current philosophy of the nation, regardless of whether they correspond to his or her personal set of ethics. Recent episodes have revealed the vulnerability of foreigners *and* nationals who find themselves caught between their own sense of hospitality and the logic of immigration policies.

In February 1997, "l'affaire des sans-papiers de Saint-Bernard" had disappeared from the headlines for a few months, but the image of CRS riot police breaking down the door of a church with axes had been broadcast several times by all the major audiovisual channels, and the pictures lingered in French memory as one of the current possible definitions of how the state meant to define hospitality. On February 4, another apparently self-contained

element was added to the growing cultural file on hospitality and its definitions. This time, one single individual was on the spot, and she was a French
citizen. Here is how the *Nouvel Observateur* told the story, a few weeks after
Jacqueline Deltombe's arrest. In other words, here is one of the narratives
easily available to the French at the time:

> Jacqueline Deltombe's crime: she put up one of her friends, Hélène Herbaut
> and the latter's Zairean partner, Tony M'Bongo Bongolo, an undocumented
> immigrant, in the four-bedroom flat that she shares with her own Zairean
> partner, her daughter, and her two nieces. Which, according to the ordi-
> nance of November 2, 1945, modified by the August 24, 1993, Pasqua law
> on immigration, is punishable by a five-year prison sentence and a Fr
> 200,000 fine. Yes, five years in prison for having neglected to ask a stranger
> for his identification papers. The discrepancy between the crime and the
> severity of the punishment was such that the prosecutor himself pleaded for
> clemency. He did not ask for any penalty to be imposed on Deltombe at the
> public hearing on January 28, arguing that "it could not established that she
> had deliberately broken the law." One week later, she was nonetheless found
> guilty as charged. (Backmann, 44)

The short article does not give lay readers a clear indication of the legal
intricacies of the case: unless they already have a knowledge of the workings
of the French juridical system through personal or professional experience,
they are likely to be more alienated than informed by the references to the
successive phases of the trial. For example, we may find it difficult to understand the discrepancy between the prosecutor's plea for clemency and the
fact that Deltombe was found guilty a week later. But what the article does
convey very powerfully is a sense of how a citizen's life can suddenly be
turned upside down as the result of a conflict between two definitions of
hospitality. If we have never considered that possibility, we may discover
that the state has a right to interfere if it claims that the official laws of hospitality (and especially its limits) are being transgressed by an individual.
Even if we do not understand the technicalities of the trial, it is easy to em-
pathize with how Deltombe felt when the journalists mention that she was
held in custody for twenty-five hours, that her home was searched, that she
was handcuffed, that there were insults and a body search.

The whole disciplining apparatus that transforms a human body into an official criminal is present here, and the process marks a personal trajectory with an indelible scar that will last forever, not only in the person's memory, but also in all types of records that could come back to haunt her when she least expects it. The article points out that she lost her job (at a time when unemployment was one of the most often cited causes of fear and anxieties among the French) and makes it clear that the system was able to punish her even before finding her guilty.

What this isolated but much publicized episode demonstrated loudly was that the nation expected each individual to abide by the state definition of hospitality, even if the rule encroaches upon the sphere of the private. Like certain sexual practices that are not protected by the right to privacy, owing, for example, to the existence of anti-sodomy statutes in some states, hospitality has never been an exclusively private practice. Legislators always limit the individual's right to protect someone. The law will intervene in certain cases, such as the harboring of criminals and minors (Schérer 1993, 18).

Such limitations to the law of hospitality (or the right to be hospitable) are a reminder of the possible ambivalence of a hospitable gesture: the concept of *détournement de mineur* protects the guest from the host, while the interdiction against the harboring of criminals protects the state from a private relationship between the host and the guest where the host's house becomes a self-contained territory above the laws of the Republic. But whether the law seeks to protect the guest from the host or the host society from a supposedly dangerous guest, the problematic element in each case is that hospitality is linked with identity. In both cases, before granting hospitality, one must ascertain to which category the guest belongs. However, the categories in question have been defined by the state, which then imposes its own identity politics on the host.

Besides, the implied consequence of the state's right to interfere in the definition of what constitutes an authorized guest is that the host's house is a subset of the national territory and that private gestures of hospitality are always a subcategory of national hospitality. But whether or not we accept the logic of such limitations, the idea that identity checks must precede the granting of hospitality remains an explosive issue because it forces the host to adopt the attitude and methods of professional identifiers (the police, investigators, customs officers, etc.). "Criminality" is not a characteristic that can be read on the body. The law makes it clear which guest-host relationships are illegal but does not specify how the goal is to be achieved, and one of the undesirable consequences of this principle is that hospitality is here inextricably linked to each individual's ability to interpret, to decode the other's body.

In the case of illegal foreigners, it is even more problematic to be forced to make no distinction between hospitality and identity. By enforcing article 21 of the 1945 ordinance, the court was implicitly saying that it is the individual's responsibility to find out about the guest's legal status. In other words, that article suggests that the way in which you define hospitality within the confines of your own home should be policed in exactly the same way as bureaucracies or immigration officers control national borders. The host must see him or herself as an immigration officer and must visualize the threshold of the house as the equivalent of a national frontier. But the whole idea of identity policing is incompatible with forms of hospitality inspired by a model where the host makes a point of not even asking who the guests are until they have been properly fed and bathed.

Apparently, however, it is not so easy to enforce a law whose practical consequences remain relatively invisible until a specific event brings to light its most restrictive applications. From the Deltombe affair, many citizens could have drawn the conclusion that it was acceptable and even mandatory for any host to act as an immigration officer. Instead, the case functioned as a symbolic turning point and generated a national controversy about the relationship between state hospitality and civic responsibility. That hospitality can be reduced to a philosophical and political double bind (both mandatory and forbidden) was both proposed and contested by the Deltombe affair. Like any news item that becomes a test and a challenge to the values of the Republic, Deltombe's personal tragedy had many conflictual repercussions: among other things, it demonstrated that the government could not expect to enforce such logic without triggering great discontent. Even though the court had stipulated that Deltombe would not have to serve the sentence, her story was suddenly treated as a matter of principle.

Maybe because the violent expulsion of the *sans-papiers* from the Church of Saint Bernard and the resulting feeling of powerlessness and inadequacy among militants were still very much present in people's minds, or because

Deltombe's arrest coincided with the election of a National Front mayor in Vitrolles (Bouches-du-Rhône) in February 1997, her story became a symbol. The Deltombe affair profoundly modifies the symbolic and structural take on the definition of hospitality by turning a binary opposition into a triangle: as long as events are constructed as a conflict between the state and immigrants, even if associations and intellectuals take sides publicly, the cultural representation of the issue is that the government is fighting for its own definition of hospitality, while the immigrants are trying to contest its limits. The stranger and the state come face to face, while the rest of the nation watches. Whoever is not an undocumented immigrant or a political leader does not have to take sides and can certainly remain silent if he or she wishes to do so. The Deltombe affair makes indifference or detachment impossible, drawing every citizen into a potentially devastating confrontation with the representatives of a state that now makes it clear that its definition of hospitality is prescribed to every single individual. In other words, the opposition between the immigrant and the state is replaced by a triangular structure where the guest (the legal/illegal immigrant) and the host (whether or not he or she enjoys the privilege of bearing a French passport) is accountable to the state, whose definition of hospitality now dictates everyone's practice. The feeling that French citizens could afford to be indifferent to the state's official definition of hospitality was probably always an illusion anyway, but the Deltombe affair turned indifference into curiosity, curiosity into concern, preexisting concern into indignation, and well-formulated indignation into a strong desire to mobilize and express disagreement publicly.

Suddenly, it was clear that hospitality (and not only immigration) was constructed as a question directly related to the law rather than to apparently private notions of generosity and goodwill. The constant and obsessive reference to the law to explain collective and individual behavior that many find inhuman or unfair could be seen as a symptom of the deterioration of the situation: it is a sign that other implicit laws of human conduct (including what we think are the "laws of hospitality") are being canceled out. When demonstrators gathered to support the "sans-papiers de Saint-Bernard" outside the church they occupied, the minister of the interior consistently responded with appeals to the "law," of which he appeared to be the sacred guardian. And as the authors of *Les lois de l'inhospitalité* point out, reducing the whole debate to a legal question is a way of marginalizing not only the immigrants, who are outside of the circle of citizenship, but also those citizens who wish to question the contents of the law. "Doesn't the insistent reference to the law seek to marginalize those who criticize it, those bad citizens, outlaws if you will? To go beyond a discourse guaranteed by the law is to point to hidden political agendas. It is to make it apparent that beyond the fate of foreigners and immigrants, the present and future of European societies is at stake" (Fassin et al. 1997, 6–7).

Constant reminders about the "law" seek to exclude ordinary people from the process of redefinition of the very model of hospitality that the state pretends to have adopted as the model of its constitution, and simultaneously to exonerate them from the responsibility of searching for their own context-specific definition of hospitality. Derrida also emphasizes the exclusionary logic of texts encoded in a language that is notoriously hermetic. Criminalizing an individual is easier when he or she is not conversant with the legal jargon, and the problem is compounded when the foreigner's limited mastery of the national language disempowers him or her at the symbolic and practical level. As we shall see, mastery of French predetermines the roles of guest and host in Merzak Allouache's *Salut cousin!*[7]

Chemillier-Gendreau goes even further when she suggests that the excessive reference to "The" law may hide the fact that one law is in competition with other (international or moral) codes, and that the constant reiteration of its supposedly ultimate authority masks the fact that it is itself a transgression of other laws. She claims that some of the elements of the French government's politics "made it apparent that the ritualistic invocation of the 'law' by the architects of this policy concealed the violation of international agreements on human rights, and especially the right to a private life or to the status of refugee" (Chemillier-Gendreau 1998, 12).

In that context, it is worth noting that Deltombe's arrest coincided with a decision by the minister of the interior, Jean-Louis Debré, to introduce a new bill whose most visible element was immediately perceived as an attempt to police further individual practices of identity. One of the most unpopular clauses of the new bill would have made it mandatory for anyone receiving an immigrant in their own home to declare his or her departure to the authorities. This new disposition was going to be added to the already long list of procedures that complicates the life of an immigrant requesting a visa for a short visit, complications that the general public had been able to ignore because they never felt that their own freedom was infringed upon.

The sudden movement of protest that greeted Debré's new proposal was not so much directed at the latest development, but, retrospectively, at the whole principle of a law that had to do with the way in which the government encoded legitimate hospitality. A last-straw effect provoked a sudden anger against the so-called *certificats d'hébergement* (certificates of lodging) that, paradoxically, did not constitute a recent element of the law. The *certificat d'hébergement* was one of the documents that an immigrant had to provide prior to obtaining a visa. Originally approved in a climate of complete indifference in 1982 (Bernard and Herzberg 1997a), it was supposed to ensure that immigrants would be hosted in decent conditions.[8] The administration's role was thus theoretically ambiguous and potentially repressive: on the one hand, it was the guardian of an ideal form of hospitality (it had to make sure that immigrants would be treated with dignity on French soil), but, on the other hand, it was clear that the clause was motivated by a fear that hospitality offered to immigrants by immigrants would degenerate into promiscuity and encourage substandard dwelling practices. The principle would have been noble if administrations had been able to offer better hospitality than the people they disqualified: instead, after ascertaining that some strangers would not benefit from "decent" housing because the homes of the relatives or friends who offered to share their accommodation did not meet official standards of "normal" comfort, administrations would simply reject visa applications. In other words, the state policed hospitality as granted by individuals but did not offer its own when it was found lacking.

Besides, it had become clear to activists and associations that certain mayors refused to provide *certificats d'hébergement* under more or less fallacious pretexts. At best, the desire to verify that immigrants would be well received resulted in humiliating and inhumane procedures that exposed the host to unpleasant visits by bureaucrats armed with tape measures. In an article published a few months after *l'affaire* Deltombe, Philippe Viledier denounced the grotesque contradictions of such inhospitable attempts at preserving degrees of hospitality:

"My mother, a sixty-seven year-old widow who lives in the Constantine region, was coming to visit me. I went to city hall with my lease, a piece of ID, my electricity bill, my pay slips and the OMI fiscal stamp. My request was registered, and I was told that someone would call me a week later. And someone from the Migrations Office did call and asked to check my flat. She checked out each room, asked to see where my mother would sleep. I experienced her visit as extremely humiliating." The young woman who tells the story is Algerian and a professor of mathematics at the University of Lyon. She has lived in France for more than ten years and, as a professor in a higher education institution, she obviously has all the necessary documents. She started the procedure to allow her mother's visit in December 1996. In March, the visa had still not been granted. (Viledier 1997, 17)

In December 1997, when the *certificat d'hébergement* was abolished by 86 votes to 35 and replaced by a simple *attestation d'accueil*, Jean-Pierre Chevènement, the new minister of the interior, called it a "useless, pettifogging formality" ("formalité tracassière et inutile") and observed: "When you have your relatives over, no one checks how many beds you have" (Montvalon 1997).

Ironically, the example of a supposedly absurd situation given by Chevènement was remarkably similar to the experience of the young Algerian woman waiting for her mother's visit.[9] The minister only alluded to the possibility of someone counting the beds in one's house to better dismiss and ridicule the notion as a scandalous and ludicrous encroachment on the citizen's right to define hospitality the way he or she wants. But the right of citizens to receive their relatives as they see fit does not extend to immigrants. In order to guarantee a hypocritical definition of decent hospitality, the state denies immigrants the right to conceptualize not only "normal" hospitality, but also generous hospitality: I may choose to extend an invitation even at a moment when I am aware that the presence of "too many" relatives will considerably reduce the space enjoyed by each of the members of the household. Naturally, it is assumed that hospitality granted by the upper-middle-class minister can never contaminate the nation and hospitality itself with squalor (or filth or noise or smell to list the stereotypical accusations made against immigrant neighbors). Even if a minister decides to invite more of his relatives than he can really accommodate (say, more relatives than the number of beds in the house), it would probably be interpreted as an even more heroic form of hospitality. Bourgeois standards would suddenly appear less of a golden rule, it would be a cute and youthful regression to the good old times when "we" were all younger and more adventurous. Or perhaps it is the case that the minister finds it completely unthinkable to take into his house people who could not sleep in their own bed (have their own room, their own bathroom, their own house, their own nation), and in that case, we still have a right to ask whether we want to share this definition of what it means to extend hospitality.

Chevènement's remark also indicates that the principle of the *certificat d'hébergement* rests on the assumption that "your relatives" does not mean the same thing for the audience he was addressing (the representatives in the Assembly) and for all French people. If he transgresses implicit bourgeois codes of decency and comfort, the gesture is almost a form of refinement that transcends the norm ("let's pretend that we are all camping, that we are above such material considerations"), but if an immigrant tries to do the same thing, it is immediately assumed that he or she is secretly plotting to impose his or her own barbaric norms and that hospitality is degraded, parodied, sullied.[10] When Jacqueline Deltombe was arrested, the principle of the *certificat d'hébergement* suddenly appeared as an intolerable imposition, symbolizing national inhospitality and the inauguration of a punishable crime of hospitality. Even if Deltombe's case was not directly related to the issue of the *certificat d'hébergement*, her tragedy was read as an example of what everyone could expect if the infamous "lois Debré" went unchallenged.[11]

In *Adieu to Emmanuel Levinas*, Derrida forcefully rejects the very concept of a *délit d'hospitalité* and talks, instead, about "crimes against hospitality": "Yes, crimes *against* hospitality, to be distinguished from the 'crime of hospitality,' as today it is once again called in French law, in the spirit of the decrees and the ordinances of 1938 and 1945 that would punish—and even imprison—anyone taking in a foreigner in an illegal situation" (1999a, 71, translation slightly modified).[12]

Even before the publication of Derrida's book, on February 11, fifty-nine outraged film directors went public, urging the French people "to disobey rather than to abide by inhumane laws." Whereas "associations had tried in vain, for months, to alert a passive public opinion to the dangers of Debré's bill" (Viledier 1997, 17), the directors' intervention immediately captured the nation's attention. They may have succeeded because their appeal belongs in a firmly established tradition of manifestos by French intellectuals in moments of crisis and was immediately identified as a legitimate call to action, even if political leaders tried to dismiss it as a meaningless outburst on the part of emotional and irresponsible intellectuals. The directors' rhetoric was powerful enough to move the debate away from a fossilized definition of the "law" by implicitly aligning them with the memory of Emile Zola's "J'accuse" during the Dreyfus affair and with "Le manifeste des 121" during the Algerian war of independence, and by referring to Henry David Thoreau's 1849 essay on civil disobedience. They succeeded in establishing a new ethical pole that proposed a well-formulated alternative to the state definition of hospitality:

> We, French directors declare: We are guilty, everyone of us, of having recently put up illegal immigrants. We have not denounced our foreign friends. And we shall continue to welcome, not to denounce, to befriend and work with our colleagues and friends without asking for their identification papers. After the judgment passed on Madame Jacqueline Deltombe on February 4, 1997, where she was found "guilty" ["*coupable*"] of having allowed an undocumented friend from Zaire to stay at her place, and according to the principle that the law must be the same for all, we demand to be indicted and judged too. Finally, we urge our fellow countrymen to disobey rather than to abide by inhumane laws.[13]

By generalizing guilt ("we are all guilty") and putting quotation marks around the word *coupable*, the authors of the manifesto expose "guilt" as a construction and present it as a desirable alternative to informing. Their vocabulary forces us to choose between "guilty hospitality" and the unglamorous role of the police informer. Hospitality is now on the side of "humanity," even if it must also be on the side of disobedience. The hiatus between politics and ethics has become a gaping chasm. The public is not asked to help bridge the gap but to take sides.

The invitation to accept that hospitality and "guilt" can be on the same side also proposes a very specific agenda. An ethical model is offered, a model that treats guilty hospitality as the response to an unacceptable definition of what it is to be a national, a legitimate host, the owner of the house. By implying that the host is guilty in the eyes of the state, the manifesto invents the figure of an illegitimate, illegal host, corresponding to that of the illegal immigrant, the illegal guest. Paradoxically, the situation recreates a balance between the owner and the person who shares the privilege of ownership. The manifesto points out that there are very strict limits to the power granted to the person who owns or legitimately occupies the house. Owning is not synonymous with the freedom to share, to use the premises as one would like to. This suddenly revealed fragility or vulnerability of the legitimate occupant of the land destabilizes the concept of host by depriving that position of much of the power that it normally has. The stereotypical host may be imagined as a rich bourgeois who condescendingly flaunts his wealth, whose willingness to welcome a poor relation becomes a specific form of almsgiving.

For that logic, the illegal host substitutes a will to question his or her own legitimacy, to view it as a contingent privilege owing to an accident of birth, the historical context of changing laws. René Schérer notes that hospitality varies according to how dwelling is defined. He distinguishes between the legendary hospitality of nomads, peasants, and the recent urban variations of the model. By choice or by necessity, some urban communities do not settle down and accept a semiclandestine, fluid relationship to the place they live, often temporarily. René Schérer calls this the "Come stay with me, I am staying at a friend's house" ("Viens chez moi j'habite chez une copine" [Schérer 1993, 34]) syndrome. The allusion to one of Patrice Leconte's films contextualizes the model and defines it as a playfully dissident tactic. Inviting someone else without consulting the friend whose apartment you are borrowing may be seen as an indelicate gesture, a casual appropriation of what is not yours to offer. Like the parasite who makes himself or herself too much at home and empties out your fridge, the guest who thinks of himself as the host seems to abuse the power that you have given him or her. On the other hand, he or she demonstrates the relativity and arbitrariness of your right to share magnanimously the house, the housing estate, the neighborhood, the nation. By pointing out that they were willing to be called guilty of illegal hospitality, the fifty-nine directors were pointing in the same direction.

The artists succeeded, perhaps beyond their wildest hopes, in mobilizing French public opinion, eventually forcing the government to amend its law. As *Le Monde diplomatique* put it, their public intervention caused "an insurrection in people's consciences."[14] Relayed by interactive technology (the Worldwide Web and faxes), the manifesto soon took the form of an endless list of signatures, a "tidal wave of petitions," as the new magazine *Saga* called it,[15] page after page of names published daily in *Libération*. The call to disobey had become a petition signed by thousands of celebrities and anonymous citizens alike.

It is, however, to be noted, that what the film directors defended with passion was a very elitist definition of hospitality: their insistence that, as artists, they had to work with foreigners almost made it sound as though they did not want to be inconvenienced by petty administrative details because they were important people. The allusion to foreign directors ("colleagues and friends") was a much-needed reminder that all foreigners are not poor and helpless, and that an "illegal immigrant" is sometimes a celebrity who has failed to get his or her visa renewed. But because this category of foreigner is still (realistically) perceived as an exception to the rule, the directors' attempt to bring the problem home almost invited a theory of the exception.

This double-edged representation of the immigrant as a desirable, sophisticated, and educated other found its way into Patrick Weil's report, *Mission d'étude des législations de la nationalité et l'immigration* (Weil 1997), the document that would pave the way for Chevènement's bill, a series of texts designed to amend the Pasqua and Debré laws. The recognition that France needs to attract educated foreigners implicitly creates yet a new split on the margin of illegality: an official construction of the difference between a desirable illegal immigrant and an undesirable illegal immigrant.

Chemillier-Gendreau reads this development as the continuation of a form of selection disguised as international "cooperation":

> This cooperation/selection requires that we negotiate with states of emigration to attract "good" immigrants, those who have skills useful to our economies. Some go as far as to theorize the principle, imagining a system of quotas per country and per category of skills. Obviously, this is no longer cooperation, but rather the continuation of a process of domination. The

Chevènement bill tacks within that logic [*louvoie à l'intérieur de cette logique*]. Without fixing the number of foreigners of one type or other whose entry and residence is authorized, the bill offers intellectuals, researchers, and students an opening that is persistently denied others and does not hesitate to justify doing so in the name of French national interests. (Chemillier-Gendreau 1998, 221)

The other ironic aspect of this elitist conception of hospitality is that it is politically self-defeating. A government may well be willing to welcome students and scholars out of a misguided belief that their faithfulness and loyalty to the system can be bought through education. The principle reveals a strange blindness to history. Students from colonized countries always quickly grasped the mixed messages and contradictory lessons that the motherland wanted to teach them. Like any group, they were not homogeneous and some opted for dissident readings. As Mahamet Timera puts it in his analysis of African immigration in France, the migratory project follows four major paths, and "education, the oldest and most consistent project, [has fed] independentist or assimilationist political and cultural movements since the end of World War I."[16]

I do not want to overestimate the role that intellectuals played in the struggle for decolonization, but I cannot help thinking that the generation of Aimé Césaire, Léopold Senghor, and Frantz Fanon, who had access to Western culture, used their knowledge in ways that had not been foreseen and certainly would not have been approved by conservative thinkers. Similarly, today, the protectionist point of view according to which students and intellectuals are less likely to challenge France's identity than less educated immigrants is probably an illusion. In other words, if students' access to the country is facilitated only because a conservative logic assumes that they are more civilized, less exotic, more likely to assimilate, then not only is the argument particularly cynical, but it is also misguided.

It is also to be noted that once the movement of protest started by celebrities had exhausted itself, some of the energy of their generous indignation lived on in the form of amended texts and perhaps a certain hesitation to assume systematically that xenophobic measures would win governmental approval. But one of the (predictable) ironies of this powerful chain of solidarity is that it forgot about the original victim. In the background, while the manifesto monopolized the media's attention, the legal system continued to operate according to its own logic, confirming the law's right to brand Deltombe a criminal. The appeal court ruled that: "Mme Deltombe was perfectly aware that Tony M'Bongo was an illegal immigrant. . . . She knowingly and deliberately did what was in her power to protect him against controls, assuring him of regular shelter in her home" (Bernard and Herzberg 1997a).

The original verdict was confirmed. I wonder how strong Jacqueline Deltombe would have to be in order not to experience a certain degree of bitterness and resentment. Perhaps inhumanely strong.

CHAPTER TWO

Deportation and Generosity: Hostile Hospitality in Didier van Cauwelaert's *Un aller simple*

How do European governments conceptualize what they call "hospitality" when they draft immigration laws and when they allow the concepts of asylum, of illegal immigrants, to change according to a constantly evolving political context? What consequences does the official discourse on immigration have for the private practices of individuals who live within states, or within local communities defined by their regional, cultural, or ethnic identities? At historical junctions, when frontiers and nations are redefined, do the "laws" of hospitality change? And will the slow creation of what some critics have called a new "fortress" Europe (see, e.g., McClintock 1995, 13) lead to radical definitions of the very concept of hospitality in communities that states have long marginalized and pushed to the periphery of their own national criteria of identity? In this chapter, I propose to examine those questions from two different perspectives: in a first part, I concentrate on the historical context that anchors my reflection in the present situation and ask what theoretical issues are raised by the need to define different types of

European political, ethical, and commercial hospitality. In a second part, I look at the contradictions generated by the impossibility of choosing any one single definition of hospitality. Such frictions are beginning to be inscribed in literary texts and testimonies, especially in one recent novel that reconsiders the definitions of the guest, of the host, of invitations, of parasites, and of hostages: Didier van Cauwelaert's 1994 Goncourt prize–winning novel *Un aller simple* (One-Way Ticket).

Frontiers on the European continent have been drastically altered in the past ten years. This is due partly to the collapse of the Berlin Wall, to wars (in the former Yugoslavia, for example), and, more peacefully, to the implementation of treaties signed by the members of the European Community (Wihtol de Wenden 1999a; Crépeau 1995). Three successive treaties marked the 1990s as a decade devoted to the redefinition of frontiers and characterized by an international obsession with immigration. While far-right parties ride the hobbyhorse of immigration and xenophobia in the hope of recruiting disillusioned voters, committees and task forces, associations, and ministers have continued to redefine citizenship, sovereignty, the foreigner, and what it means to migrate. In a simultaneous gesture of opening and closing, Europe is currently stressing the concept of "freedom of movement" within its redefined borders, which means increasing controls on the outskirts of its new symbolic territory, in a general atmosphere of mistrust and suspicion that treats all non-Europeans (especially African, Middle Eastern, and Asian outsiders) as potentially undesirable parasites.

The three treaties in question are the 1992 Maastricht treaty, the Schengen agreements, and, finally, the 1997 Amsterdam treaty that encompasses the previous ones. The Maastricht treaty, which emphasizes the economic identity of the new European market, created a supranational territory designed to improve the circulation of goods rather than of people, which means that the issue of hospitality was deemphasized. Yet some of the "titles" clearly signaled the intention to move from the European Economic Community to the European Union, from EC to EU. Titles V and VI made it clear that the free circulation of goods was only a first stage, and that the member states planned to institute common foreign and security policies (which includes harmonizing laws on immigration, although the issue remains invisible in title V).[1]

The Schengen agreements went further and marked the limits of a new zone of cooperation within which freedom of movement was guaranteed to individuals, provided that they were able to cross the reinforced frontiers of the Schengen community. Signed in 1985 but implemented only five years after the 1990 convention regarding the application of common policies, the Schengen agreements contributed to the creation of fortress Europe, whose philosophical (and therefore political and practical) goal was increased freedom within the Schengen bloc and reinforced control on the supranational border line. Cooperation between EU states takes the form of international systems of identification and data collection that leave many non-Europeans and Europeans alike worried and suspicious of the new computerized Big Brother, the so-called S.I.S., or "Système d'information Schengen."[2]

Ratified on June 17, 1997, the Amsterdam treaty is a rewriting of the European constitution. Regarding migration policies, the following is stipulated:

1. Open frontiers for people in the European Union:

   Identity checks at the internal frontiers of the European Union will be abolished over the next five years, except at the borders of Ireland and the United Kingdom. Controls at external frontiers, ports and airports will of course be maintained and will be implemented with equal vigour throughout the European Union.

2. A European policy on visas, asylum and immigration:

   Over the next five years, the member states of the European Union will harmonise their rules on issuing visas and granting asylum to people from outside the European Union. This also applies to the rules on immigration. For instance, minimum European norms will apply to the reception of asylum-seekers, and every member state must provide at least adequate food and accommodation.[3]

The 1992 Maastricht treaty, the implementation of the Schengen agreements in 1995, and the 1997 Amsterdam treaty are forcing Europe to reinvent or adapt the notion of hospitality in a way that both draws on, and departs from, a cultural norm that is only vaguely present in Europeans' minds but exists nonetheless (a tradition of hospitality that eclectically combines Greek, Roman, and Judeo-Christian references).[4]

One factor further complicates the relationship between hospitality and immigration, and I would like to keep it in mind before turning to Cauwe-laert's *Un aller simple*: in many cultures, the definition of hospitality seems to be closely linked to the definition of transaction, exchange, and gift, and to the ways in which one can distinguish between gifts and economic ex-change. This is why it is almost impossible to talk about hospitality without mentioning generosity and economy. The dominant patterns of exchange between individuals will represent the horizon of the debate on hospitality. Hospitality is always caught between two ideals: on the one hand, we can imagine it as an infinite, unconditional, selfless, and endless gift (of your time, of your space, of your resources), or, on the other hand, it can be con-ceptualized as a well-balanced exchange of mutual services. So the way in which a group defines what is owed to each individual and what belongs to the category of excess conditions is how hospitality is conceived. A direct consequence of this is that private and state hospitality are also to be com-pared with professional hospitality: the model of the hotel, of the hospital, and all similar institutions that provide hospitality as a service also represent poles of attraction or of repulsion that have to be kept in mind when meta-phors are used to describe the situation of immigrants.

Un aller simple received the Goncourt prize in 1994, right after the birth of the 1993 Pasqua and Méhaignerie laws, two sets of new policies that re-stricted access to French nationality for children of immigrants and gener-ally enforced more and more restrictive policies, whose objectives were to convince the public that the government's goal was "zero (illegal) immigra-tion" (the qualifier "illegal" was sometimes dropped during Pasqua's public speeches) (Naïr 1997). Cauwelaert is a French writer based in Nice. Written in the witty and humorous tradition of Emile Ajar's *La vie devant soi*, *Un aller simple* tells the tragic story of Aziz, a young man deported to Morocco by the French police, who think that he is an illegal immigrant. The French government also assigns a "humanitarian attaché," Jean-Pierre Schneider, to accompany Aziz back to his village of origin in Morocco to help him "rein-sert" himself. This unlikely pair are on a collision course with absurdity, be-cause the village in question does not even exist. The name was invented by the person who forged Aziz's passport. Aziz was born in France, quite possi-bly to French parents, but he cannot prove it because he has spent his youth and adolescence among Gypsies, who adopted him after his parents died in a car accident: "The car was an Ami 6, of the Citroën race, so they called me Ami 6 in memento. Those are my origins, if you will."[5]

This novel addresses the direct consequences of immigration policies on a character who is not an immigrant but who is not technically a national either,[6] a character who could be any one of us, because no one knows who he really is, because he symbolizes the principle of substitution, of interchangeability. As Derrida would say, that is the principle of the hostage: "The hostage is first of all someone whose unicity endures the possibility of a *sub*stitution" (1999a, 55).

Emphasizing the possibility of substitution is one powerful way of questioning the legitimacy of identities and nationalities, and in *Un aller simple* the author carries the idea to interesting extremes. Jean-Pierre, the official representative of the French government, has left his family, never to return. He dies in Morocco, and when Aziz decides to bring the body back to Jean-Pierre's parents, a rather surrealistic coincidence occurs. First, Aziz rents a van that happens to be of the same "race," as he puts it, as the vehicle of his origins: like the car in which his parents died, it is a Citroën. Besides, for reasons that I don't really want to talk about, in order not to spoil the story, Aziz never gets around to telling Jean-Pierre's parents the truth. He cannot reveal that their son is dead. So, just as Jean-Pierre was taking Aziz back to an imaginary village, Aziz invents a story to substitute for Jean-Pierre's actual fate. He pretends that he is being held hostage (another role of interchangeability) by ferocious Moroccan terrorists. And as if that story had acquired a life of its own, when Aziz leaves the parents' house, wondering what he is now going to do with Jean-Pierre's body, he realizes that the Citroën has disappeared. It is as if the vanishing of the second Citroën ultimately closes a strange circle of hospitality. Jean-Pierre, who insisted on giving Aziz his real country, who wanted to use his own voice to tell Aziz's story, is eventually enabled to speak about Aziz/himself through Aziz, who now undertakes to finish the novel that Jean-Pierre was trying to write: "Jean-Pierre wanted to write a novel where he would say 'I' with my voice. In the end, I think this novel is being written. I even have a hunch that the author feels more and more at home in my body" (118).

The policemen who deport Aziz need the media and the government to believe that "justice" has been done, that order has been restored, that the illegal immigrant has been returned to his country of origin, but that story, in its simplicity, in its purity, cannot be told. Not only because Aziz is the essence of irregularity but because the novel insists that irregularity, homelessness, rootlessness are, if not interchangeable, at least shared by the would-be immigrant and the most documented of all characters, that is, the official representative of the French government on a mission to enforce its immigration laws. The tone and irony of the demonstration serve, not to minimize Aziz's scandalous victimization, but to discredit any attempt to justify the *attaché humanitaire*'s sense of legitimacy.

A crucial aspect of the novel, from which all the other features can be derived, is that Aziz has spent his childhood among Gypsies, an archetypally diasporic people. And Aziz is like his community of adoption in that he is both potentially always homeless and perfectly well integrated. This story is that of a guest among guests. Complex relationships of hospitality develop between Aziz and the Gypsies, and they are mirrored by relationships between Aziz and Marseilles, or France, and between the Gypsies and the French. The novel shows how homelessness can always be combined with, rather than opposed to, belonging. *Un aller simple* shows to what extent outsiders are also insiders, to what extent homeless individuals can also be hosts. And when I say "to what extent," I should really say "according to which different rules and conventions" this may happen.

For this novel is obviously not a study of Gypsies, and if the reader is looking for a reliable ethnographic document, he or she is bound to be disappointed. *Un aller simple* is nothing like Isabel Fonseca's *Bury Me Standing*, for example, or recent French films on Gypsy communities such as Tony Gatlif's trilogy.[7] Nor does the author seek to usurp the role of the native informant, as some postcolonial subjects tend to do (Spivak 1999). What Cauwelaert's novel does achieve, however, is an exploration of the constantly interlocking identities of communities perceived as "ethnic" by the dominant French constructions of Frenchness. Even if Aziz is a fictive Moroccan, even if the Gypsies, here, are also a fiction, and even if the French are also exposed as stereotyped by their own narratives, each group interacts with the others, as a minority or a majority, depending on the context.[8]

As we have seen, the traditional vision is that only the owner of the land has the power to grant hospitality. That element of (often illusory) power carries the risk of allowing perverse forms of hospitality to develop, as where a host flaunts his bourgeois wealth to his poor relations or a king levies exorbitant taxes partly to organize ritual "largesse" in which he literally throws gold coins out of the window (Starobinski 1997). In Cauwelaert's *Un aller simple*, the Gypsies do not grant hospitality because they are in power or because they can afford to raise another child. They even lie to Aziz, pretending that he was found on the back seat of a stolen car. In an ironic manipulation of the old cliché that Gypsies steal children from Christians, the novel explains that Aziz is "a foundling by mistake" ("un enfant trouvé par erreur" [5]).

What is particularly unexpected and also humorous in this novel is that there is no attempt at idealizing the Gypsy community that plays the role of host when the unnamed child loses his parents. No exoticism turns the Gypsies into a better model of solidarity that survives in spite of pressures to assimilate into a Western culture that has forgotten ancient laws. What *Un aller simple* describes is hostile hospitality, a strange mixture of the contradictory etymological roots of the word "host" (*hospes* and *hostis*, "host" and "enemy," hostility and hospitality, belong to the same family). In *Un aller simple*, the Gypsies' hospitality is a form of acceptance that is never unconditional, that is always likely to be denied. In other words, the type of hospitality granted to Aziz by the Gypsy community is far from ideal.

First of all, the gesture of welcoming is not unanimous, to say the least. There is disagreement within the community, the majority of which don't want to take care of the child that the "old Vasile" brings back to the neighborhood after the car crash. Only Vasile wants to adopt the baby. "There were no identification papers in the glove compartment, so [Vasile] thought that I was a sign from heaven. Nobody contradicted him because he was already very ancient at the time, and according to our customs, it's the senile old farts who are wise" (6), the narrator explains.

I am not sure that the old man is supposed to be read as a typical Gypsy. Cauwelaert's novel is marked by facetiousness, and I doubt that we should interpret this as a critique of real Gypsies. Yet old Vasile does represent one model, one tradition that could be European, if Europe were not reneging on that ideal. Vasile's definition of hospitality goes back to ancient Greece, where the foreigner was supposed to be treated as if he had been sent by the gods. Vasile wants to respect a law that has obviously fallen into disuse but that his presence can keep alive for a few more years. This is the type of hospitality that Homer's *Odyssey* talks about, a law that demands that you receive strangers without even asking who they are, regardless of whether they are deserving or not, poor or not. There is an element of constraint in this obligation (the fear, for example, of offending a god), but this definition of hospitality makes it an infinite gift; it is not measured or justified by economic or political interest. Plato "puts hospitality at the head of the list of duties prescribed to citizens. It is a sacred duty that cannot be infringed upon under penalty of incurring the wrath of the gods," René Schérer says (1993, 11).

Vasile's beliefs, however, are not shared by his community. If the Gypsies respect his desires, it is out of a mandatory deference to his status as an elder. Their compliance with his demands is almost disrespectful. Isn't it rude to be polite out of politeness?[9] It is clear that their willingness to obey Vasile is mixed with contempt. Here Vasile is treated both as a senile old man whose opinions are not valued and as the representative of a class to which tradition grants power.

The contradiction between several sets of values is not resolved: the novel does not condone the systematic alliance between age and power (even Aziz knows that his protector is *gâteux* [senile], as he puts it), but it does not present the old man's definition of hospitality as old-fashioned and no longer valid.

The community as a whole only grudgingly accepts Vasile's law of hospitality but does not believe in it, does not understand it. Yet an omniscient voice, almost behind the narrator's back, suggests that the old man knows exactly what he is doing even though his beliefs have become incomprehensible to his people. He views the child as a heavenly messenger, as a Christlike figure whose lack of conventional origins is the very reason why he should be treated as a divine guest. When Aziz learns the truth about how he was accepted by the Gypsies, he visits the old man to thank him. But neither this I-narrator nor the community seem capable of understanding the theological terminology with which Vasile responds to Aziz's thanks: "Begotten not created, of one substance with the Father, by whom all things were made" ("Engendré non pas créé, de même nature que le Père, et par Lui tout a été fait" [11]).[10] The voice that defends hospitality is both on the side of senility and on the side of wisdom.

Later, when Aziz must seek the clan's approval to marry Lila, Vasile's status and senility are mentioned again to explain the results of the vote: "There was a vote in the elders' caravan. I won by two ballots, both cast by old Vasile, who does not remember his name but has the right to vote twice because of his age" (32).

This type of election could be seen as a parody of democracy, in the sense that Aziz does not have the support of the group. The result of this vote, which supposedly agrees to an intercommunity marriage, to cultural hybridity, underlines the fact that Aziz owes his precarious position to one individual and not to the collective will of the people. Here, hospitality depends on one person's vote, a situation that the novel describes in all its ambiguity, preserving the contradiction between the cause and the consequence: the cause is Vasile's apparently irresponsible vote, the result is the granting of the ultimate form of hospitality (the right to mix blood lines) by a reluctant group. This is not a happy moment of consensus but a moment when a community grudgingly obeys a law of hospitality that it no longer believes in. I wonder if Cauwelaert is suggesting that it is still possible for a group to grant hospitality even if that choice is not the most popular option, even if the community as a whole does not seem to believe in hospitality. Needless to say, the parallel has interesting consequences in a country where right-wing and left-wing governments turn the so-called "immigration problem" into an electoral platform. Here, hospitality is not a gift, it does not mean acceptance, and it is not the same thing as love. It coexists with exclusion and it can be betrayed.

As I suggested in the introduction, women are often a barometer of hospitality, because groups do not let them act as agents capable of granting or denying hospitality. In other words, they sometimes constitute part of the exchange of favors that the guest and the host negotiate as gifts, signs, and symbols. The idea that women are exchanged seems primitive and old-fashioned, and we would, I suppose, be quite happy to imagine that such sexist practices only occur in countries that we continue to think of as underdeveloped and undercivilized, including when such countries supply immigrants who become, for the West, the stranger within. In the case of Cauwelaert's novel, the first part, which takes place within the Gypsy community, may deceive the reader into a narrowly ethnic condemnation of the way it treats women. What happens to Aziz and to Lila might well be interpreted from a traditionally Eurocentric and pseudoanthropological point of view.

Aziz and Lila have fallen in love, but both characters seem convinced, from day one, that they will never be able to marry, because a Gypsy woman must marry a Gypsy man. Even after Lila's official fiancé is killed by a security guard, Aziz is still not accepted as a potential suitor, and without ever spelling it out, the omniscient voice makes it clear that the clan is responsible for Aziz's arrest in the middle of the wedding ceremony and his subsequent deportation.

It is fair to say that Aziz is not an anti-sexist hero in this story: he is not excluded from the group because of his willingness to fight for women in general, or even for Lila in particular. As for Lila, she is so resigned to her fate that she cannot even imagine a different scenario. Aziz is not a dissident force in this instance; he is not trying to break any rule, to go against tradition. Some readers may find it implausible that he does not fight against or even protest sexual taboos, or that he readily agrees to "buy" his woman from her brothers for "a dozen Pioneer CD players and forty Bose speakers" (32). The specific brand names and the choice of the objects that will constitute the woman's price give a new twist to this supposedly timeless fashion of exchanging females for goods and reminds the reader that these Gypsies are also postindustrial capitalists. Aziz abides by the laws not because he accepts their logic but because they are laws. He says: "Sometimes, the Gypsies are weird: they would rather a woman spent all her life alone, in dishonor, bringing them shame, than sell her at discount to a *gadjo* who will erase the stain by taking her far away" (32).

So it is not because he represents ideological dissidence that he is suddenly excluded and expelled, that hospitality is suddenly denied in the cruelest way. He has not betrayed his hosts' trust. But his foreignness sets limits to how much he can ever hope to belong. At the very moment when a man and a woman are acting as subjects who want to personally redefine the laws of belonging, the group intervenes, using the woman as pawn in a game where men impose community practices of hospitality. In this case, the Gypsy community even goes further, in that it appeals to the larger inhospitable group (the French) to do the dirty job. One law of inhospitality is used to enforce another law of inhospitality. Individual subjects are not free to rewrite the agreements.

The structure of this betrayal is fascinating in itself. It reminds us that the opposition between minority and majority is not enough to predict structures of alliances and solidarity. We know that in France, during the period when immigrants were relegated to overcrowded shantytowns, even hospitality among immigrants sometimes meant ruthless exploitation (Rosello 1997). Here Cauwelaert cautions the reader against the idealization of minority practices. And the fact that Cauwelaert first places this Russian doll model within the Gypsy community is an interesting narrative setup: readers tempted by an exoticized reading that concludes from the passage that this is a Gypsy problem are in for a surprise, because in the second part of the novel, when Jean-Pierre, the humanitarian attaché, starts telling his story to Aziz, we realize that the same abuse of power has taken place within the French administration: in Jean-Pierre's case, a man (his direct supervisor) who wants to sleep with Jean-Pierre's wife, Clémentine, has shamelessly used his authority and the official discourse of immigration and cooperation to get rid of him. On the one hand, Jean-Pierre parrots the government's official party line. Just like Aziz, who was willing to buy Lila and to provide the agreed number of stolen car radios, Jean-Pierre does not even try to rebel against the immigration politics adopted by his community. He knows the mantra of inhospitality by heart:

> the government has inaugurated a procedure that is not only inscribed in a discourse of dignity but also seeks to be effective at the level of results, for the ultimate goal is not to make you leave a country that asked you to come when you were needed, but to show you, with the necessary help, that now, *your* country needs you, because the only way of stopping migrating flows from the Maghreb is to build a future *in your country*, through a politics of incentives to development both at the industrial level and at the level of human resources and . . . (52–53)

At this point in his tirade, Jean-Pierre stops abruptly. The interruption (Aziz says he "breaks down") is motivated by the fact that he was going to admit that a recent TV show called "Marseille, ville arabe" is the real motivation for the operation launched in Marseilles. Naturally, his rehearsed discourse is completely irrelevant, because neither Aziz nor his ancestors are part of this "you" that "we" needed. Yet it is interesting to note that the official hypocritical recognition of a debt is used to skirt better the issue of reparation. Not only is the discourse of reverse hospitality (we are making you feel at home in your own country) tainted with sordid media manipulations, but the novel also exposes the sheer irrelevance of this collective dogma at the level of individuals.

This paragraph is a wonderful parody of what the French call *langue de bois* (bureaucratic cant), but Cauwelaert's critique of devious hypocrisy goes even further: here, he insists that it is perfectly plausible to allow this official discourse on state inhospitality to coexist with a more private narrative of inhospitality and betrayal that involves different actors. In this case, one individual's agenda drives the implementation of the larger project, corrupting and undermining its most basic foundations. Jean-Pierre confesses to Aziz that his position as *attaché humanitaire* is the result of a personal/professional dispute with his supervisor, Jean-Pierre's wife's lover: "He's her lover, Loupiac. The assistant media director at the ministry. He sent me on a mission to get rid of me" (74).

Paradoxically, Jean-Pierre's situation is quite comparable to Aziz's: both men are kicked out of the community by rivals who covet their lovers. To be fair, Jean-Pierre left of his own will: "I was quite clear about it: as soon as she told me she had someone else, I left! I took a suitcase, my word processor, and I checked into a hotel" (74). And when he asks Aziz if he should have rebelled or resigned himself, nothing suggests that he appreciates the irony of his companion's answer. Aziz is obviously speaking as much for himself as for Jean-Pierre when he says: "I answered that life did not always give you enough time to react, and one had one's pride" (74).

One of the most vexing and invisible problems raised by immigration laws is the existence of an unacknowledged level of human interpretation between the legislation and the administrator who applies it and makes judgment calls. If the philosophy of the law is supposed to be self-evident, it is clear that its implementation is always mediated by culture, that is, today, by a generalized atmosphere of suspicion and xenophobia. Cauwelaert's novel goes even further. It suggests that policies are also betrayed by private agendas that uncannily reveal the self-serving and egotistical logic that generated the law. Jean-Pierre and Aziz are both victims of forms of institutional sexism, which they are paradoxically willing to accept.

Conclusion

Un aller simple suggests that state or community inhospitality is sometimes used as a pretext for perpetuating certain unwritten laws. By crossing the issue of hospitality with questions of nationality and ethnicity, by introducing a minority group and a minority character whom it casts as a stranger among strangers, *Un aller simple* reflects on the current struggle for recognition in Europe by both supra- and subnational identities. The description of unexpected forms of hospitality (and hostile hospitality, especially, cannot be confused with acceptance, love, and affection) redraws certain boundaries and forces us to rethink the intersection between hospitality and generosity, hospitality and self-interest. Sometimes, hospitality is a dissident option, the choice of one individual, who may not be able to impose his or her convictions for very long but can still make a difference. Again, that suggestion is most relevant in contemporary France, where the media have publicized a series of cases revolving around the issues of sanctuary and the possible sanctions incurred by individuals who harbor undocumented immigrants.

Finally, *Un aller simple* offers a glimmer of hope on a realistically overcast horizon. The novel knows that all identities primarily consist of narratives, but it does not stop at this potentially apolitical postmodern frontier. For example, the fact that Aziz is "Moroccan" on his documents is not explained away simply in terms of "reality" versus "narrative." Aziz knows that he had a choice between several narratives, and that the decision to become "Moroccan" was both contingent and overdetermined: contingent because no one knows where Aziz was really born or who his parents are (and the likelihood of him being Moroccan is slim), but also overdetermined because there was a reason why he did not get a fake French passport: it would have been more expensive than a fake Moroccan passport. This economic consideration underscores the fact that there is also a hospitality of money or cultural capital, and that some narratives are more equal than others. Each human being has a right to a nationality, but it is clear that some nationalities are more desirable than others, and that global citizenship does not exist. Aziz's passport is the emblem of the contradictory mixture of contingency and overdetermination that presides over the state's philosophy on jus soli, immigration and naturalization.

The novel thus moves away from the more conventional discourse of hybridity that insists, for example, that each subject's legitimacy as a national is relativized by the arbitrariness of narratives of citizenship. Granted, at a certain level, we are all hybrids. Yet that realization alone (and many critics have pointed it out) does not solve the problem of disempowerment and disenfranchisement (Ha 1995; Kortenaar 1995). Cauwelaert turns the tables on hybridity: the point is not so much that we are all strangers; in fact, it is almost the opposite. Aziz discovers that anyone can be a host, but that being the host always involves some kind of appropriation of a territory, or perhaps of a body. He discovers that he is both from nowhere, from an imaginary Moroccan village, and very much from Marseilles, and also that he can literally become Jean-Pierre, a Lorrain ostracized by his family. This is not celebrated as a solution; it is inscribed as the cause of tremendous confusion and anxiety. For example, when he discovers that he is about to be deported to a village that does not exist Aziz says: "I'm sorry. I don't mind being exemplary, but I lived all my life in France as a foreigner, and I am not about to start over as a foreigner in a country where I would be the only one to know that I am not at home" (41–42). Yet, at times, this very possibility of being inside without owning or outside without being excluded is also a source of pleasure. It is the infinite hospitality of knowledge. At school, Aziz discovers that he can cherish countries and nations to which he does not belong: "The greatest reward for me was to learn about the geography and the climate of a country, not because it is where you come from but simply because it exists" (15).

CHAPTER THREE

Host(esse)s Granting and Refusing Hospitality
Across National and Ethnic Lines

At the beginning of Karim Dridi's film *Bye-bye*, two Algerian brothers, a young adult and a teenager, reach Marseilles after driving all night. They are expected by a family, whose members are soon revealed to be their cousins, uncle, aunt, and grandmother. For reasons that are not quite clear at first, it becomes obvious that they are going to stay a while, and when Ismaël, the elder brother, promises not to bother them for too long, his uncle, sounding very offended, repeats several times and very loudly that his house is their house and that they can stay as long as they want, adding that he is the one who makes the decisions. Whether or not his indignation is a genuine reaction of surprise at the apparently Westernized Ismaël's fear of over-staying his welcome, or whether the tone is part of a ritualized exaggeration of goodwill is hard to determine, but what I find striking in this scene is that the film lets us compare and confront different constructions, different definitions of hospitality, showing that the conventions accepted as normal by each character are not necessarily shared by others. A generation of Arab

63

immigrants, their children, and the so-called host nation have to come to terms with at times profoundly different and incompatible expectations about how to share space or how to conceptualize hospitality.[1]

As is the case in countless narratives of hospitality, here, the man of the household is the one who grants the right to stay to his guests, and he bases his generosity on the certainty that no one will question his authority in his house. The two guests, as well as the rest of the family, are supposed to acquiesce and to recognize his power to act as host and to extend his hospitality to the two Parisian relatives. He briefly announces what kind of restructuring his decision entails: his son will give his room to the guests and sleep in the living room. Part of the father's prerogative is thus to displace the practical burden of hospitality onto a less powerful member of the family: his child, not he, will have to give up some of his space to accommodate the new housemates. His male authority is challenged by the son, however, who strongly objects to the request and starts arguing, in spite of the father's growing anger at his rebellious attitude. The discussion threatens to degenerate into a full-blown quarrel until the mother intervenes. Only after she impresses upon the reluctant host that their cousins are only going to stay two weeks (a limit that she unilaterally introduces into the equation) does he grudgingly agree to obey the laws of hospitality, which, she says, cannot be transgressed without bringing shame to the family.

What is most interesting about the mother's intervention is that she both appeals to a law of hospitality that is ethnically encoded (and therefore presumably shared by the whole family) and completely modifies the original contract proposed by the father (who was apparently enforcing the very same law): originally, the master of the house officially and formally grants an indefinite right to the two cousins: they can stay as long as they want, he insists. And the authority that is capable of guaranteeing that privilege is his own supposedly unquestioned status as head of the family. But as the passage makes clear, neither his power nor the family's hospitality is really infinite, and the mother's negotiation seems to indicate that other imperfect yet more consensually reached agreements are also acceptable, and perhaps more in keeping with contemporary situations. Her son finally agrees to sleep in the living room, although he clearly resents the two cousins' intrusion, and it is more or less tacitly agreed that the reason why this is tolerable is that he can look forward to the two guests' departure in the not-so-distant future. As for the father, he is profoundly displeased by the mother's success and vociferously objects to what he (rightly) perceives as a refusal to follow his orders unconditionally. Instead of being satisfied that his plan will be implemented, he angrily asks the son why he says yes to the mother and no to him, adding, in case we have any doubt that he feels horribly threatened, that *he* (not the mother) is the breadwinner and the boss. Obviously, to be recognized as the all-powerful host is at least as important as making sure that his guests are comfortable, whereas the mother, while reaching the same conclusions about how the house will be reorganized, seems to privilege different priorities. I am not even sure whether the reference to how "shameful" it would be not to follow the custom is a genuine fear or whether this is part of a strategy to protect the son from the father's anger, but the net result is that she succeeds through persuasion, whereas her husband's authoritarian attitude has failed.

But what might be even more remarkable in this scene, and what the father may really be complaining about, is that the mother does take on the role of "host": she may pretend to be deferring to her husband's will but she is the decision maker. She is not treated as a servant who is implicitly or explicitly expected to take care of the guest's needs while the master of the house gets credit for his hospitality.

Far from being an exception in the French cultural landscape, this scene asks questions also dealt with in other contemporary novels, autobiographies, and testimonies written by children of immigrants: *Bye-bye* raises complicated theoretical issues about the difficult intersection between ethnicity, gender, and hospitality, especially when different generations are negotiating the transmission of a cultural heritage. In this chapter, I propose to unbraid the tightly woven narratives of gender, ethnicity, and immigration in order to think about what happens when this cluster of concepts intersects in difficult circumstances. By difficult, I mean a moment when two traditions of hospitality, that is, two potentially different sets of customs, are in contact. Whenever any type of exchange between people occurs (be it commercial exchange or a gift or a ritualized transaction), different laws of hospitality may clash, sometimes violently, especially if the situation takes place in a country where individuals are represented as belonging to separate "cultures," separate "communities."[2] Between French persons of European origin (who have forgotten that their ancestors were not always French), and French persons of Algerian origin (who are not allowed to forget that their parents or grandparents are Algerians), a level of misunderstanding may well persist even if cohabitation has more or less ensured that each individual knows that hospitality is not universally defined. It would be simplistic to assume that there is a simple coexistence of two modes of hospitality: the traditional French one[3] and a traditional North African one, imagined as the sophisticated and delicate custom of nomads and desert people. First of all, the two models I am alluding to are closer to allegories than to systems of laws that individuals are taught to practice: it may not be very useful to imagine that models of hospitality are monolithic and strictly walled off by the limits of ethnic or national identity. If we choose to make such generalizations about "French" hospitality and "Arab" hospitality, we have to resign ourselves to producing a series of statements whose "truth" masks profound discontinuities: "France" is not going to be a reliable monolithic entity, and the point of François Maspero's *Les passagers du Roissy-Express*, which I propose to analyze in this chapter, is that Paris is as remote from the residents of its *banlieues* as the typical "peasant" once was from nineteenth-century urbanites. And even without being anthropologists, we can guess that the lifestyle of Mauritanian nomads has little to do with that of the inhabitants of the suburbs of Algiers.[4]

On the other hand, there is every reason to compare practices within or between identifiable systems as long as we do not assume that individuals are naturally, biologically bound to a given pattern. Generalizations about, say, "French" hospitality and "Moroccan" hospitality allow us to describe vastly different expectations regarding hospitality and sometimes to declare some forms of it more desirable than others. For it is not enough to dismiss such constructions as myths: first of all, because myths are part of a national legacy that in practice determines what is acceptable or unacceptable. In the next chapter, we shall see that Jean de la Fontaine's fable about the Town Rat who invites the Country Rat may well be an old-fashioned generalization about rural authenticity versus urban decadence, but that it continues to be culturally understandable, relevant to some situations. Besides, such stories also influence children who attend French schools, presumably seeping into their conscious and unconscious minds, to resurface later as individual practices, even if the intertext has long been forgotten.

The second reason not simply to dismiss any construction of ethnic hospitality as a potentially harmful and useless stereotype is that conflicts often result from a lack of understanding of the neighbor's laws of hospitality, even if the laws in question are only imagined and misconstrued. As was demonstrated by Jacques Chirac's infamous little sentence about how the noise and smell of the immigrant neighbor drive the French worker crazy, today the illusory and perhaps comforting distinction between the next-door neighbor and the exotic foreigner is no longer operative.[5] In other words, in contemporary France, it would be illusory to assume that even an imagined Arab hospitality and French hospitality can remain completely separate.

Yet it would be simplistic to assume that two sets of distinct laws can co-exist without influencing each other, at least at the level of cultural knowl-edge, and there are also differences within each of those two sets of laws. Whom you invite, for how long, and how you treat your guests while they stay varies tremendously not only from group to group but also from class to class within the national or ethnic group. How then, does gender inter-sect with ethnicity? How do women negotiate the cultural and ethnic line? Does their femininity remain an invisible marker? Do they provide us with new models of cross-hospitality, with new stories and new laws?

To explore this issue, I would like to turn to two examples from two dif-ferent books. I first focus on a text that is, by now, rather well known in fran-cophone studies: *Passagers du Roissy-Express*, a travel narrative / guide book in which François Maspero (a writer and ex-publisher) and Anaïk Frantz (a photographer) decide to take a trip through the Paris *banlieues*, a nondestina-tion that allows them to explore and discuss the artificial binary opposition between exotic spaces and a familiar point of origin (Ridon 2000). In *Pas-sagers du Roissy-Express*, an exchange between two women of different ethnic origin is on the verge of leading to a moment of hospitality, but their com-plicity is interrupted by Maspero's decision to move on. After analyzing the muffled conflict that the scene generates between the main protagonists, I turn to another example, in which the failed moment of hospitality is appar-ently more brutal and more ostensibly racist, or at least xenophobic: in *Mé-moires d'immigrés*, a collection of interviews compiled by the daughter of Al-gerian immigrants, Yamina Benguigui reminisces about her childhood and tells the story of a misunderstanding between a little girl of Algerian origin and a European neighbor who does not recognize that the former is trying to share a ritual gift with her. By comparing the two episodes of failed hospitality, I would like to analyze the promises and limits of cross-cultural encounters, but also to reflect on the possibilities offered by the narrativization of such episodes: by telling their tales, both Anaïk Frantz and Yamina Benguigui slightly modify the original situation and manage to bridge cultural gaps at the very moment when they denounce their existence to the reader.

Madame Zineb's Tea: Hospitality in the banlieues

Maspero and Frantz's atypical destination questions simple definitions of tourism and complicates the relationship between different types of travelers and migrants: citizens of modern postindustrial states often go abroad as tourists, and the hospitality they receive cannot (always) be dissociated from forms of tourism that they control and have invented for their own comfort. Tourism reinvents hospitality or modifies the relationship between private and commercial practices. Migrants, on the other hand, often have to rely at first on the generosity of members of their community who arrived before them. And the hospitality they enjoy is not necessarily approved by the authorities, which creates a tension between the laws of hospitality recognized within ethnic groups and the government's conception of state hospitality across nations. Frantz and Maspero alter this logic by changing the structure of traditional trips: their internal trajectory preserves the structure of encounters between different ethnic groups that neither tourism (which sometimes artificially highlights but mostly downplays cross-cultural encounters) nor migrations promote. Maspero and Frantz's experiences raise interesting questions by constantly testing the frontier between services and generous invitations, and by bringing to the surface invisible discrepancies between their expectations as educated Parisian nomads and the forms of hospitality that they discover when they meet people whose ancestors or parents were Italian, Algerian, or Senegalese, to name but a few of the nationalities they encounter.

Commercial hospitality pretends to believe that money and consumption can adequately substitute for knowledge of local laws of hospitality. From one MacDonald's or Hyatt to the next, Western tourists trade a bill for the predictability of a certain familiarity, a level of comfort that shields them from the reality of their relative or absolute cultural incompetence. But the price of that type of commercial hospitality is the absence of a learning experience. The tourist is protected from being a guest who is at the mercy of the other's generosity. As we saw in the Introduction, the principle of receiving someone presupposes that the host constitutes himself as the owner of the land, or at least of the house to which he welcomes you.

Naturally, ethnicity and femininity do not operate along lines of alliance and solidarity in this domain. During the colonial period, even if a woman was as good as owned by the plantation owner, she could still compensate for her powerlessness by terrorizing her slaves.[6] Today, the continued devalorization and feminization of housework sometimes lead to a trading between gender and ethnicity: the woman of foreign origin ends up cleaning house for the European woman and reproducing neocolonial patterns.[7] Commercial hospitality, which is more likely to be suspected of cynicism, and which we regard as a parody of "real" hospitality, has at least one redeeming aspect—it makes the power relationship between the guest and the host more chaotic, less potentially unilateral, although it preserves a nostalgic simulacrum of cultural authenticity: folkloric performances are organized for the hotel guests, and the employees' uniforms mimic supposedly traditional outfits.

One of the problems that we may encounter when we become strangers in a strange place is that we are not sure that our own models of hospitality are transferable. We are not sure either that they are *not* transferable. Or, to formulate differently, one of the problems that tourism creates is that it brings different sets of laws of hospitality into contact. To make matters worse, because hospitality is also a form of generosity, it can or should never be reduced to a law prescribed by unwritten rules of etiquette. In hospitality, there is always some excess, a gift that goes beyond what is strictly enforceable. But when two communities meet, or when one individual from one community finds him- or herself in a different group, the likelihood that both societies define hospitality in exactly the same way is remote. In the context that I am exploring, similar problems will be raised, albeit with different manifestations, depending on whether we are talking about tourism or immigration. A crucial consequence of both phenomena is that some individuals are forced to compare or sometimes confront different practices of hospitality, different conceptions and expectations about what it means to be the host, the hostess, the guest.

In Maspero's book, the situation is complicated by three elements. First of all, because of the rather atypical form of traveling chosen here, commercial hospitality and individual hospitality are constantly interwoven, and commercial hospitality is examined through the anthropologist's lens rather than consumed as a service. Secondly, because of the almost parodic structure of the trip, no clear boundary between tourism and immigration can be established. If, for the native whose land is invaded by a tidal wave of condescending Westerners, the tourist, as Jamaica Kincaid suggests in *A Small Place*, is an ordinary man turned into a monster by virtue of the relative increase of power that displacement confers on him, "an ugly, empty thing, a stupid thing, a piece of rubbish pausing here and there to gaze at this and taste that . . ." (Kincaid 1988, 17), then Maspero and Frantz are not exactly tourists. Yet they are not immigrants either: even if they try to construct the *banlieue* as a space of difference (partly to test that stereotype), the impression that they are abroad, elsewhere, can, at any time, be relativized and rationalized. They are, after all, French Parisians who can go home whenever they wish to do so. They do, however, accept that, as city dwellers, they lack a degree of cultural competence in the *banlieues*. They do not try to impose their norm; they are aware of their vulnerability, and they meet people who are likewise vulnerable.

Thirdly, the series of encounters between the two travelers and their human objects of study is complicated by the fact that the person who accompanies Maspero is a woman and a photographer. Frantz's gender is humorously and self-consciously problematized from the very beginning of the journey, as if she knows that her presence implicitly modifies the genre of the travel-narrative-by-two-explorers: when Maspero first calls her and asks, "How she felt about this idea he had, yes, a rather strange and perhaps a bit of a foolish idea," Frantz replies, "I'm your man" (Maspero 1994, 10). This woman, who is Maspero's man, is also a photographer, whose pictures, according to Maspero are atypically nonpredatory: "They never took people by surprise, were never muggings, They were not pictures taken on the sly [*images à la sauvette*] or rapes" (Maspero 1994, 11, translation modified). The woman as photographer is thus defined as the opposite of the stereotyped (often) male photographer who steals images from his subjects as if he were robbing them of their soul.[8] Franz also blurs national and ethnic frontiers: her identity is constantly defined as a form of movement or in-betweenness. The text gives us a brief portrait at the beginning of the trip, but this narrative résumé insists less on hard facts and figures than on a general attitude and mentality: Franz lives on the margins, constantly challenging the categories of a world defined in terms of class, nationalities, ethnicities, and even geographical neighborhood: Anaïk lives on the impasse de l'Ouest, but she spent her life on the frontiers. "For that she might go to Africa, as she did one year, but might just as easily not leave the XIVth arrondissement in Paris" (Maspero 1994, 11)]. Her family name, Frantz, may suggest that her ancestors were born outside of France, but *Les passagers du Roissy-Express* never gives us any indication of her ethnic background or personal history. And yet, the story does insist on her identity: Frantz is the archetype of the stranger: she is either never at home or at home everywhere. The story takes great pains to identify her as a woman who spends her whole life crossing borders, reaching beyond the frontiers of social classes and ethnic groups: her identity is formulated in terms of movement rather than in terms of rootedness. Regardless of how long she spends anywhere, Frantz is a traveler, a nomad whose imagined community consists of "bizarre people, mostly—what are usually called dropouts, misfits, even tramps" (Maspero 1994, 11). A photographer who does not know how to sell her pictures, and whose professional identity is, consequently, relatively unstable and unimportant, Frantz works in a "contact zone" (Pratt 1992) that makes many of her potential customers uncomfortable with her photographs: "All too often, her photos provoked displeasure and irritation: why photograph *that*? 'That' was precisely the world right under our noses, which we never see: the frontier world that every one of us finds a bit scary, even very scary" (Maspero 1994, 11–12). From the very beginning, the reader is thus warned that what Frantz will show us is not necessarily what we wish to notice, and that her presence is a promise of unconventional encounters. She is both a woman and a man, a French speaker who has chosen images as her language of predilection, and her own background serves as a catalyst in making the reader aware of the photographed subject's identity.

But just as her position as a frontier dweller challenges the very construction of national and ethnic identity, her voice is not easily perceptible within the economy of the book, and the reader is implicitly encouraged to keep in mind this oblique positioning when the time comes to interpret the various episodes that take place during the trip. While *Les passagers du Roissy-Express* as a whole is clearly the result of a close collaboration, the separation between Maspero's and Frantz's voices is not always obvious. Frantz is solely responsible for the photographs, but the text is a braid of their perceptions (although it looks as if Maspero was ultimately in charge of the prose). At times, it is very difficult to know who is speaking, whose opinion is being expressed, because the text does not present us either with a first-person narrator who calls the other "he" (as if Frantz were the narrator) or with a first-person narrator who consistently calls the other "she" (as if Maspero were). At times, a sentence informs us that "François" did or said something, letting us assume that Frantz might be the narrator, but then, another sentence starts with "Anaïk" and seems to indicate that Maspero has taken over as the narrative voice. So that when whole paragraphs or pages do not refer to either of the characters by name, it is not clear whether we should assume that the text speaks for both of them or for one dominant narrator. An interesting textual hybridity results from this ambiguity.

More important, the text does not try to pretend that the two travelers always agree, and one particular scene raises interesting questions about hospitality, or more specifically about a breach of etiquette, a moment when hospitality is offered and refused. Toward the beginning of their journey, Frantz and Maspero find themselves in the vicinity of the famous housing estate in Aulnay known as "les 3000," an archetype of what was built during the 1960s, which the media tend to treat as a symbol of all architectural and social disasters.[9] Frantz and Maspero carefully avoid assuming too much about this infamous *cité*, however, and the text emphasizes history, on the one hand, and personal encounters, on the other. One particularly ambivalent moment occurs when Frantz meets a woman and asks her whether she can take a picture.

The woman is described as "a lady dressed in a long, glinting silk tunic, her head covered by a scarf" (Maspero 1994, 34). In other words (but these words are precisely not used), here is a woman whose physical appearance would usually lead the onlooker to think "Islam, tradition, Arab, North Africa."[10] Cultural reflexes might also make us suspect that such a traditional woman would probably traditionally resent, or at least be suspicious of,

Frantz's desire to photograph her. French literature tends to propose that hypothesis as a piece of exotic knowledge that the educated traveler should possess: I am thinking, for example, of Michel Tournier's *La goutte d'or* (1985; trans. as *The Golden Droplet* [1987]), where the hero leaves his oasis to be reunited with his picture taken (stolen) by a blond tourist. Mme Zineb complicates our assumptions about "tradition" and "Arabs vs. photography," however, by accepting graciously, and by interpreting the gesture as a mark of friendship and affection:

> "It warms my heart, you asking to take my photograph." She's feeling down. . . . She invites them up for a cup of tea. Anaïk hesitates. François refuses because time's getting on, it's turned seven and they still have some way to go. Or, as Anaïk later complains, because he was embarrassed. They'll send the photos. They'll come back and see her. They swap addresses and telephone numbers. Madame Zineb has a sad smile. (Maspero 1994, 34)

An informal but genuine exchange occurs between the two women: we may assume that Mme Zineb wants to reciprocate in some way and to show her hospitality by inviting Frantz and Maspero into her home, by offering them tea. Yet the moment of complicity between the two women of different ethnic origin does not last: Mme Zineb's invitation is declined, not by Frantz but by Maspero, whose excuse seems to contradict the rationale of the trip. The idea that they must go on, almost for the sake of going on, rather than accepting this woman's invitation, runs counter to their original plan to meet the inhabitants of the *banlieues* with whom, as Parisians, they cannot associate on a daily basis.

The text does not try to hide a moment of discomfort and conflict between the two travelers. The reader can never tell for sure whether he or she has access to the voice of a man or that of a woman, and I would suggest that this hesitation adds to the depth of the narrative. Even if I wish to avoid the simplistic equation between women's texts and feminine (let alone feminist) writing, it is interesting to focus on those moments in *Les passagers du Roissy-Express* when the two voices openly disagree about which rules, which conduct to adopt. Fruitful tensions reveal that the account is not monolithic, and that individual interpretations are superimposed on collective cultural reflexes.

Here, for a few crucial seconds, Frantz is silenced: Maspero's reply does not take into account her desire to accept the woman's hospitality. At the same time, the disagreement is not buried, and the text allows Frantz's voice to reemerge by spelling out the contradiction: the sentence starting with "Or . . ." ("Or, as Anaïk later complains, because he was embarrassed") is an unexpected addition that proposes a less flattering version of Maspero's act. What Frantz interprets as his "embarrassment" is not denied; it remains a working hypothesis, an accusation, a reproach that he does not wish to answer, allowing the reader to suspect that he may have unconsciously accepted responsibility for Mme Zineb's sad smile. Why did Frantz want to accept? Why did Maspero refuse? The text cannot quite articulate an explanation, but at least the tension between the two reactions is preserved faithfully, as is the consequence of Maspero's poorly motivated refusal: the comment about Mme Zineb's sadness signals a debt he has incurred. The passage preserves the memory of a moment of failed hospitality, when two women apparently share the same unwritten assumptions and desires, a complicity that seems to go beyond cultural boundaries but curiously stops on the border of gender.

For example, immediately after telling us about the incident with Mme Zineb, the omniscient narrator inserts a parenthesis that was obviously added after the completion of the book: a voice that says "she" when talking about Frantz tells the reader that six months after the trip through the *banlieues*, the photographer returned to "les 3000" and, in the absence of Maspero, was finally able to accept Mme Zineb's invitation: "October 1989: return to the 3000. Anaïk took Madame Zineb her photos, and this time they all had tea together [cette fois, elles ont pris le thé ensemble]" (Maspero 1994, 34).[11]

It occurs to me that the presence of this passage within the economy of the travel narrative metaphorically reproduces a moment of hospitality that took place in spite of Maspero's refusal and embarrassment: after the journey is completed, a foreign element is added to the body of the text, as if hospitality was given to a stranger for a short while. The paragraph is framed by a parenthesis, as if to mark the limits of a right to visit rather than a right to stay indefinitely, but it still gives an idea of who Mme Zineb really is: we find that she has a husband and children. Her happiness and her sadness are received into the text in the same manner as Frantz is welcomed as a guest. Maspero remains in the background, neither giving nor receiving hospitality, but allowing the story to entertain possibilities that he cannot quite imagine, to express forms of generosity that are foreign to his instincts, to his perception of the world.

These two brief allusions to Mme Zineb might be read as isolated moments, and the episode as scarcely worth noticing, if, twenty pages later, another disagreement did not confirm that the issues of who accepts whose invitation and who interprets behavior as welcoming or threatening are crucially linked to the overall goal of the trip to the *banlieues*. The disagreement between Frantz and Maspero is more than simply a matter of whether or not to accept Mme Zineb's invitation: they differ fundamentally in their gut reactions to the presence of the unknown—what we might call their instinct, or their unformulated appreciation of foreignness. When strangers meet strangers, each becomes not only both a potential host and a potential guest, but also, at least for Maspero, a potential enemy: the old Latin equivalent between the host and the enemy continues to lurk behind each generous attempt at meeting the other on his or her ground, and suspicion may, at any time, poison the budding relationship between tourist and native, between national and immigrant, between the nomad and the sedentary.

Hospitality requires a level of trust that the text redefines as a rhetoric of positive suspicion: when faced with the unknown, interpretations replace unmediated, or apparently unmediated, understanding. In order to want to be a host, in order to accept invitations, those interpretations of the other's intentions must be favorable, to the point of what one might call extreme naiveté. In a sense, infinite hospitality (greeting the stranger whoever he is, wherever she comes from) must deploy infinite naiveté, or perhaps a certain indifference to the possibility of seeing one's hospitality abused. Maspero and Frantz represent the two poles of a rhetorical and ideological spectrum: he is on the side of cautious analysis; she is hesitant, as with Mme Zineb, but still gives the stranger the benefit of the doubt. In the following passage, compare the rhetoric of opinions, of likes and dislikes, used by Maspero, and the generous but tentative assumptions with which Frantz responds to her companion's anxieties: at some point, Maspero is suddenly seized by what he calls *vertige sécuritaire* (a "security attack"), a form of paranoia that puts him on his guard, that makes him uncomfortably vulnerable:

He does not like the fact that all the time they were talking to the two young women, three or four idle youths had been circling them and discussing something. He doesn't like the fact that these boys have followed them, even walking in front of them at times, right down the avenue; that they watched Anaïk taking photos; that they called others over. Nor does he like the way Anaïk leaves her large bag wide open. "Maybe," she says, "they want me to take their photo but daren't ask?" Maybe. (Maspero 1994, 44)

Maspero says three times that "he does not like" something. Frantz is apparently oblivious to the threat that he perceives, and when she tries to interpret what scares her friend, she does so according to her own generous logic: the explanation may be that the stranger is shy. Shyness is a form of reserve, not a threat, and it would easily disappear if she offered the young men the same attention and respect she gave Mme Zineb. Her "maybe" contrasts with Maspero's reiterated dislike of the situation and preserves the space of doubt, error. Similarly, when Mme Zineb offers them tea, Frantz hesitates, a space of indecision that Maspero interrupts, upsetting a careful and delicate exchange between people who may not share the same rules. By refusing the invitation, Maspero saddens the host and refuses to enter into a pact of gratitude in which Mme Zineb would be the creditor.

Similarly, while Frantz is ready to give the gift of her art to shy teenagers, François suspects them of inhospitality. He almost accuses them of being thieves, but he does so indirectly, via a rather authoritarian and sneaky comment on Frantz's open bag: he implicitly suggests that she is putting them at risk, that she should obey his laws of caution. Her "Maybe," however, makes a suggestion too: Frantz implies that more thinking, more interpreting remains to be done, that the situation is not clear and that more communication is needed to ascertain everyone's real feelings. His skeptically repeated "Maybe," on the other hand, is a grudging concession to the fact that he cannot rule out her interpretation but stops short of crediting it with verisimilitude.

In this exchange, the reader realizes that everything is linked, and that a whole system of hospitality/inhospitality is being discussed, even if the two travelers seem to be exchanging banalities. Twenty pages after the encounter with Mme Zineb, Frantz suddenly demonstrates that Maspero's comments on her bag are indistinguishable from an overall system of which she disapproves. "Even so," she reiterates, apparently out of the blue, "It is not good. We really should have had tea with Madame Zineb" (Maspero 1994, 44; modified translation). Mme Zineb, already a distant memory in the reader's mind, reappears like the ghost of failed hospitality.

This time, doubts and hesitations have disappeared, replaced by a certainty: "It is not good." And like Maspero, she repeats her statement, as if she cannot forgive herself. Through her analysis of the situation, the text proposes a law of hospitality that regulates the guest's conduct. According to Frantz, the two travelers are guilty of transgressing this unwritten law, and her subsequent return underscores the less than trivial nature of this transgression.

Frantz seems to know that the refusal of hospitality has consequences that do not easily disappear. In *Les passagers du Roissy-Express*, the potentially devastating and lasting outcome remains an intuition, a vaguely formulated statement of disapproval. But other stories go even further and articulate Frantz's intuition: in Yamina Benguigui's *Mémoires d'immigrés*, another failed moment of hospitality leads to the burial of one generation's form of generosity.

Cakes Offered, Refused, and Buried

Yamina Benguigui's *Mémoires d'immigrés* is a series of interviews that also function as an autobiographical search for forgotten or uncelebrated roots: through her questions to two generations of immigrants and children of immigrants, Benguigui both elicits answers and triggers a flow of memories within herself. Those memories are then woven into a narrative that gives them meaning and reestablishes their legitimacy (Durmelat 2000). For example, while she is interviewing Naima, who reminisces about the "fête de l'Aïd," a moment when her father would recover some of his dignity, Yamina is suddenly taken back to her own childhood and to a moment of alienation, a moment of failed hospitality, when the little girl had to negotiate misunderstanding and hostility.

> When the time had come to celebrate Aïd, in one of those generous moments that were so typical of her, my mother asked me to go to the neighbors' and to bring them a plate of little cakes that, according to the

custom, is given away in memory of a dead relative. "Go knock on her door and make sure to tell her that the cakes are a gift from Uncle Moussah." "Yes, mom," I had replied, a docile thirteen-year old little girl. And I still see myself, petrified with fear, ringing the doorbell, carefully holding the plate to avoid dropping the cakes, and to this day, I can still hear the hostile and shrill voice asking: "Who is it, who is at the door?" "It's me, Yamina, your neighbor's daughter, my mother told me to bring cakes from my uncle Moussah!" "You can tell your mother that I don't know that uncle of yours" retorted the neighbor's voice. I remember shrugging my shoulders and thinking: "How could you know him, he is dead." The following year, I had made another experiment and knocked on another neighbor's door. That one had a house and a beautifully tended rose garden, but I was no more successful. So the following year, when a similar plate was inflicted on my poor sister, we both agreed to bury the cakes in a vacant lot, far away from home. I can't help smiling when I remember that story. (Benguigui 1997, 183; my translation)

Mme Zineb's encounter with the two travelers results in a sad smile (*un sourire triste*) that haunts Maspero. Here, the level of communication between the two protagonists is even more rudimentary. The conversation takes place on each side of a closed door, not even on the symbolic threshold where boundaries are not always crossed but at least exposed as permeable. The little girl never sees the neighbor. The Medusa-like, terrifying grown-up who can "petrify" children remains a "voice," whose tone clearly signifies that no hospitality will be granted. The woman does not even know that she is refusing a gift. According to her, this little foreigner is transgressing a rule that everybody should know: people must be acquainted before offering each other cakes.

Her simplistic analysis of a situation that she does not understand forecloses the possibility of further exchanges at the very moment she thinks that she is communicating: she gives the little girl a new message to take back home: "You can tell your mother that I don't know this uncle of yours," but this pseudoreply is meaningless. Rather than continuing a conversation, it forces the cross-cultural dialogue underground: the girl's reaction to the message will not be formulated. The neighbor's perspective is that she has had the last word (the little girl does have an answer to the insulting and paternalistic lesson, but she keeps her thoughts to herself). She shrugs off the incorrect interpretation and refuses to continue to act as the misunderstood messenger.

The courier withdraws from a place of mediation, and three voices are now cut off from each other, that of the mother: "and make sure to tell her that the cakes are offered by my Uncle Moussah"; that of the neighbor: "You can tell your mother that I don't know this uncle of yours"; and that of the little girl, whose remark is never voiced: "How could you know him, I thought, he is dead." The fact that she talks to herself forever excludes the other woman from a new system that she could have learned. The gift, which might have been followed by an explanation of a religious and cultural custom if the woman had interpreted her surprise as ignorance and not as the result of a breach of etiquette, remains incomprehensible. "Petrified" and silenced by the woman's inhospitable misinterpretation, the messenger is reduced to a form of powerless superiority: she knows better, she is bilingual and bicultural, but she cannot educate the other.[12] Mutatis mutandis, she is in the same position as the teenagers whom Maspero interprets as a threat. As a result, the gift fails. Uncle Moussah, whose memory the act of generosity celebrates, is relegated to a past that cannot be commemorated.

At the end of the paragraph, the narrator manages to alter the pessimistic logic of inhospitality imposed by the neighbor. Unexpectedly, the two sisters succeed in turning miscommunication into a creative counterpractice: they invent a new ritual, they bury the cakes. Intended to resurrect Uncle Moussah symbolically, or at least to keep his memory alive, the cakes are entombed, not to reappear unless the same complex ceremonies and counterceremonies recur between the mother, the neighbor, and the mediators. The burial is a complex gesture, because it is both a failure and a success: it cannot be reduced to the disappearance of the objects or of the conflict that they symbolize, because the cakes are not destroyed, eaten, or thrown out. Although we often equate the idea of "burying" emotions and feelings with unhealthy forms of denial, I would argue that this burial is not a metaphor for repression: it is a forceful and highly charged symbolic act.

From a purely economic perspective, after all, if the cakes had been eaten, part of the original logic would have been respected: they were meant to be eaten. At a superficial level, the little girls waste food, a sacrilegious act even for those who live in the midst of abundance. At another level, eating the cakes that were supposed to be given in memory of the uncle would be another form of sacrilegious transgression. The children do not eat them, because for them this is no ordinary food; it continues to represent something that can only be given, even if the gift is refused. Once the original ritual fails, once the neighbor sends them away, they do not throw out the cakes. They have to improvise. They bury the uncle, his memory, but also the gift, its refusal, the failed moment of communication between two women. The main purpose of this clandestine ceremony is not explained: is it because it is more important to shield the mother from the knowledge that her gesture of generosity missed its mark, or is it to protect the messengers from the consequences of their failed attempt at translating their own law of hospitality? The children do not want to go back home with the refused gift. Consequently, the mother will never know what happened.

The latent conflict between two laws of hospitality is never completely smoothed out, and worse still, the refusal of the gift may have killed a custom for good: we can assume that Yamina Benguigui, if she has become a mother herself, has thought twice before entrusting her own daughters with a plate of cakes to be offered to a neighbor. One word, in the paragraph, suggests that the narrator does not completely forgive the mother for failing to realize that she was sending a member of her family on an impossible mission: the second year, "a similar plate was *inflicted* on my poor sister" (my emphasis). The responsibility of translating the untranslatable is "inflicted" on the sisters, a burden of which the mother remains unaware.

But the encounter is not an altogether sterile misunderstanding: the spurned gift becomes or remains an object sacralized by shared customs: even if only the two little girls participate in the burial ceremony, their recreated microritual bonds them as witnesses. They can remember and commemorate the event in all its complexity, in all its contradictions. The two sisters perform a sort of improvised but serious ceremony that replaces other types of initiation practices: they initiate themselves into the world of mediators, which they already inhabit and will inhabit until their deaths.

The ritual shared by the two mediators is not collective and not legitimized by an ethnic, religious, or cultural community. The comfort that individuals may seek in the feeling that a whole society would recognize and affirm the gesture is lost. In that sense, the burial of the cakes is simply a parody, or a mournful repetition of the original ritual gift. The burial of the cakes is both like and unlike the death of the scapegoat, the Freudian murder of the father: here, what is buried stands for what was already dead. In that sense, the ritual is both less and more efficient than the original that it replaces and is meant to unite a whole people: the two sisters create their own commemorative ceremony, but they cannot share it with the rest of the community, or with their French neighbors, who interpret them as foreign elements. And not only does the Frenchwoman remain ignorant, but the mother is not told that her gift was not accepted.

Conclusion: The Gift of Postcolonial Texts

Both Maspero's and Benguigui's books thus tell stories of ambivalent moments of relative failure and relative success. In both cases, a woman tries to offer a symbolic gift across the ethnic and cultural line, but within a community of neighbors who share the same space. In both cases, that hospitality is refused, but the refusal is followed by a complex process of negotiations, whose delicate and sophisticated nature the text explores.

In *Les passagers du Roissy-Express*, the text carefully documents a moment of discord between the two travelers and consents both to the friction and to its unilateral resolution when Anaïk Frantz returns to the scene alone and finally accepts the invitation that François Maspero had refused. The original refusal is not erased, but at least the text allows for the possibility of some sort of reparation and, more important, it enables the situation to evolve, communication to improve, and hospitality to be better understood, accepted, and reciprocated, even if in asymmetrical ways. Just as Madame Zineb welcomes Anaïk into her home, the story welcomes Madame Zineb into this multifaceted history of the Paris *banlieue*, where she becomes an important character.

In *Mémoires d'immigrés*, the moment of failed hospitality is even more problematic in its cruelty and violence. If Madame Zineb's invitation is declined, the little girl's offer is much more violently rejected by the neighbor, who does not even consent to open her door. And the woman who refuses the gift is not offered a second chance, so that the cakes are finally buried. On the other hand, the publication of the story goes beyond the addition of parenthetical remarks and moves toward imaginative forms of resolution of the conflict. The narrative magnifies the private ceremony between the two little girls and makes it public, shareable by a new community of readers who belong to different ethnic and religious groups. The children, who have never told their story, have become grown-ups and, as readers, can now participate in the commemoration of what has become an episode from the past.

Both texts function like a new gift, a new invitation, or, perhaps, a new plate of cakes that is dug up from its symbolic grave to be offered both to the Frenchwoman and to the mother in a gesture of reconciliation. Neither passage is intrinsically tragic in tone. In *Les passagers du Roissy-Express*, Madame Zineb smiles, even though sadly. In *Mémoires d'immigrés*, the narrator smiles too: "I can't help smiling at that memory." At one level, it is legitimate to wonder if this amusement is an idiosyncratic reaction (other children must have gone through the same experience and come out deeply hurt) or the result of the adult's critical distance between the present and her vulnerable childhood. But one of the forms of hospitality that we, as readers, owe to the text is to allow for the possibility that the story is indeed amusing and did not elicit an irreparable sense of shame.

The two stories tell bittersweet fables of half success and half disaster, and they both also manage to do the work of mediation that the little girls could not do from behind a closed door. Publication has opened a door between two communities that cannot easily talk to each other. *Mémoires d'immigrés* can welcome both the mother and the neighbor as mediating texts capable of understanding both positions: the mother could not share the precious legacy of Aïd because she did not know that mediators must translate rather than repeat words too faithfully; she expected her daughters to use *her* words: "make sure you tell . . . ," and the child, who describes herself as an "obedient daughter," accepts that role without succeeding in conveying the message of generosity. The neighbor has not learned about a custom that she might have appreciated and perhaps even adopted. And she has certainly not understood that she was being rude, and that two laws of hospitality have brutally clashed.

But the moment of failed hospitality also leads to a complex reshuffling of positions of power and knowledge: as Marcel Mauss puts it, in one of his lesser-known texts, depending on how gift-giving is performed, power is gained or lost either by the recipient or by the giver.[13] Here, clearly, only the mediator is in a position to understand why generosity is refused and why it becomes a burden. The neighbor, by refusing the gift, wastes a chance to learn, but so does the mother, who never realizes that her gift was perceived as a threat. While the episode of the cakes unfolds, neither the giver nor the recipient of the gift is capable of establishing a meaningful relationship, because both ignore the rudiments of the other's code, and there is no one to explain it to them.

What the text does for its readers is to put the two codes in contact by explaining the meaning of the two women's behavior: the link between baking the cake and the memory of Uncle Moussah is spelled out to readers who don't know anything about Aïd, although the text refrains from didacticism and does not impose a discourse of universal hospitality. The telling of the story also speaks to Muslim mothers who might send out their little girls with plates of cakes without ever thinking that the gift may not be received as graciously as they would hope, because it is part of a set of laws of hospitality and generosity that are not shared and will not be understood. The remembered episode is a cautionary tale that warns mothers that their messenger may be incapable of transmitting their message of generosity and may return with a message of hostility.

While the gift of the cakes by the little girl may be perceived by the mother as a moment when a law of hospitality is learned and perpetuated, the story tells us that, for the child, this was a moment of discontinuity: in the intradiegetic episode of the cakes, the uncle's memory is in danger of being erased. He is buried a second time with the cakes. But in *Mémoires d'immigrés*, the uncle is resurrected again, his memory being associated with tender memories of complicity that the narrator shares with her sister. Readers may imagine that Benguigui's mother and all those who may perform the same social function never find out about their messengers' sobering experiences. They may also imagine that even the publication of the written version of the story will not change anything for the mother: perhaps she will not read it; perhaps, for one reason or another, she cannot read such texts. But the possibility exists that this trio (the mother, the neighbor, the daughters) will come to occupy the position of readers who, by discovering that they were involved in a complex and polyphonous dialogue, will also be reunited by a mental act of recognition, especially if they share the narrator's amusement. The story creates a new space of encounter, the space of the book where different communities are shown to cohabit, even if imperfectly and uncomfortably.

This area of utopian encounter may be called the space of "translation," even if only one language is apparently spoken by the three main characters; the situation permits of "a translation other than the one spoken about by convention, common sense, and certain doctrinaires of translation" (Derrida 1998, 10). As readers, we may suddenly remember previous experiences and be given a chance to reinterpret the dynamics of hospitality and inhospitality between cultures. Just as the original actors of the texts may eventually occupy the position of readers, readers may realize that they once were in the situation of the characters described in the stories. And the complex reappraisal that may then take place is the ultimate gift of successful postcolonial texts that create new spaces of safe experiments where women of different ethnic backgrounds might have a chance to rethink cross-cultural laws of hospitality.

CHAPTER FOUR

Immigrants and the Logic of Interchangeability: Merzak Allouache's *Salut cousin!* and Jean de La Fontaine's "The Town Rat and the Country Rat"

After *Omar Gatlato*, the film that made Merzak Allouache famous, the Algerian director regularly attracted critics' attention with films that tended to redefine the expectations of Algerian viewers and filmmakers alike (Bensmaïa 1981; Djelfaoui 1981).[1] On the international scene, Allouache's work is not as well known as it deserves to be, but two of his recent films attracted critical attention, *Bab el-Oued City* in 1994 and his 1996 *Salut cousin!* (*Hey, Cousin!*) the subject of this chapter.

In *Salut cousin!* Allouache focuses on the encounter between Alilo, an Algerian visitor to France, and Mokrane, or Mok, as he prefers to be called, the child of Algerian immigrants, and on the type of hospitality that the latter can grant to the former. The film examines what happens when individuals wish to grant hospitality but the state has the power to thwart them. Allouache suggests that in such cases, hospitality can never be more than half-successful and half-disastrous, because host and guest are not at liberty to define their own roles on the chessboard of international and individual hospitality: while the presence of the two characters seems to promise a simple distinction between a host and a guest, the identities of the heroes prevent them from adopting such roles.

Remarkably, the issues explored in *Salut cousin!* (hospitality between cultures and within minority communities) are not only the main theme of the movie but also a metaphoric enactment of the conditions of production and distribution of Allouache's work in the mid 1990s.

Hospitality: Filmmaking in France and Algeria

Salut cousin! was a fall-back plan for the filmmaker, and the cultural and political context that forced the director to give up his original scenario is interestingly woven into the plot of the film. I first wondered whether hospitality would be a significant concept in *Salut cousin!* when I read that the scenario of Allouache's latest film had replaced an earlier one: according to Marie-Paule Marchi, the Algerian director had been planning to make a new film on the situation of contemporary Algeria but was not able to work in his country:

> For the moment, after *Bab el-Oued City*, Merzak cannot go back to Algeria. He had a project on a serious subject, on the media and the murders of journalists in his country. For reasons of realism and truth, it was out of the question to film outside of Algeria. But since Merzak wants to bear witness and because he is teeming with ideas, he very quickly bounced back with the scenario of *Salut cousin!* (Marchi 1996)

Like so many Algerian writers and artists, Allouache was one of the large group of intellectuals who had to protect themselves by fleeing their country for fear of reprisals. *Bab el-Oued City* is the story of a young baker whose short nights are always interrupted by a loudspeaker that broadcasts fundamentalist speeches directly into his room. Exasperated by the noise (as well as, or perhaps rather than, by the ideological content of the message), Boualem disconnects the loudspeaker and throws it into the sea, unaware that Islamists will regard this as blasphemy. The situation deteriorates so rapidly that Boualem is eventually forced out of the country: one of the last sequences shows him on a ship to Marseilles, a series of images that both ironically rewrites the nostalgic endings of many colonial and postcolonial films (from *Pépé le Moko* to *The Lover*) and constitutes a sadly prophetic intuition for Allouache himself. A few years later, he would have to give up on the privileged vantage point of his native Bab el-Oued to follow his hero into exile, and to weave his social critique of Algeria into a different plot.

His unequivocal condemnation of the role played by Islamic fundamentalists in *Bab el-Oued City* thus turned Allouache's native Algeria into a dangerous and inhospitable land for him. It would, however, be a gross simplification to imagine that France was able to provide shelter and unproblematic hospitality. Generally speaking, it is worth noting that Algeria occupies a specific place in the debate about political asylum, and that the alarming situation in that country has finally led French jurists to redefine the concept of "asylum": traditionally, political refugees are viewed as the victims of persecution by a state. But when the danger comes from independent movements such as the FIS (Front Islamiste de Salut), until recently, the legislation did not allow individuals to claim refugee status.[2] That specific situation was addressed by the report prepared by Patrick Weil in 1997 as a preliminary to the Chevènement laws. Weil recognizes that the current status of "asylum" forecloses certain types of claims and proposes that the notion of *asile territorial* (territorial asylum) be added to the category of "political refugee":

> For example, in Algeria, democrats persecuted by fundamentalist Islamist movements cannot be granted the status of refugee. Similarly, when a civil war or an ethnic conflict breaks out in a country, the persecuting agent cannot be equated with the state.
>
> In practice, however, some cases are brought to the attention of the minister of the interior by the director of OFPRA [the Organisation française pour la protection des réfugiés et des apatrides, or French Office for the Protection of Refugees and Stateless Persons], who takes into consideration the reality of dangers justifying the need for protection although they fall outside the criteria that automatically lead to the granting of refugee status. In such cases, a form of territorial asylum can be granted by the minister of the interior. (Weil 1997)

Allouache's situation is one of the individual trajectories that regularly force communities to redefine the meanings of words such as "hospitality" and "asylum." Furthermore, the period when *Salut cousin!* was shot and distributed was particularly sensitive in France: in 1995, a series of terrorist attacks on RER trains in Paris triggered a wave of panic that resulted in a high level of police activity. It is easy to imagine that the whole community of Algerian (or Arab-looking) immigrants in France suffered because of their physical resemblance to the imagined Arab terrorist. In other words, although France may have seemed an obvious destination for the francophone Allouache, he was no doubt perfectly aware that exiled Algerians were not always welcome there. When the film was made, both France and Algeria were alienating and inhospitable lands for him.

Besides, the film industry and its international structures were not very good at compensating for the hostility of inhospitable states: in spite of its presentation at Cannes and of the fact that it won several prizes, *Salut cousin!* did not immediately find a distributor.[3] Allouache was caught between two inhospitable lands when he wrote the story of the cousins Alilo and Mok, two outsiders, one of whom (Mok) firmly believes that he is an insider. Given the conditions of production and distribution of Allouache's film, it is all the more remarkable that he should have chosen to make a film about two cousins, one of whom depends on the other's hospitality. One of the most interesting features of the several layers of narratives to be found in *Salut cousin!* is that they make contradictory or at times incompatible statements about the role of each cousin, and especially about who is the guest and who is the host: in the film, a tension persists between stories told in the visual realm (the treatment of certain objects by the camera) and stories told by more overtly oral narratives (to be found in the plot, but also in the sound track and the literary intertexts). The contradictory narratives constantly reassess the responsibilities ascribed to each role (guest and host). Perhaps, in the end, the film expresses doubts as to the possibility of immigrants ever occupying the position of hosts.

I therefore propose to compare the visual and narrative treatment of symbolic animals whose role and functions are deceptively attached to each of the protagonists. One rather obvious layer of the film narrativizes the two cousins' story as a retelling of Jean de La Fontaine's fable "The Town Rat and the Country Rat." If we follow that grid of interpretation, the two

cousins more or less naturally find themselves identified as the Country Rat and the Town Rat. But another tightly interwoven story undermines the clarity of our interpretive process by adding to the first pair of animals other highly charged symbolic objects that we can also attach to one of the cousins: a fish in a fishbowl (for Mok) and a suitcase (for Alilo). The constant superimposition of the two narratives allows Allouache to present us with a double and contradictory portrait of the main protagonists as host and guest.

In *Salut cousin!* the two cousins find themselves reunited in Paris for a few days. Both are of Algerian origin but one is a *beur* (or child of North African immigrants living in France), while the other, Alilo, lives in Algiers. Alilo has come to Paris to pick up a suitcase of haute couture merchandise that his boss will sell on the black market as soon as his courier has brought it back to Algiers. Remarkably, although this practice, called *trabendo*, is commonplace, Mok does not even know the meaning of the word, obliging/enabling Alilo to explain it to him (and, presumably, for French moviegoers).[4] Alilo stays at his cousin's apartment and becomes better acquainted with Mok, who was born and raised in Paris and does not seem to have ever ventured outside the city. The film thus sets up an original dialogue, not, stereotypically, between a "French" character (presumably of European origin) and an "Arab" (about whom it is often culturally irrelevant to ask whether he is French or not, an immigrant or not), but between two Arabs whose trajectories are radically different. *Salut cousin!* thus moves away from the comforting familiarity of plots where "France" meets "Algeria" (or other minority communities) along visible, clear-cut racial, religious, and cultural lines. It is also an implicit critique of the commonplace representation of immigrants as divided into "first" and "second" generations.

Second-Generation Mediators: Perpetual Guests

Since the end of World War II, France has tended to think of its immigrants in terms of "generations": the large population of North African immigrants recruited by industrialists who needed a cheap and compliant labor force to build cars or erect the high-rises of future *banlieues* is still routinely (and unrealistically) imagined as a "first" generation. Their precarious conditions (they did not always speak French; they lived in shantytowns, some-

times for as long as fifteen or twenty years; they were expected to accept the most arduous and least-paid jobs) are often contrasted with the fate of their children or grandchildren, whom the collective unconscious lumps together as the "second" generation.

Paradoxically, not all "first generations" of immigrants are equally remembered as such, and only some ethnic or national groups seem to produce a "second generation." It would be foolish to assume that all the Italian, Polish, or Spanish immigrants who came to France at the beginning of the twentieth century have gone back "home," and yet no Polish or Italian "second generation" seems to have materialized in the French cultural unconscious. As Gérard Noiriel suggests in his *Le creuset français*, the term *seconde génération* started to be used with reference to the children of immigrants from the Maghreb toward the end of the 1970s and has gained cultural currency without being backed up by valid statistical data or solid "scientific research" (Noiriel 1988, 211). Observing that the term is usually almost exclusively (and illogically) employed to refer to *beurs*,[5] he proposes adopting a historical approach to reach a definition that will "protect the concept from polemical uses" (211).

More important, this so-called "second generation" has apparently been invested with the mission of testing the principle of "integration": struggling against stereotypes and assumptions, the members of this almost undefinable community sometimes propose their own labels, such as *beur* or *rebeu*,[6] and sometimes reject the very principle of labeling, underscoring the absurdity of an ideology that sees immigration as a hereditary feature. Their voices contribute to the debate on French hospitality. As books such as Benguigui's *Mémoires d'immigrés* and Maspero's *Passagers du Roissy-Express* demonstrate, the children of North African immigrants are often held responsible for the success or failure of cultural exchange or cohabitation: they are seen as mediators, as go-betweens, whose seemingly natural function is to occupy the no-man's-land between the perpetual host and the eternal guest, or rather, between hosts who never envisage renouncing their privilege (i.e., French people of European origin) and guests who are never allowed to become hosts (i.e., the children of immigrants who have inherited their parents' disenfranchisement). There is no name for that position between the guest and the host. This mediating position is not recognized, and it is never

clear whether immigrants' children are the equivalent of translators, of ushers, or of ambassadors.

France is no exception here. Many Western countries of immigration think in terms of waves, of generations, and I would like to argue that narratives that posit the existence of a "second generation" of immigrants are worth looking into because they smuggle in curious assumptions, which then circulate in a country's political and cultural unconscious. I suspect that the "second generation" discourse does much more than merely state the obvious.

The point of discontinuity between an immigrant and his or her family can be articulated as a set of manifest differences. In France, it is not rare for the children of immigrants to speak French without any "foreign" accent—they will, in fact, probably have picked up the regional accent of the area where their parents settled, enabling them to go unnoticed among the "autochthonous" population;[7] their cultural references will be those of their peers (school tends to enforce cultural norms both through the teaching of mandatory programs and because of teenagers' ritualistic encoding of relationships);[8] their "difference" from an imagined native identity might become so imperceptible that they will not even be identified as part of the "second generation" that they are supposed to embody.[9] Yet, even if it is fuzzy, invisible, and inconsistent, the idea of a "second generation" does not lose its relevance and power: it allows us to continue to think of "immigrants" as guests and of "us" as hosts. If we think of immigrants' children as "mediators" between "us" and "them" (rather than, for example, as part of "us"), the parents will continue to be seen as newcomers (even if they have been in the country for thirty years). Besides, mediators do not really become hosts; they are not unconditionally placed in a position that would allow them to invite new guests.

The notion that children are mediators between two cultures already implies that we see them as operating in some sort of limbo, as not enjoying (having, being part of) "a" culture, "their" culture. Portraying them as "in between" or "neither here nor there" (Bhabha 1994; Laronde 1993) is judicious because it reflects the limits of some nations' hospitality, but it does not take into account the fact that parents too (be they immigrant or natives) were always in-between (between social classes, between regions, or perhaps between religions), and that even dominant groups are the product of many hybrid networks, that their allegiance or lineage is anything but simple and straightforward.

If we expect children of immigrants to be (more) tolerant (than we are) of new immigrants, if we express consternation when a so-called second-generation immigrant votes for a political party with a strongly anti-immigrant platform, are we not implicitly saying that the politics of the children of immigrants ought to be determined by a feeling that their own situation is still precarious, that they are still expected to prove themselves as real citizens, and that their right to grant or refuse hospitality is not yet automatic? I am obviously not saying that I condone in any way the type of intolerance and selfish thinking that would lead an individual to resent the presence of the "next" wave of immigrants, but I don't think that anti-immigrant attitudes on the part of the children of immigrants is any worse than the intolerance of a "Français de souche" (autochthonous French person). It is tempting, however, to use such thinking to justify the hostility of others toward immigrants, as if inhospitality were somehow more acceptable when enacted by people whom history has made national hosts for more than one generation. Forgetting that the position of the "children" changes radically with time (within their lifetimes), the national imagination forces them into the sometimes infantilizing role of translators by interpreting them as the hyphen between their parents' assumed cultural incompetence and the dominant norm: they remain children long after they have become parents, just as they are children of immigrants before being citizens. Moreover, the translator occupies an ambiguous position in the rarely perceived continuum between host and guest. Paradoxically, the translator is a guest invited to better exclude those who are encoded as others: for the translator allows the host to get away with not speaking the other's language and contributes to the creation of a context where the newcomer who does not speak the dominant (linguistic or cultural) idiom is expected to find a way of communicating with a host who shows no intention of learning the other's language.[10]

If we perceive children as caught in an inherited game of who is the host and who is the stranger, we perpetuate the distinction between the host and the guest even after everyone's situation has changed so much that the guest has become the host and vice versa. At one level, the constantly reinforced opposition between *banlieues* and urban centers (even if everyone knows that *banlieues* are not exclusively constituted of immigrants, and that Paris is home to many foreigners), between *beurs* and "Français" (even if some *beurs* are Français and if all "Français" are not Europeans) perpetuates the notions that once a host, always a host, and that guests pass on the gene of guesthood to their offspring. And this level of reasoning coexists with a very articulate discourse of "integration" that posits that it is desirable for the children of immigrants to become part of the nation, and therefore, supposedly, to be in a position to welcome other immigrants, to act as the host.

What is thus exceptional in Allouache's film is that he does not focus primarily on the opposition between the first and second generations. He shows that a *beur* can precisely not count on any accumulation (of knowledge, stability, power) as long as French society systematically tries to elide the consequences of time and persists in thinking in terms of dynasties of immigrants.

Allouache avoids the trap of thinking in "second-generation" terms by choosing his characters within what some people think of as the "same" culture and the "same" generation in order to point out the inaccuracies of assumptions about those forms of "sameness." The two cousins are both of Algerian origin, and they are the same age. But even though *Salut cousin!* does address the issue of how immigrants relate to their parents and to their relatives (Alilo insists on paying a courtesy visit to Mok's parents), the film departs radically from the model proposed by Benguigui in which children are go-betweens. *Salut cousin!* is also significantly different from recent "*banlieue* films" such as Mathieu Kassovitz's 1995 *La haine* and Jean-François Richet's 1995 *Etat des lieux* or his 1997 *Ma 6-T va crack-er*: in those films, most of the main characters were born in France, and the narratives concentrate either on the relationships between youths of different ethnic backgrounds (the typical *blanc-black-beur* trio) or on the teenagers' conflicts with the police or other grown-ups.[11] Allouache neither particularly insists on the diversity within the *beur* community (as Malik Chibane had done in *Hexagone* in 1993) nor focuses on a character's return to what Gisèle Pineau somewhat ironically calls the "pays pas natal" (non-native land) (Pineau 1996, 269). Unlike films such as Mahmoud Zemmouri's *Prends dix mille balles et casse-toi* in 1980 or Rachid Bouchareb's *Cheb* in 1991, *Salut cousin!* is neither about

Mok "returning" to Algeria (even if that is what takes place at the end of the film) nor about Alilo's decision to settle in France (even if he is indeed forced to do so in the end), but about the relationship between two cousins.

If Mok's physical appearance identifies him as an "Arab," his own self-identification is obviously more complex. But there is a certain rigidity about his choices: he rejects what has to do with Algeria and a supposedly identifiable Algerian origin. In his eyes, Algeria is a dangerous country that he has no desire to visit. He even wants to put as much distance as possible between himself and his own recent past (life in the *banlieue* where he grew up). In a scene that the end of the film retrospectively ironizes (since Mok will eventually be deported to Algeria), he insists that he will never go there. When Alilo is about to leave, he says: "Write to me when you get there. Watch out in Algiers! And come back . . . because I am not about to set foot in your *bled* [godforsaken village], with what is going on there" (Allouache 1996, 60). He feels no solidarity with other immigrants, especially if they come from Algeria: when Alilo mentions that he has seen someone he knew in Barbès, Mok expresses anxiety and reiterates his "French" identity:

Mok: I'm talking about all those weirdoes who come from the bled . . . and who are going to make trouble for us.
Alilo: What kind of trouble?
Mok: Mind you, I don't give a damn! I'm French. (17)

I am not sure that the point, here, is to criticize Mok's alienation and refusal to defend his own people: rather, the film denounces the illusion that different experiences of immigration systematically lead to the forming of alliances and communities, and it also demonstrates the limits of the opposition between the native's knowledge and the foreigner's ignorance. Each side of the paradigm is carefully negated: not only is the native's superiority relative and hardly worthy of admiration, but it is often nothing more than the acting out of a strong confidence in one's ability to survive in Paris. Conversely, the visitor's supposed ignorance is challenged by Allouache's portrait of an individual who is quick at decoding grids and readily adapts to references that he perceives as different from but similar to his own.

From the very beginning of the film, Mok makes a point of showing off his Parisianism, and his views soon become prescriptive. As the host, he wants to teach Alilo how to behave properly in Paris, as if his guest's gauche manners somehow reflect poorly on his own personality. When Alilo has to go to hospital in the middle of the night because he has eaten too many bananas, Mok takes care of him, but later he complains about the breach of etiquette: Alilo's antics, he asserts, are endangering his reputation. "Look, it's not very nice of you to kick up such a fuss in my neighborhood" (12). The fact that he expresses himself in juvenile street slang does little to hide the fact that Mok's fear is the equivalent of the old worry, "What are the neighbors going to think?" In this example, the host internalizes a definition of his role as the guardian of native norms: he feels responsible for policing the guest, for making sure that he conforms. The interpreter of the law of hospitality becomes the guardian of the law. Like the figure of the poor relation, Alilo is systematically underestimated by his cousin. Alilo is routinely if subtly infantilized, and the host, who implicitly adopts the role of parent, resents the risk of being shamed by poorly brought-up offspring.

For the fine line is easily crossed between a host's generous desire to decrypt a foreign reality that might make the guest uncomfortable and the temptation to reencrypt the world as a set of rules that must be respected: even though all Candides are usually presented as clever decoders whose foreignness gives them an edge, they are also at the mercy of an unscrupulous host, who may choose to make them toe the line of their own reality rather than marvel at their fresh perspectives. Mok does not have any scruples and eagerly blurs the line between host and instructor or initiator: he presents his cousin with long lists of dos and don'ts, whose absolute truth the narration undermines, exposing them as contradictory or sometimes wrong. In a scene that lasts only a few seconds, Mok manages to propose two perfectly contradictory rules of how to cross the street in Paris. If the spectator identifies with Alilo, he or she may well reflect, anyway, that foreigners know how to cross a street, especially if, like Mok's cousin, they live in a city such as Algiers. But even if Mok's condescending contempt were not immediately apparent, the rapidity with which the script makes him change his mind from one side of the street to the other is an obvious critique. Comically, Mok first recommends extreme caution when crossing streets in Paris, "because they drive like maniacs around here" (19), but once he reaches the middle of the busy crossroads, apparently carried away by a wave of enthusiasm and passion, he proceeds to walk right in front of

incoming traffic and, to a concert of angry horns, lamely explains to his as-
tonished cousin, "Come on! Come on! That's how Paris is, got to be quick"
(19).

When Mok does not contradict himself blatantly, the film uses another
character to sow doubts in the spectator's mind and to provide the spectator
(and Alilo) with an alternative position: when Alilo explains to his new friend
and neighbor, Fatoumata, that Mok has described their *métissé* "arrondissement" as "the up-and-coming Paris neighborhood" (11), she replies: "Mok's
daydreaming! This is Moskowa, the home of poverty" (57).

Mok also lies about his family, and his fabrication is particularly revealing, because it is a perfect stereotype: according to Mok, his father is unemployed, his mother is depressed, his two brothers are probably going to die
of AIDS or of an overdose, and his sister has become a prostitute. All the elements of a typical *banlieue* tragedy are present, as if Mok had plagiarized
the worst tabloids or a sensationalist TV documentary. The narrative is a
sort of perverse form of mimicry: even if his own life contradicts the popular discourse about *banlieues*, Mok has more or less schizophrenically internalized the scenario of the undesirability of his (social and ethnic) "origins."
Alilo will have a hard time adjusting to reality when he finally meets Mok's
family and discovers a perfectly integrated and relatively happy household:
the father is retired, the mother mostly worries about her (imaginary) excess
of weight, she does cry a little when Alilo mentions her two sons, but it turns
out that she has been missing them since they emigrated to the United
States to work in films. As for the daughter, the dialogue comically nurtures
the misunderstanding for as long as possible: she does find her job very
"physical" and admits that the neighbors were surprised at first, but, like
Alilo, we finally realize that it is not because she is a prostitute but because
she drives a taxi.

Allouache has thus chosen to portray his host as a decidedly unreliable
native informant. Mok is a mythomaniac liar, and the film makes it clear that
his version of reality is challenged and contradicted both by himself and by
others. As a result, *Salut cousin!* manages to attack the implicit equation between hosting and native legitimacy from two different theoretical angles:
by exposing Mok's native knowledge and competence as flawed and over-
estimated, the film suggests that one can be a (good or bad) host without
claiming the status of native informant. Secondly, it reminds the audience

that even the host who feels most secure in his rootedness and his right to use the property as he wishes can entertain dangerous illusions about how safe he really is: at the end of the story, the policemen and women who barge into Mok's apartment and literally shove him out of the country do not even bother to give him an explanation: to a distraught Mok who asks, "Deportation . . . But . . . but what are you talking about?" the policeman simply replies: "You know full well what it's about" (64). Mok is supposed to have internalized the reasons why the system is kicking him out and to agree with the conclusions that lead to his deportation. As spectators, we are not sure "what it's about," although a few ominous signs have warned the spectator that Mok has been in trouble for a while: his girlfriend has revealed to Alilo that Mok is expecting to be tried for his involvement in a tragedy. As is often documented in *beur* novels and films, Mok was once refused entry to a bar, and his enraged friend Roger tried to avenge him by setting fire to the place. In the ensuing car chase, he lost control of the car and is now paralyzed. Invisible and mute, this well-meaning French friend, the host who did not see why he could not share his privilege with another host, rather than view Mok as a guest who cannot bring other guests, is now an albatross. Although full of good intentions, his anti-racist friend could not help Mok. His anger made his situation much worse, and he is now completely silenced and the indirect reason for Mok's deportation. But the film presents the event as an always indirect cause; Roger is not the only culprit. As in Louis Malle's *Au revoir les enfants*, where the young Jewish student is betrayed by his friend's concerned gaze (Higgins 1996), it is impossible to know exactly who to blame, to pinpoint which single act leads to Mok's deportation. We also know that Mok, using a fake ID, has accepted money from an Algerian father who wanted to marry his daughter to a citizen or a legal immigrant. In other words, he has sold the privileges of the host under false pretenses.

From the very first scene, the logic of Allouache's film thus mixes two stereotypical plots: the encounter between foreigner and native, but also the relationship between what the French would perceive as two "Arabs." And the story sets up a rather sharp contrast between the two cousins: Mok is a sophisticated Parisian who is starting a singing career; Alilo is an ignorant and naive Algerian. Mok is a Westernized Arab who takes pride in his perfect French and ridicules his cousin's Algerian French; Alilo is gentle, straightforward, and none too articulate. Mok is a cool artist who raps on La Fontaine's fables; Alilo is an unemployed *trabendiste*. As one critic puts it, this is the story of a "French *beur* who views his Algerian cousin as an amiable primitive" (Ferenczi 1996, 32). Mok is the host, and Alilo is his guest.

Immigrants as Guests, Hosts, and Parasites: The Town Rat and the Country Rat

The consequences of the two cousins' relative positioning are implied in a first level of discourse that I would like to analyze here: the constant allusions to Jean de La Fontaine's writings, and specifically to "The Town Rat and the Country Rat," an intertext that invites us to identify Mok and Alilo as the two heroes of the fable. Critics and reviewers have rarely resisted the temptation to summarize the plot with reference to the fable: *Le Film français* reviewed the film as follows: "Alilo, the Country Rat, has just arrived from Algiers for his little deal, and he marvels at the capital. Mok, the Town Rat, his cousin, a second-generation immigrant and Parisian to the core, welcomes him."[12] "The seven members of the 'Cinestival' jury fell in love with this fable of the Country Rat and the Town Rat," said *La Marseillaise*.[13] More surprisingly, but still in the same vein, the *Nouvel Observateur* chose to evoke Tex Avery's rewriting of both "Little Red Riding Hood" and "The Town Rat and the Country Rat" instead of the original intertext. "Do you know Tex Avery's 'Little Rural Riding Hood,' where a redneck country wolf comes to visit his cousin, a refined town wolf?" (R.A. 1996). As even those readers who are indeed more familiar with Tex Avery than with La Fontaine may remember, the original fable tells a tale of failed hospitality:

> Town Rat once graciously
> Asked Country Rat to dine
> On ortolans left over
> By the household. On a fine
>
> Turkish cloth the plates
> And knives and forks were laid.
> I leave you to imagine
> How merry the two friends made.

It was a handsome spread,
All that a rat could wish,
Yet someone marred the mood
Half way through the main dish.

Their ears pricked up a sound
At the dining-room door. Cat![14]
Town Rat bolted for cover,
Followed by Country Rat.

The scratching ceased, the prowler
Moved off. At once the host
Led his friend back to the field:
"Now let's finish our roast."

"That's enough, thanks," said the other
"Tomorrow you'll be my guest.
It's not that I am critical of
The food—you served the best.

But at home I eat in peace
And nobody interrupts.
Goodbye then. And to hell
With pleasure that fear corrupts.

(La Fontaine [1668] 1979, 1.9)

To be fair, critics were perfectly justified in invoking the fable so system-atically and in assuming that Alilo and Mok play the roles of the two rats, because the film employs the fable as an implicit grid of interpretation: the dialogues between the two cousins are saturated with references to La Fontaine: while he cooks for Alilo, Mok rehearses his hip-hop version of "Autrefois, autrefois le rat des villes. . . . " (Once, once, Town Rat . . . [Al-louache 1996, 20]), and later, he tries out his texts on an audience of teen-agers. Whenever Alilo mentions his cousin (to his business partner, to his parents, to Fatoumata), he talks about Mok's career: "He sings with ani-mals" (35), "He works with a machine, and with Monsieur La Fontaine for the lyrics" (56), and he tests people's reactions, as if he cannot quite decide what to make of his cousin's choice. When he picks up his suitcase from Maurice, a Jewish *pied-noir* consumed by nostalgia, he asks him:

> *Alilo:*   Monsieur Maurice! I'm sure you know La Fontaine . . .
>
> *Maurice:*   The fountain?
>
> *Alilo:*   Yes!
>
> *Maurice (ironically):*   Women's wear?
>
> *Alilo:*   No! No! La Fontaine, the guy who writes little songs about animals. He's clever . . . he talks about animals but he's talking about us. (44)

It is thus tempting to imagine that the film invites us to see Mok as the Town Rat whose love for the big city makes him ignore his potentially dangerous situation, and Alilo as the supposedly more genuine Country Rat: is Alilo a sort of *ingénu* whose native Algeria symbolizes a potentially more natural and more humanly meaningful alternative to Parisian hospitality?

Language and Hospitality

The film, however, complicates the equation by dealing with its implicit model in an ambiguous and interestingly contradictory way, for the relationship between the fable and each of the characters is decidedly asymmetrical. Given their different cultural backgrounds, Mok and Alilo cannot be equally influenced by the literary intertext, and Allouache's film takes advantage of this imbalance to explore the relationship between language and hospitality, and to criticize Mok's neocolonial belief in his own linguistic superiority. *Salut cousin!* suggests that hospitality necessarily entails an element of linguistic flexibility, which raises the issue of the relationship between hospitality and language (including the language of cultural references).

The allusion to an archetypal French author serves to mark the difference between Mok, who has gone through the French educational system and knows all the fables inside out, and Alilo, who, although he vaguely remembers one of the fables, obviously does not identify with the protagonists and does not presuppose that everyone knows La Fontaine. Here is how Mok first explains his work to his cousin:

> *Mok:*   Right now, I am working on Jean de La Fontaine's texts. The Cicada and the Ant, d'you know it?

Alilo: Oh, yes, I know him from school! When it's on the tree with a piece of cheese in its mouth.

Mok: No, you stupid idiot! [—Oh Putain de nullos!] You're too much! That's The Crow and the Cheese. (Allouache 1996, 12)

Alilo and Mok have enough literary references in common to discuss the same author. What differentiates them is their attitude toward the canonical text mentioned by Mok. Mok treats La Fontaine's fables as raw material. His slightly pompous formulation (he is "working" on "texts") implies mastery and the ability to invest in what Pierre Bourdieu would call "cultural capital." His "work," the spectator soon finds out, consists of using La Fontaine's fables as the basis for rapped compositions. Alilo, on the other hand, does not "work" with La Fontaine; he merely remembers learning some of his fables at school.

Alilo makes no extravagant claim about his knowledge of the fable. To a literary critic, his way of telling the story may appear simplistic and unsophisticated ("When it's on a tree with a piece of cheese . . ."). The two cousins do have the same common literary denominator. They share at least a minimalist canon. But no sense of cultural community can stem from this common reference, because Mok feels superior to his cousin. He acts like a schoolmaster lamenting a student's ignorance: contrasting comically with his pretentious "I am working on La Fontaine's texts," his reaction ("Putain de nullos!") to Alilo's response is a brutal shift in register, back to Parisian youth slang.

In fact, one of the differences between Mok and Alilo is the latter's lack of familiarity with the cultural references that Mok shares with his neighbors, his public, and his family. What makes him an ironic "Country Rat" is that he does not understand his role in the economy of the fable that the film surrounds him with: La Fontaine is not hospitable to him, because no agency within the film takes the trouble to make him aware that a literary model hangs over his head like a sword of Damocles.

The problematic difference between hostile and hospitable cultural references is depicted as one element in the more general issue of language: in the film, the host has internalized the superiority of "his" French, and he constantly makes fun of Alilo's difficulties in understanding. A sad parody of the colonial master, he never notices his own ignorance and gets angry just as quickly when Alilo says something that he does not understand as when Alilo does not understand what he says.[15] Alilo is perfectly willing to spell things out: "Hang on, don't get mad! I'll try to explain" (20), he responds to Mok's puzzlement over whether the motive for his cousin's trip is business or pleasure (10). Mok, on the other hand, gets angry when he has to "translate" his own words. Mok gives us the impression that his guest is expected to make the effort, and that, as host, he has a right to refuse to go beyond his own linguistic habits. Besides, he does not try to hide his contempt for his cousin's ways of talking.

When Mok reminds his cousin that *he* does not speak Arabic, he seems to take strange pride in that ignorance. On the one hand, if I suppose that Mok speaks (or ought to speak) Arabic simply because it was the native language of his parents, or at least of one of them, I ignore the complex realities of language acquisition (even if both parents speak a different language at home, it does not necessarily follow that a child will "absorb"—or should absorb—that language, especially if school reinforces another language). Mok has chosen to cut himself off from the possibility of bilingual hospitality—he has no notion of *bilangue* (Khatibi 1990).

Jacques Derrida recalls being taught in French when he was growing up in Algeria after World War II and notes that Arabic, far from being the most "obvious" foreign language, was practically impossible for him to learn, because the whole system excluded it from the realm of the learnable: "We knew that it was allowed, which meant everything but encouraged . . . Arabic, an optional foreign language in Algeria!" (Derrida 1998, 38–39). And several tactics can be equally effective in imposing "law as language":

> Every culture institutes itself through the unilateral imposition of some "politics" of language. Mastery begins, as we know, with the power of naming, of imposing and legitimating appellations.
>
>   This sovereign establishment [*mise en demeure souveraine*] may be open, legal, armed or cunning, disguised under alibis of "universal" humanism, and sometimes of the most generous hospitality. It always follows or precedes culture like its shadow. (Ibid., 1998, 39)

Law is internalized "as language" by Mok, who does not seem to see any contradiction in the fact that he is refusing to meet his cousin halfway: his cousin must learn French (and *his* French) if he wants to communicate. And even if I don't want to presuppose that Arabic is a "natural" language for Mok, his insistence that he has not taken "Arabic" as a first foreign language sounds too contemptuous not to be suspected of being a form of postcolonial mimicry.

His intolerance is all the more ironic in that Mok's own French is idiosyncratic or, rather, typical of his generation, his neighborhood, and his social class. His brand of French slang would probably sound unacceptable to the guardians of standard French.[16] And yet he does not seem conscious that his resistance to Alilo's French makes him provincial and parochially attached to what is, after all, his own version of what is "French." Whenever Alilo asks for explanations, he expresses annoyance and irritation: "Look, you're a pain! Why do I have to explain everything?" (Allouache 1996, 19). The unfairness of his impatience becomes even more obvious when Alilo is puzzled by typically *verlan*, or back slang, expressions that even a francophone foreigner would be unlikely to know: when Alilo fails to understand the remark, "Laisse béton, ils doivent pioncer" ("Forget it, they're probably asleep"), Mok exasperatedly answers: "Fine, OK! *Pioncer* . . . sleep . . . Look, it's a drag to have to explain every word I say . . . I speak French don't I?" (21). In standard French, of course, *béton* means "concrete" (the building material), but "Laisse béton!" here is back slang for "Laisse tomber!" ("Drop it!"), and short of adopting a normalizing attitude, it is difficult to point out that Mok's prescriptiveness is illegitimate.

Interestingly, although the film is critical of Mok, it does not idealize Alilo's language, which is not equated with a more culturally "authentic" dialect or vernacular, to be saved from the bulldozers of colonial education. Alilo's French does not appear to function here as the equivalent of the Caribbean creole extolled in *Eloge de la créolité* (Bernabé, Confiant and Chamoiseau 1989) or of the language that the hero of Bernard Dadié's autobiographical novel *Climbié* (Dadié 1955) could not speak at school for fear of being punished with the dreaded "symbol."[17]

The film does not clearly indicate whether it wants to celebrate Alilo's brand of bilingualism and his type of Algerian French (or French Algerian) or if it wishes to expose Alilo's simplistic vocabulary and often grammatically incorrect syntax as the mediocre result of postindependence Algerian educational efforts. Cultural theorists disagree on the issue of language:

Ahmed Roudajia laments the "Franco-Arabic and Arabo-French gobbledy-gook that even students speak," saying, "This type of esoteric and some-times hilarious conversation enacts on a daily basis the cultural and linguis-tic tragedy experienced by Algeria since its independence."[18] In another essay in the same book, Ghania Mouffok and Luc Chaulet criticize the "myth of a pure Arabic language that would have united people from the Maghreb and the Machrek" (Mouffok and Chaulet 1992, 46); in spite of failed state intervention, they write, one language has emerged that allows intercomprehension between all the populations that independence has brought under the same flag: the woman in her apartment, the Kabyle from the mountain, and the intellectual who was trained in French. The authors call that language *l'algérien* and observe: "Whenever 'Algerian' was able to fall through the net of censorship and self-censorship, this language, that turns its back on French, on Arabic, and on Berber, and that decision-mak-ers despise, was able to find favorably disposed audiences" (ibid.).[19]

To some French speakers who are not aware of the Algerian linguistic de-bate, Alilo's language may appear uncomfortably hybrid and alienating. But rather than providing a didactic explanation, rather than putting forward his own views, Allouache prefers to force us to pay attention to the issues of asymmetry and power that complicate the relationship between Alilo and his cousin: the type of linguistic intolerance that Mok displays when he speaks with Alilo is the same type of hasty rejection that he suffers from when *he* alienates his public. His "work" on La Fontaine's "texts" gets no re-spect from a crowd of suburban youths who make fun of him for being too literary, too close to what they associate with school, schoolteachers, work. "Yecch, it stinks! Out, out!! . . . We aren't in elementary school any more" (Allouache 1996, 21). What Mok probably identifies as a highly sophisti-cated adaptation of classical material is thus dismissed by a *banlieue* audience that stereotypical thinking might have led us to imagine to be his "natural" public. It is not clear whether the film wants to show that Philistine reac-tions are not the exclusive province of bourgeois audiences,[20] or whether Al-louache is making fun of his own characters' lack of artistic talent, but one irony supersedes other hesitations: the hostility displayed by the young teenagers who refuse to listen to Mok is strangely similar to Mok's own im-patience with his cousin. Linguistic codes are part of the symbolic territory that Mok tries to police as host, and he does not seem aware of the irony of his double standards.

Not realizing that, like Alilo, he is "lost in translation" (as Eva Hoffman puts it), Mok dismisses his cousin's efforts to communicate and regularly makes fun of him. As Derrida observes, however, the issue of language cannot be dissociated from the most basic level of hospitality, and one who rejects the other's language is already rejecting him or her:

> Among the serious issues that we are dealing with here is that of the stranger's discomfort with our language. A foreigner always runs the risk of being made powerless by the judicial system of the nation that welcomes or expels him or her: the stranger is first and foremost a foreigner in the judicial language that articulates the duty of hospitality, the right to asylum, its limits, its norms, its police, etc. He or she must ask for hospitality in a language that, by definition, is not his or her own, that is imposed by the master of the house, the host, the king, the lord, power, the nation, the state, the father, etc. They impose a translation into their own language, and that is the first type of violence. The question of hospitality starts here: must we require the stranger to understand us, to speak our language in all the meanings of the words, in all its possible extensions, before being able to, in order to be able to, welcome him or her? (Derrida and Dufourmantelle 1997, 21)

Allouache's film shows that the host's linguistic violence can exist as a series of layers of intolerance: Mok's linguistic inhospitality is mirrored by France's inhospitality to some French speakers. The "judicial" or official language is a sort of passport that opens or closes doors, and its power is always differential.

Rats and Parasites

As far as Mok is concerned, translation is always one-sided and always a cause of impatience and irritation, but the film does not let him get away with this pseudosuperiority: the literary intertext constantly reminds the viewer that even the supposedly sophisticated Town Rat is sometimes treated as a bothersome parasite. More generally speaking, the host is not allowed to be the only powerful speaker whose idiom must be the immigrant's and his or her translators' ultimate target language.

In other words, contrary to what a superficial reading of the intertext suggests, *Salut cousin!* has no interest in confirming the binary structure of the fable, in which the Country Rat is either the grateful or the ungrateful guest of the Town Rat. Mok can certainly, at first, be read as a sophisticated host—a denizen of "Paris branché" (plugged-in Paris), as he puts it—who will show his naive guest a good time. If we remember the end of the fable, however, we also have to assume that the feast will be interrupted. La Fontaine's fable suggests that there is something fake or incomplete about the Town Rat's hospitality, and that he should have warned his guest that he is not master of the situation. The threatening presence of the real owner of the house hovers over the scene, and it is clear that this powerful but invisible presence only allows the subaltern rat to partake of human leftovers. In the fable, the Country Rat objects to the dangerous way he is entertained and says he could have offered simpler but more wholesome hospitality. But, as Michel Serres had already observed in his study of "interrupted meals," the fable presents us with a whole gallery of portraits that can all be placed in the category of "parasites": "The city rat invites the country rat onto the Persian rug. They gnaw and chew leftover bits of ortolan. Scraps, bits and pieces, leftovers: their royal feast is only a meal after a meal among the dirty dishes of a table that has not been cleared. The city rat has produced nothing and his dinner invitation costs him almost nothing" (Serres 1982, 3).

What is interesting in Serres's formulation is that he seems to blame the Town Rat for practicing a type of selfish hospitality that does not require any effort: he did not prepare the meal; the rats must content themselves with feasting on what the actual host and his guests have left uneaten. Mok as Town Rat is thus sharing a cultural meal that he has not cooked; he is inviting his cousin to live like a parasite. Yet, if we insert the fable into the context of the film, the Town Rat's invitation can also be seen as a confession of powerlessness. Although he brags about his familiarity with "Paris branché," Mok is hardly in control of his life, and he must survive on crumbs left under the table after more legitimate meals. No matter how much he wishes to share with Alilo (and there is an obvious element of bragging in his generosity), he can only give him what society lets him have access to. Many, like him, find that they cannot "produce" much of anything because they are unemployed. In *Salut cousin!*, Mok is about to start an apparently high-risk career as a singer, and even his impresario cannot be eliminated from the list of parasites who organize the distribution of cultural, financial, and political crumbs.

Mok's powerlessness is relative, however, and I would argue that it does not altogether foreclose the possibility of hospitality: in spite of a relatively narrow room for maneuver, the Town Rat has skills, and he takes advantage of his knowledge. He knows how to be in the right place at the right time to benefit from the "ortolans left over," and it is not exactly true that it does not cost him anything: he is willing to share his resources with Alilo, who will get something out of his stay in Paris.

For the film does not buy into the idea that a return to the "country" (including one's country of origin) is always an idyllic return to peace and uninterrupted legitimacy: in the fable, the opposition is ultimately used to criticize the Town Rat's unjustified feeling of superiority. The fable suggests that if hospitality is threatened by a force that the host cannot control, if the power invested in the host is not absolute, and if another level of ownership can, at any time, claim the land (and therefore access to food, to resources, to recognition), then, it is corrupt and unacceptable. As the Country Rat puts it when it refuses to return to the feast after the cat's appearance:

> It's not that I am critical of
> The food—you served the best.
>
> But at home I eat in peace
> And nobody interrupts.
> Goodbye then. And to hell
> With pleasure that fear corrupts.

Here, the film departs from the fable. Contrary to his literary model, Alilo never tries to portray his native Algiers as a haven of peace. He does mention what the international press loves to cover (violence, danger), but he is also particularly critical of gender relationships at home. When he does reluctantly speak of his life in Algeria, he explains that, in Algiers, if he as much as speaks to a woman, he cannot ever marry her, because she will be considered a fallen woman. Besides, he sadly remarks, it is a non-issue anyway, because he has no money and no flat. In Paris, he falls in love with Fatoumata, with whom he moves in at the end of the film. Another type of hospitality is thus inaugurated, between a sub-Saharan African woman and an Algerian male, who own nothing but the desire to stay together, as if hospitality here were a mutual decision to cope with the absence of legitimacy and recognition by a larger group.

Salut cousin! thus does not necessarily glorify the Country Rat's desire for peace and honest simplicity. Serres's insight is to recognize the ambiguity of the host's position: the Town Rat is itself a parasite, the Country Rat is also a parasite, but so is the ultimate host (perhaps a *fermier général*, or tax collector?) whose meal is being devoured. *Salut cousin!* uses the fable in a different way, however: of course, it is possible to see the world as a collection of parasites who imagine themselves as host(-parasites) or guest(-parasites), but the film also suggests that it is the prerogative of dominant societies to impose a logic of interchangeability between powerless individuals who can, at any time, be reinterpreted as guests and not as hosts by the powers that be. Only if we place Mok in the context of French immigration policy do we see that the presence of a second, more legitimate owner deprives him of the pleasures of entertaining Alilo as his guest.

To make that point, the story must reveal the limits of the literary intertext and highlight its contradictions. This is done by the addition of another (visual) interpretive grid that competes with La Fontaine's fable in the film. If we pay attention to visual layers that seem irrelevant to the plot, a new level of meaning points up the tension between the dialogue, which emphasizes the literary source, and the representation of another creature in *Salut cousin!* that contradicts the lesson offered by the "rat." That creature is Mok's goldfish, a constant presence that comments on his life and decisions and offers us a completely different version from his own narrative and the lesson of the interrupted meal.

Mok's Goldfish and Alilo's Suitcase

When Alilo first walks into Mok's apartment, the first brief interaction between the two cousins and the fish is a way of laying down ground rules between the host and the guest. Then, throughout the film, the fishbowl appears in the frame whenever an important scene takes place inside Mok's apartment. When Mok cooks for Alilo, the fish is in the foreground, and it is visible in the scene when the community rallies around Alilo after he is beaten up by skinheads. The fish is also the fake protagonist or parodic witness in an important scene where Alilo finally rebels against Mok's lies and disobliging inventions about his family. Finally, when the police come to deport Mok, three shots give the viewer three different perspectives of the fish in his bowl: when the police knock on the door, a closeup of the bowl shows us the fish bumping its head against the glass, seemingly struggling to escape. Before he consents to leave the apartment, Mok insists on feeding the fish one last time. A bird's-eye view of the fishbowl is the last shot of the apartment after Mok's departure.

In the first scene, while Alilo is trying to establish some sort of contact with the fish (he dips his finger into the water and taps on the glass), Mok insists on laying down the rules: as the host, he explains how things work in his territory. The fish's name is "Personne" (Nobody), he says, and Alilo should never feed it, because it requires special food. He also reprimands Alilo for trying to talk to the fish through his fingertapping: "Are you trying to traumatize him or what?" Alilo is thus told off for trying to interact in a way that he thought was friendly and welcoming. Mok makes it clear that he is in charge, that he knows the codes and the law. Food and friendliness are governed by the host, who expects the guest to follow his recommendations.

This first scene is important, because it prepares us for the film's portrayal of Alilo as a bad guest who will, in Mok's absence, do exactly the opposite of what he is supposed to do: after finding out that Mok has been lying to him about the family, about his own story, Alilo becomes a rebellious guest. The "bad" guest is, in fact, pointing out to the spectator that the host was being unreasonable, and that the whole relationship of power between the host who knows and the guest who must learn should be redefined.

In this scene, Alilo suddenly becomes the host: he is alone in Mok's apartment waiting for his cousin to come home, and he decides to cook for him, buying groceries, including a single banana, at the local market. The "Spaghetti à la thaïlandaise" that Mok has cooked for his (skeptical) cousin on the evening of his arrival is here replaced by a typically Algerian dish. And not only does Alilo take the place of the host in cooking for Mok, but he also deliberately breaks the rules by feeding the fish a big chunk of bread. He is quite aware of what he is doing: when he feeds the fish, he angrily calls Mok a *salaud* (bastard) for feeding it "dust" and not proper food. Mok's fancy fish food is thus dismissed as phony.

Alilo even rebaptizes the fish in this scene, a symbolic reappropriation that also satirizes Mok's ambitious dream: he addresses the fish as "M'sieur Cousteau." The name is not insulting or cruel, and the allusion to Jacques Cousteau, a contemporary media personality, is consistent with Alilo's international TV references. But it denotes a different type of imagination, a different way of positioning oneself on the chessboard of literary and cultural allusions: "M'sieur Cousteau" is certainly less glamorous or perhaps less pretentious that the fish's "real" name, the name picked by Mok, "Personne," one of the numerous literary references (in this case to Homer's *Odyssey*) that his cousin does not seem capable of appreciating or even of identifying. Throughout the film, the fact that Mok has to explain the meaning of words and allusions puts Alilo at a disadvantage. Yet, in spite of his impression that he "is" French, and that, unlike Alilo, he speaks the language fluently, Mok cannot legitimize his presence on French soil. Calling his fish "Personne" not only conjures up the figure of a homeless traveler but indicates a knowledge of situations where linguistic cunning alone will allow the hero to fool the dangerous comrades of the outsmarted and wounded Cyclops. If we accept that the fish is a degraded portrait of his owner and a comment on his precarious relationship to his less than perfect environment, the name "Nobody" is a sad vision of the distance between Mok's self-aggrandizing portrait of himself and the reality of his powerlesness. If Mok is indeed *personne*, it because the system treats him like an interchangeable Arab, even if he sees himself as "French." The image of the lonely fish stuck in its bowl is seen from the perspective of an all-powerful camera, and it provides a tragic contrast with Mok's voice, heard on the soundtrack, emanating from the answering machine, triggered by Alilo's call. Mok's voice suddenly seems like the fish speaking, delivering a couple of uncannily appropriate quotations: "Qui veut voyager loin ménage sa monture" ("He who wants to travel far looks after his mount" [Racine, *Les plaideurs* 1.1]),[21] and "Rien ne sert de courir; il faut partir à point" ("It's no good rushing; what counts is getting a good start" [La Fontaine 6.10]). These snippets about the art of traveling and getting somewhere take on a rather sinister meaning, especially when followed by Mok's supposedly reassuring message: "I'm not home . . . but don't worry, I'll be back soon" (Allouache 1996, 64). The supposedly streetwise urban rat has underestimated his resemblance to the only creature whose life is apparently not worthy of being turned into a fable, but whose fate closely matches that of its owner: forgetting that he is prisoner of a glass wall, he entertains the illusion that he can grant hospitality, but the end of the film reminds him that his situation was always one of precarious dependence.

In the economy of the film, the tragic implications of Alilo's voice resonating in Mok's empty apartment are slightly compensated for by the message itself: Alilo announces that he cannot go back to Algiers because his suitcase, which he has left on the platform, has been destroyed by the police. And although he starts his sentence with an ominous "It is a tragedy" (echoing the very first conversation between the two cousins, when Alilo explains that he has lost the address of the owner of the suitcase), the spectator knows that he is not devastated to be forced to stay a while: to Mok, he explains that the destruction of the suitcase forces him to stay in Paris for fear of his boss's reprisals, but he also confesses coyly that he is in love with Fatoumata and has accepted her hospitality.

In a ruthlessly symmetrical pattern, the film swaps the two characters: Mok, who felt most rooted, most secure in his identity as a Parisian *beur* is suddenly made transient and forced into exile, while his counterpart, whose presence was always construed as a detour, a forced delay caused by a comedy of errors, ends up staying in France for the foreseeable future.

The moment of substitution when the two cousins suddenly exchange their respective identities as traveler and resident does not come as a complete surprise to the spectator who has followed the evolution in the relationship between the characters and the objects that the film assigns to them. While the film suggests that the recurrent image of the fish can be read as a visualization of Mok's fate, it also pairs Alilo with a visual unit that accompanies him through Paris, the constantly reappearing and disappearing suitcase, a piece of luggage that redefines the definition of baggage and carefully exposes some apparently innocent assumptions about the connection between a suitcase and its owner, a suitcase and the person who carries it, the contents of a suitcase, and a person's identity.

From the beginning of the film, Allouache makes the point that Alilo's

suitcase is the only object that has any significance, and that it will not function as the traditional piece of luggage that we have come to recognize as
the mark of the traveler. Normally, the presence of a suitcase is already a discreet request for hospitality: its bearer will need a space to put it down at the
end of the day. As for the contents of the case, they represent what is left of
"home," what can stand for home: what is inside the suitcase simultaneously
underlines the absence of home and the idea of what home is (now reduced
to a collection of things).

In Alilo's case, however, the suitcase plays a completely different role.
Alilo does not carry it with him from home and ends up not taking it back
with him to Algiers. In other words, the presence of the suitcase paradoxically corresponds to the duration of his trip (it disappears when Alilo decides to stay in Paris), but in a strange reversal of traditional narratives, it is
because the suitcase disappears from the picture that the trip is over rather
than the other way around. In fact, the suitcase is a constant source of concern and curiosity; it makes people talk and ask questions; it forces some
characters to go somewhere, to wait, to act, to choose: it is a catalyst. It generates questions about identity and dwelling, staying and going, being a
guest and being a traveler, about the circulation of objects and the circulation of people.

Each traveler has his or own way of using a suitcase and ideas about how
best to treat this home away from home. Some do not unpack until the nostalgic desire for an exotic destination has receded. Some unpack right away
because they can't bear the sight of the suitcase, the thought of its tempo-
rariness, because putting the suitcase away out of sight is evidence of (sedentary) normal life. Each departure has its rituals and its representational cli-
chés too: how many films show a woman throwing a suitcase on a bed and
filling it haphazardly with clothes when a relationship is about to end melo-
dramatically? In many cases, the size, quality, quantity, and shape of the
piece(s) of luggage serve as visual or textual shortcuts to give us information
about the type of the journey and the identity of the traveler: the suitcase is
the only thing today's affluent tourists and the refugees fleeing across France
in 1940 have in common. And in *Salut cousin!* the omnipresence of the suitcase brings back ghostly memories of the war of Algeria, when the revolutionary slogan "La valise ou le cercueil" (The suitcase or the coffin) confronted Algerian *pieds-noirs*.

In itself, the suitcase does not connote tragedy or happiness. Like hospitality, it is the locus of an ambivalent space that creates the possibilities of generosity, of (ex)change, of an enriched relationship, but also of abandonment and cruelty, of betrayal and loss. If the fishbowl represents the limits of the host's safety (Mok has a home, but he is a prisoner of this carefully invented bowl, out of which he probably will not survive), the suitcase also emphasizes the potential fragility of the guest, as well as his relative freedom and mobility.

Historical intertexts also remind us that suitcases sometimes ironize the notion that a journey implies a return. Even if representing death as a final trip is a banal cliché, the presence of a real suitcase that has survived its owner often functions as a reminder of unspeakable physical and mental cruelties. When the trip has no real destination except nothingness, suffering, and death, the suitcase only reinforces the abject hypocrisy of the rhetoric of deportation. Many families deported by the Nazis were allowed to hastily pack a suitcase when they were arrested, and we can imagine what it may have meant to be able to carry the suitcase as far as possible, as far as the system that would crush them permitted, as long as it was possible to sustain the slightest illusion that this trip would be of the kind from which the traveler is allowed to return.[22]

In Allouache's film, the suitcase is not linked with such excruciatingly painful situations, and, even if Mok's secret is a tragedy, it has nothing to do with that specific motif. The treatment of the suitcase in *Salut cousin!* seems particularly inventive in the context of North African immigration literature and culture: in *beur* literature, in testimonies and films, the suitcase is never innocent. It is a constant reminder that whether or not they have French nationality, people of North African origin, and even their children, will be treated as guests, whose rights are limited by the host's rules ("Don't feed the fish"; "Don't cross the street"; "Cross the street").

According to recent published and audiovisual testimonies, the generation that French popular culture continues to refer to as the "second" generation of Arab immigrants was tormented by the frustrating persistence of eternal suitcases: here, the perversion of the traditional trip did not lie in the absence of a meaningful destination but rather in the fact that the parents refused to interpret their children's home as a final destination. With hindsight, their children now realize that the dream of a return to Algeria was a carefully nurtured illusion, but for years the paradox of a long-term but precarious stay persisted without being named, without being organized by a coherent narrative. But when is it clear that the notion of returning is an illusion? When does the carefully preserved mobility of those who don't buy furniture and deprive themselves of comforts become an unrealistic dream that destroys the present instead of preparing the future? And the longer one lives out of a suitcase, the more difficult it becomes to give up on all those years of investment in a better future elsewhere.

Children who were born and raised in France may have trouble understanding that their parents or grandparents did not have a choice and were forced to keep everything they had in a suitcase because they lacked proper accommodation. Recruited by French industry at a time when France suffered from a severe housing shortage, some North African immigrants both symbolically and literally lived out of their suitcases for years. Recent accounts of life in *bidonvilles* have finally told the stories of children whose belongings fit into cardboard boxes or suitcases, out of which the mother extracted perpetually crinkled clothes (Lallaoui 1993; Lefort 1980; Begag 1986; Benaïcha 1992).

In Yamina Benguigui's *Mémoires d'immigrés*, the perpetual feeling of uprootedness is symbolized by the overwhelming presence of the never-disappearing suitcase: "My brothers and sisters grew up clutching suitcases. Me too" (Benguigui 1997, 9). With one hand on the handle of the suitcase, the children of immigrants are caught in an eternal no-man's-land: they are not going, they are not staying, they are in the state that Hélène Cixous calls *Algériance*, a perpetual process of departure and infinitely deferred arrival that the suffix *-ance* implicitly connects with Derridean *différance*, or postponement of interpretation (Cixous 1998, 153). Neither quite host nor quite guest, the character whose hands clutch a suitcase is supposed to acquire the identity of the Town Rat, whose meals are always potentially interrupted by the real master of the house.

In Allouache's film, however, the omnipresent object redefines the role of the predetermined suitcase. Here, it is not the emblem of the traveler but of the businessman: what is inside the suitcase is what counts, and that does not belong to Alilo. He does not even travel with his suitcase: when he arrives at the station, his bag is so small that he could almost be a commuter who has just alighted from a suburban train. And the end of the story aligns his identity with the first images of the film: the suitcase miraculously disappears, literally in a puff of smoke, liberating Alilo from the past, from Algeria, from his business deal, and from being a migrant.

The association between the suitcase and business is established from the very first encounter between Mok and Alilo. Whereas the typical traveler arrives with a suitcase, Alilo picks up a suitcase that he has not packed. He does not own the contents either. When he returns, he will give the suitcase to his boss, and his job will be done: in other words, the suitcase is never connected to his identity, unless we consider that his business is a professional identity (a weak identity in this case and also part of a parallel economy). The ambiguity is used by Allouache to create comic moments of (mis)reading and ambiguities: for example, Alilo is puzzled by his African neighbors, who constantly carry tiny business cases. He wonders what could be the point of carrying such small suitcases, into which hardly any merchandise can fit (some Rolex watches perhaps?) Mok has told him that his neighbors work in "international trade," but the explanation seems implausible to Alilo, who defines business as the carrying of one suitcase from one country to the next.

The fact that he does not own the contents of the suitcase makes him an improbable traveler and even gives one of the minor characters an opportunity to express stereotypical homophobia: in one particularly unpleasant scene, Alilo, who has left the suitcase at Mok's place, comes back to find that someone is trying to take it from him. Mok has accumulated gambling debts he can't pay, and the creditor has come to his flat to demand his due. Thinking that there may be valuables in Alilo's suitcase, he opens it and pulls out an expensive woman's dress. When Mok begs him not to take the suitcase because it belongs to his cousin, the man answers: "C'est une tante ton cousin?" ("Is your cousin a queen?"). The question is implicitly cruel because it is clear that the thug is throwing a generally hostile blanket over homosexuals and transvestites. In the French dialogue, the homophobic insult is perhaps slightly redeemed by the fact that the retort is also a linguistic pun on the parallel between "cousin" and "aunt" (*tante*), as if Mok had simply lied about the nature of the relationship that connects him to Alilo. But Serge's nasty question also serves to confirm an assumption that we presumably share: the contents of the suitcase represent or at least give an indication about the identity of the bearer of the suitcase. As a passport metonymically replaces your identity when you present it to the immigration officer, what is inside the suitcase is supposed to represent who you are. Here, the implausibility of the connection between the red haute-couture dress that Serge extracts from the suitcase and the image of a "male" cousin makes him question Mok's story: as if when a suitcase does not contain what people expect you to own, or wear, it can no longer be yours.

The suitcase is contaminated by the suspicion that Alilo suffers from some form of troubled identity. His relation to his own suitcase is so problematic that, throughout the film, the way in which he relates to this disappearing object marks the different stages of his progressive incorporation into a Paris of sorts. At first, it is even missing altogether, because Alilo has lost the piece of paper that indicated where he was supposed to pick it up. Alilo does not have an address, and he does not have a suitcase: in other words, the object that the film will progressively connect to Alilo in the same manner as the fish is Mok's emblem first identified as a structuring absence, a crisis ("It's a tragedy," Alilo says when he meets Mok for the first time). The suitcase is either absent, confusing, or threatening.[23] At the end of the film, Alilo finally stays in Paris for good, while Mok is deported because of a final incident that involves the wretched suitcase: viewers who saw the film when it first came out would have needed no reminder that a suitcase left alone on a platform would immediately have aroused suspicion. In 1995, Parisians were used to the visible anti-terrorist "Plan Vigipirate" and to the spectacle of sealed trash cans. And one of the very last scenes of *Salut cousin!* ironically comments on the counterproductive effects of paranoid associations between foreigners, travelers, and potential terrorist threats. That sequence is particularly interesting from a visual point of view: Alilo and Fatoumata are together on the platform. Alilo is about to depart, and she meets him just in time to declare her love and force him to do the same. The couple enter the frame from the left and move away from the camera, with their backs to us, their silhouettes diminishing progressively as the camera moves back, away from them. At first, a tiny portion of the frame (to the right and at the bottom) is occupied by the top of Alilo's suitcase on the platform. As the camera moves back, the proportion between the size of the camera and the two characters is reversed. From the right bottom angle, the suitcase gradually invades more and more of our visual space, until it almost hides the two characters. It is not clear whose point of view the camera is adopting, and only later do we find out whether this particular angle has any significance at all. What the spectator may notice at that point is that the suitcase is left alone (that Alilo is separated from that part of his identity, and that he finds himself in the same position as he was when he arrived a luggage-free traveler) and that from one point of view, the suitcase is becoming bigger and bigger, as if someone is paying more and more attention to it, rather than to Alilo.

That particular hypothesis is later confirmed when the suitcase has completely disappeared from the frame, to be replaced by Alilo's voice on Mok's machine: he announces, once again, that the situation is "very serious," and that he cannot go back to Algiers because the police have destroyed the suitcase. Paradoxically, then, it is the misreading of the suitcase as the property of a dangerous terrorist that prevents Alilo's return to his own country and forces him into illegal immigration. Just as the so-called Pasqua laws were accused of creating illegal immigrants by endlessly complicating access to regular status, a paranoid reading of the suitcase (the fear of Alilo as Arab terrorist) prevents the return of one Algerian traveler who never had any intention to emigrate, whose stay in Paris should only have lasted a few days.

Conclusion

While the intertextual reference to Jean de La Fontaine's "Le rat des villes et le rat des champs" places Mok squarely in the position of the sophisticated host and Alilo in that of the more ignorant and naive guest, the film contradicts this hypothesis by attaching to each character an object whose recurring appearance tells a different story about the construction of their respective identities. While the plot and the literary references converge to separate Mok and Alilo and insist on their difference (the traveler versus the sedentary Parisian; the urban artist versus the unemployed *trabendiste*; the "Frenchman" versus the Algerian; and, finally, the host and the guest), the fishbowl and the suitcase insist on the internal contradictions of their identities and ultimately lead to the interchangeability enacted at the end of the film notwithstanding the characters' wishes. As parodic images of the two characters' situations, the fishbowl and the suitcase constitute a visual refrain or running commentary that belies both Mok's optimistic portrait of himself and Alilo's determination to go back after a few days.

Salut cousin! suggests that, in the case of immigrants, the distinction between guest and host tends to be blurred by the fact that the opposition is always inserted into a larger structure that barely tolerates the idea that an immigrant should become a host. That structure, however, cannot accommodate the relativity of hospitality, its inherently reciprocal possibilities, and the vision of a continuum between hospitality granted and received. Three images of the immigrant as guest and/or host are thus proposed in the film: the goldfish, the rat, and the baggageless traveler. The literary intertext explores the ethical dimensions of the charges of parasitism disguised in La Fontaine's fable, but the very notion of parasitism is implicitly criticized and modified by the image of the goldfish imprisoned in its bowl. The ultimate host may at any point trap and expel the "rat" from the house. If Alilo manages to protect his freedom, it is because he accepts that he is no host: his status remains eminently unstable, and he must accept being a guest; he is at the mercy of generous friends and relatives (Mok's family invite him, Fatoumata takes him in). But at the end of the film, his trip no longer has a professional purpose and the symbolic suitcase has disappeared. For him, a form of *errance* is the only solution, and his form of migration, or rather migrancy, does not come with the glamorous identity of the jet-setter or of the modernist intellectual.[24]

Salut cousin! suggests that individual hospitality is overdetermined by the way in which the state manages immigration and national identity and demonstrates that the system often leads to self-contradictory maneuvers. Not only is the state incapable of living up to its hospitality laws, but it cannot control the complex workings of hospitality between individuals. At times, it even goes against its own inhospitable dictates: in *Salut cousin!* the system exceeds its own logic by deporting a perfectly integrated *beur* and by creating the conditions that paradoxically lead to Alilo becoming an illegal immigrant. The general balance of state hospitality by the end of the film is a zero-sum game: one person leaves, one stays; statistically, nothing has happened. But the state's inhospitable suspicion of strangers is what forces the one to stay and makes him dependent on another immigrant's hospitality.

CHAPTER FIVE

Gender and Hospitality: Women as Gifts, Hostesses, and Parasites

In this chapter, I would like to adopt a perspective that will slightly modify the focus (or bias) adopted in the preceding pages: as I suggested in the Introduction, no discussion of hospitality can ignore the troubling elimination of the female figure from the primordial guest-host pair and how hard it is for women to be treated as guests. But I also knew that my emphasis on migrants (which reflects the flavor of contemporary debates) would lead me in a direction that did not automatically include gender. Political and ethical discourses tend to privilege discussions of the migrant as a metaphor for a group whose gendered characteristics are less significant than other markers (not only racial and cultural differences, but also numbers and movement). If one privileges the interaction between the national and the foreigner, if the most evident model for the guest is the immigrant, then contemporary cultural debates are bound to focus on the public rather than on the private sphere, on the collective rather than on the individual, and on a supposedly universalistic nongendered perspective rather than on the specifically gendered aspects of hospitality.

It may therefore seem rather counterintuitive to focus on the most private and domestic practices of hospitality. And yet, the decision to concentrate on what happens once the stranger has entered the home enables us to foreground concerns that we often relegate to the domain of the negligible. Those issues, once addressed, might enable us to throw some light on attempts to redefine the most general aspects of hospitality. Just as new forms of historicism and historiography have taught us that it is immensely valuable to concentrate on those ordinary people whom history tends to forget in order to privilege heroes, the will to concentrate on the humblest or most ambiguous forms of hospitality will force us to change perspective and to recognize that the relevance of certain issues might be relative. Other questions, on the other hand, will be brought to the fore and become unavoidable.

The most evident of such reconfigurations has to do with the construction of gender in the domain of hospitality. An analysis of texts or films that take place inside the house will force us to mobilize and perhaps question our stereotypes about the differences between private and public as the respective provinces of male and female. If a general discourse about immigration and hospitality tends to remain non-gender-specific (because of the strong connection between hospitality and universalistic ideals or illusions), a study of what happens once the (male or female) guest is inside the house will make it much more difficult to ignore the gender specificities of the host or hostess's role. New types of questions will unavoidably be asked, such as what happens to hospitality when it has become domestic hospitality, or, how do different cultures conceptualize a specifically feminine hospitality? More concretely, depending on what type of dwelling we envisage, how does a female guest differ from a male guest, and how is a host different from a hostess? And, as Joachim Manzi puts it, "How does one welcome, name, love the female stranger?" ("Comment accueillir, aimer, nommer la femme étrangère" [Manzi 1999]).[1]

I therefore propose to concentrate on several works of fiction (two films and one short story) that present us with case studies in which a consideration of gender simply cannot be avoided.

Women as Bad Hostesses: Sembène Ousmane's
"Black Girl" and Jean Renoir's Boudu sauvé des eaux

The first text I wish to consider is "La noire de . . . ," a 1962 short story by the Senegalese author and film director Sembène Ousmane, which he later adapted for the cinema himself. By questioning the attributes of the host and challenging us to interpret the characters as either "natural" hosts or unlikely guests, this story invites the reader to reflect on the harmful consequences of splitting the figure of the host into distinct human beings.

The story begins with a sentence that establishes a clear-cut distinction between the events of which it tells and history with a capital H. From the very first paragraph, the text both connects and differentiates the suicide of the young Senegalese protagonist and the story's historical background: "It was the morning of the 23rd of June in the year of Our Lord nineteen hundred fifty-eight. At Antibes, along the Riviera, neither the fate of the French Republic nor the future of Algeria nor the state of the colonial territories preoccupied those who swarmed across the beaches below La Croisette" (Sembène 1997, 42).

Ousmane sets his story against a background of war and decolonization: the date he chooses makes the young woman's death coincide with the end of the Battle of Algiers, with Charles de Gaulle's referendum colonial self-government within a French community, and with the resounding "No" to that question orchestrated by the Guinean leader Ahmed Sékou Touré. The date is therefore historically significant, but it is also presented as a non-issue, a frame whose presence the participants in the story choose to be oblivious to. The omniscient narrator's ambiguous gesture thus makes sure that 1958 becomes both impossible to forget and relatively irrelevant to the characters.

I suggest that this deliberately ambivalent beginning is a proposal made to the reader: like the journalists and police inspectors who are arriving at the house at the same time as the story's readers, so to speak, we are invited to decode and to interpret a specific situation. Later, when we try to understand how some forms of perverse hospitality can lead to a guest's death, we shall have to keep in mind that we were warned about the risk of separating history from what goes on in the house. The tourists who "swarmed across the beaches" (the French says "invaded the beach," and I can't help thinking that the allusion to conquerors is intentional) are models of bad readers, whose tendency is to separate the public from the private, history from stories, the house from the nation.

At the beginning of the story, the point of view zooms in on a private mansion, the dwelling place of a French family and of their young Senegalese live-in maid, who has just cut her throat in the bathtub. At the end of the story, two laconic paragraphs tell us: "'Suicide,' the investigators concluded. The case was closed. The next day, in the newspaper, on page 4, column 6, hardly noticeable, was a small headline: 'Homesick African Girl Cuts Throat in Antibes'" (54).

In between, a long flashback invites us to take the place of those "investigators" and of the "journalists" who did not know how to tell the story and who opted for absence, invisibility: the author's text is a deliberate attempt at replacing their interpretation with a different and more complex account, as if he had to write one of the possible stories of this "black girl" to resist the mimetic gesture of white witnesses who are in a rush to make the body disappear, physically and figuratively.

To the simplicity of the inquiry's conclusions, which reduce Diouana to her racial and gender identity ("a black woman") and to a feeling of powerlessness and passive fragility (she is supposed to be homesick, to suffer from a fatal case of nostalgia), Ousmane opposes a backward look that reveals violence and unconscious abuse. His determination to go back to the source of her seemingly inexplicable act reveals a logic of perverse hospitality whose consequences could easily remain invisible. I suggest that if the author implicitly rejects the distinction between Algeria and Antibes, between the international and the private, if he insists on replacing silence or journalistic shortcuts with a detailed narrative that superimposes the present on the past, Africa on France, it is because the short story as a whole wishes to promote a form of hospitality that does not completely separate the figure of the host from that of the guest, or rather objects to the possibility of splitting the figure of the host into different actors who are each responsible for distinct tasks and whose identity places them on a rigidly organized hierarchical ladder.

When is the overall figure of the host split into separate roles? It happens when an excluded third character is inserted between the guest and the host, when the servant appears on the social stage. And one aspect of the servant's identity or function is particularly disturbing, especially when he or she is required to live under the same roof as the master: although servants share with guests the right to enter the master's house, they are precisely not placed in the position of guests. Instead, servants find themselves expected to act as if they were hosts-owners whose responsibility is to attend the guests' needs, to take care of them, humbly. Even if modern guests no longer want their host to wash away the dirt accumulated on their feet after a long and tiring journey, the generous ambiguity of the host's position is that he is a master who is willing to turn into a servant, at least temporarily. Everyone knows that this interlude is not meant to last, and that even when the master consents to act as a servant, he can recuperate some of his prestige and power through more or less perverse readings of his gesture: a master who seems to lower himself in the service of his guests can derive a symbolic profit from his humility that turns his ostentatious gift into a form of investment, of "largesse." Yet, even if his discomfort is largely compensated for by the way in which he calculates the benefits he will derive from his position, it is understood that he consents to take the place of the weaker, that he uses his body to make someone else's comfortable. The extreme-case scenario transforms the host into a voluntary slave.

Ideal hospitality obtains when the definition of the host reaches the highest possible density of symbolic polysemy: the host consents to play apparently incompatible roles, those of master and slave. But one of the ways in which the host can deviate from this ideal is to avoid the element of servitude that his function requests by delegating that specific aspect of his task, by making sure that each of the different components of his role will be taken up by a different individual. And when the locus of hospitable invitations is the private bourgeois house, this division of labor is not accompanied by a recognition that the labor in question should be compensated. On the one hand, the presence of guests creates work that the master of the house is not prepared to do, but the work still has to be done by a subaltern, who finds herself transformed into an excluded third by the hospitable pact. It thus happens that when the host welcomes you and makes sure that you are comfortable inside his house, he has arranged for a system of hierarchical redoubling: the host remains in charge of the welcoming gesture, but he is no longer responsible for the work created by his desire to pamper his or her guest. He may decide on how dedicated he will be, but his hospitality will be relayed by a servant, who will mediate between the guest and the master's desire.

Until now, I have not made much of an effort to establish equality between the sexes when talking about the owner of the house. I have generally used the masculine to describe the host, avoiding the systematic use of "he or she" grammatical tactics in anticipation of the following statement: generally, it is clear that when this dissociation between welcoming and taking care of the guest intervenes, it coincides, in the bourgeois home, with a separation between masculine and feminine. And that opposition is often compounded by the presence of a servant.

I am thinking of Jean Renoir's film *Boudu sauvé des eaux*, where M. Lestingois, master of the house, is presented as the archetypal generous host. After diving into the Seine to save the homeless Boudu from suicide, he brings the man back home, and, despite the reluctance of his wife and his maid, invites him in and asks him to stay. From the beginning of this tense cohabitation, it is painfully evident that Lestingois wishes to welcome Boudu (spontaneously, it seems, as if to satisfy an instinct rather than to fulfill a duty). The two women, on the other hand, are immediately hostile to the guest, and his presence triggers a latent conflict between the male and female characters. A form of complicity develops between the owner and his guest, the masculine pair being pitted against the two women's hostility and anger. Social differences are erased by the rearrangement of hospitable roles, the two women equally losing power in front of a guest who would normally be at the bottom of the social pecking order. Madame Lestingois and her maid, Anne-Marie, unite against the stranger.[2]

Usurping the role of the owner of the house, Anne-Marie remarks out loud: "This guy is filthy. I hope we aren't going to keep him!" ("Qu'il est sale, ce type-là, j'espère qu'on ne va pas le garder"). Translating *on* as "we" is a stretch, but the French impersonal pronoun, although grammatically singular, pretends to install a communal decision, hiding the fact that the servant will have no say in the matter. As for the legitimate spouse, she objects to the idea of Boudu spending the night with them and proposes to give him money to pay for a hotel room. Her solution to the situation is to switch from private hospitality to commercial hospitality and to make it clear that her gift consists of allowing the guest to benefit from the material comfort bought by money but not from her own attentions. It is therefore tempting to conclude that the film presents "women" (or at least the two main female characters) as either incapable of a spontaneous gesture of hospitality or strangely resistant to sharing their premises. Their refusal to welcome Boudu seems petty and ungenerous, and it looks as if they are breaking the simplest laws of hospitality. But the film also gives us the necessary elements for a different interpretation of the relationship between all the characters: after all, the narrative never gives the women a chance to be "hostesses." They are both reduced to a much less glamorous role, that of domestics in the service of the owner of the house, and, transitively, of his guest. Meanwhile, M. Lestingois still thinks of himself as the host (a prestigious symbolic identity), even if he does not do his share of the chores generated by the guest's presence, extra labor that he demands from his wife and servant. To feed and dress his new "friend" (as he makes a point of addressing Boudu), Lestingois resorts to a rhetoric of demands and orders: he tells his wife and servant what to do. His imperatives are barely concealed by the hypocritical use of a paternalist tone that pretends to erase social borders between the rich bourgeois and the still dripping bum.

The host's authority shifts subtly, and seemingly haphazardly, along the chain of pronouns he uses. Moving from *tu*, when he gives an order (disguised as a declarative statement), to *mon* when he claims a new relationship with the guest (my friend), to a *nous* that pretends to include the rest of the family and recruits everyone else, as if they had agreed to anything: "*Tu* mettras un couvert pour *mon* ami Boudu qui dîne avec *nous*" ("Set a place for my friend Boudu, who is having dinner with us"). Often, his statements are even more authoritarian, starting with "Go get . . ." ("*Va me chercher . . .*") or "Go and open a can of sardines for him." And the spouse's humble position is powerfully underscored (and, I would suggest, implicitly criticized) by the unexpected attitude of this unpredictable guest, who, instead of replying to conventional codes with conventional codes, refuses to express any kind of gratitude and acts as if he were amplifying the authoritarian aspects of the master's imperatives. Not only does he rudely refuse to drink the soup that has been prepared for him, but he also demands that the woman, who has brought him fresh clothes, leave the room immediately while he changes. Modesty may be the cause of his shyness, but this in no way explains the fact that he asks M. Lestingois to make her do as he wishes, as if she did not exist, nor that he feels necessary to bark: "Et plus vite que ça" ("And faster than that") when, outraged, she does indeed get out of the room. Making a point of bossing her around, he exclaims: "Ce n'est pas trop tôt" ("High time!") when she brings him the requested sardines.

The wife, on the other hand, makes it clear that if she consents to play the role of the unwilling hostess, it is only because she considers that she does not have any choice, that she has no power: when her husband says that they are going to turn the sofa into a bed, she does not fight his decision but dissociates herself from the entire operation: "Oh, my friend, you are the master," she says. And the word "master" precisely emphasizes his authority and power rather than his kindness and generosity. At first, it is difficult not to interpret the man's attitude as the more humane and understanding—until we realize that the money that Mme Lestingois proposes to spend on a hotel room for Boudu is a substitute for her labor, not her husband's. M. Lestingois acts as if he wanted Mme Lestingois and his servant to take the place of the innkeeper or hotel employees who would be in charge of keeping Boudu comfortable, so that his wife's reference to money suddenly seems less inelegant and more meaningful.

If we agree that hospitality calls for a series of gestures that must combine the art of welcoming symbolically, as well as a more humble aspect that makes the host closer to the servant, then Renoir's film shows the hypocrisy of a situation where men's hospitality only manifests itself through a transitive form of female servitude. The figure of the host is split into two human roles: the husband monopolizes welcoming the guest and the prestige this gesture carries. Serving and powerlessness, as well as being blamed for not being more hospitable, become the lot of the two women. The legitimate wife falls into the same category as the maid (who also happens to be the husband's mistress, as if the film wanted to suggest the multifaceted resemblance between the two women).

In Renoir's film, the two female characters react to the male host's intrusion by becoming temporary and ambiguous accomplices, because they team up against the identified enemy, but, more often than not, in literary or cinematographic fictions, this relationship between women stops short of alliances and deteriorates into antagonism, each character trying to renegotiate social and gender roles in order not to combine the doubly disempowering identities of woman and servant. For the splitting of hospitality between different actors according to how glamorous the activities are can be achieved through much more complicated channels than a simple distinction between genders. Often, the lines of complicity follow social hierarchies, not gender identities.

And if the social ladder that refines gender oppositions occurs in a situation where the distinction between colonized and colonizer is added to the equation, the picture becomes even more problematic and potentially tragic, as we shall see in Sembène Ousmane's short story. Even in the *métropole*, however, it is easy to find examples of cultural productions that have tried to explore the carefully hidden tensions created by the presence of servants in the domestic space. When a maid or a butler lives with his employers, new borders are created and blurred between the inside and the outside, the family and the stranger, the host and the guest, serving and welcoming. Jean Genet's 1954 *Les bonnes* [*The Maids*] proposes that the violence of the situation will be visited on the master of the house, and more recent cinematographic adaptations of his famous play (such as Claude Chabrol's 1995 *La cérémonie*), have asked the same questions from a slightly different angle. Like Sembène Ousmane, Genet and Chabrol are fascinated by a type of relationship that blends, in a very ambiguous way, the codes of hospitality and the ethics of the workplace. The maid has the same address as her employers, lives in the same house, and shares the same food: at a certain level, she occupies the same function as the children, whose relative powerlessness is hidden precisely by the authority they may decide to exercise over the servants.

Tran Anh Hung's *L'odeur de la papaye verte* (*The Scent of Green Papaya*), a film released in 1993 that portrays events that took place in Saigon in 1950, tells the story of children whose fate has placed them in the roles of the servant and of powerful little copies of the master: Mùi, a ten-year-old child torn from her rural family, is hired as a servant by a rich family. She shares the house with the parents, other servants, and three little boys, who alternatively ignore or pester her. Tin, the youngest, is often mischievous, his childish tricks alerting the viewer to the possibility of much more sinister violence. In one particularly puzzling scene, while the little girl is scrubbing the floor on her knees, he urinates into one of the large precious vases that adorn the family house. In two other scenes, the camera compares the reactions of the young girl and her master's son to the same reality: the presence of ants in the house. First, we see a young male child, who could be ten or eleven years old, watching ants struggle and die as they get stuck in a gooey trap of melting candle wax that he is allowing to drip onto the window sill. An extreme close-up magnifies both the insects' suffering (which we might otherwise tend to dismiss) and the little boy's detached cruelty. In a mirror scene, the camera focuses on the little girl, who has a completely different reaction to the same insects: although she has only a few minutes to swallow her lunch, she takes the time to observe another colony of ants. She is mesmerized, and a sense of wonder embellishes her small face as she watches intently, without ever touching or disturbing the animals in any way. In Tran Anh Hung's film, the servant's extreme youth makes her close to the other children, but the story also insists on the unbridgeable gap between them, revealing the unfairness of the little girl's situation

Similarly, in Sembène Ousmane's short text, the reference to children is used by "Madame" as a way of pointing out that she is not responsible for Diouana's death. To convince the inspectors that the maid was well treated, she declares: "I don't know why she killed herself. She was well treated here; she ate the same food, shared the same room as my children" (Sembène 1997, 44).

The use of the word "shared" is almost perverse, because it idealizes the maid's living conditions by making her symbolically close to the children, but "Madame" does not seem aware of the irony of her remark: she infantilizes this grown woman, whom she has deprived of privacy. Diouana has no place to call her own, so she is absolutely incapable of taking on the role of host. In this case, the individual house is much more than a place where she resides: completely isolated, almost imprisoned, with no friend, relative, or even acquaintance in the town where she lives, Diouana has no choice but to treat her employer's house as her home, her neighborhood, her country even. Explaining why suicide is the only plausible hypothesis, the neighbor who found her body in the bathtub tells the inspector: "Oh! Who do you think would make an attempt on the life of a Negro girl? She never went out. She didn't know anyone, except for Madame's children" (Sembène 1997, 44). Unlike the factory worker, for example, who can make a clear distinction between home and the workshop, the live-in maid is literally (con)fused with the house she occupies. If she eats the same food as the children, if she shares their bedroom, it is not because the house has replaced the exteriority of a workplace but because the workplace has swallowed the very idea of home, excluding the possibility of hospitality. The fact that no one can be expected to harm her except herself only further demonstrates that Diouana has become invisible to everyone, that the house has absorbed her. If Genet's maids kill their employers, Diouana, who slashes her throat, paradoxically reoccupies the place of the subject by claiming her right to die. Like the Hegelian slave whose only freedom is to reappropriate his own body by destroying it, Diouana reestablishes borders between the house and herself, between her identity and that of her employers.

The story of the young maid's death might seem rather anachronistic in the context of 1958, if the role of the domestic was not filled by an exotic whom both the neighbor and the children insist on reducing to her racial identity: "la Négresse" (the black girl). The story takes place before Senegal's independence, when the inhabitants of the colonies are still referred to as "*indigènes*": the word is repeated several times in the text, although the author takes care to cordon it off with scare quotes, which is a way of politely welcoming it into his own discourse while making it clear that he does not want to be too closely associated with it. In a sense, the same type of limited hospitality is granted to Diouana inside the house.[3]

Contrary to what happens in *Boudu sauvé des eaux*, "Monsieur" is completely invisible in this story. He is not even in town when Diouana commits suicide. And the splitting of the role of the host does not involve him: here it occurs between "Madame" and Diouana rather than between "Monsieur" and "Madame." At the beginning of the text, the narrator makes an interesting proposal that places both women in relatively similar positions: they each want something from the other, and each expects to be granted her wish. It is clear, however, and the narrator underlines the misunderstanding, that each is convinced that she alone will reap the benefit of an exchange that cannot satisfy them equally. As the narration puts it: "They were not speaking the same language" (Sembène 1997, 46). For if "Madame" is ready to invite Diouana to come to France with them, if she is more than willing to pay for the ticket, it is because she cannot stand to give up on the privileges that she enjoys in Africa, and that she knows that she cannot hope to export her power to the *métropole*: she wants to be served as diligently as usual, even if the status of workers in France does not allow her to act as if she owned Diouana (The young maid does bitterly complain, at some point, that she was "sold, sold. Bought, bought" [ibid., 53]). Conversely, Diouana ardently desires to go to France, and she reacts as if she truly believes that she has been invited as a guest. She does not understand that Madame is going to take advantage of her. Far from it. In fact, she does not stop to consider that in her narrative, she is made an offer whose price is not really spelled out. Each woman has a vested interest in the exchange, and each fears, at first, that the other one is going to let her down.

> Diouana wanted to see France, this country whose beauty, richness, and joy of living everyone praised. She wanted to see it and make a triumphal return. This was where people got rich. Already, without having left African soil, she could see herself on the dock, returning from France, wealthy to the millions, with gifts of clothes for everyone. She dreamed of the freedom to go where she wished without having to work like a beast of burden. (Ibid., 1997, 46)

The paragraph underlines the ambiguity of all migratory projects and the misunderstanding between migrants' hopes and the rhetoric of governments that talk about "hospitality." Here, a human being is caught up in a political and economic logic that goes largely beyond her own wishes and hopes, but she does not seem to be aware that someone expects something of her and that two mutually incompatible projects are clashing. What is interesting in this crisscrossing is that Diouana's fantasy is to become like her master: like "Monsieur," she wants to be rich, free, capable of giving to others, capable of generosity and largesse. She is not so much interested in improving her own lot or of taking advantage of a Western nation's reputedly better standard of living. What she seeks is a complete transformation of her personality, a magic metamorphosis. Without ever saying so, the story suggests that her dream is to become a white man or to identify as a white man, to enjoy the privileges that she sees he enjoys.

Paradoxically, Diouana's desire would come true if she were indeed this family's guest, for if the host must become his guest's servant, the guest also becomes the host's master, at least for a while. But the reason Madame invites her to accompany her in France, and Monsieur will wait for her on the pier, belongs to a completely different type of reasoning, and there is no naiveté in that calculation. In *Boudu sauvé des eaux*, the role of the guest and that of the servant are respectively attributed to the man of the house and to the women, whereas Sembène's "Madame" cannot benefit from that stereotype. Her situation is much more complicated. If she insists so much on having Diouana with her in Antibes, it is because she has had a chance to discover that even a difference in social class does not give her any power over other women as soon as she is no longer protected by the colonial system.

During her first return to the *métropole*, Madame has made the painful discovery that she cannot persuade her European maid that she is not an employee whose rights are those of any worker on French soil. As soon as Madame is no longer dealing with Diouana, the relationship with the servant can no longer be confined within the semantic field of hospitality, however broadly the woman wants to define it. Between Madame and her European employee, exchanges belong to the realm of the market, of economic trade. For Madame, this is a surprise: "In France, when she hired a maid not only was the salary higher but the maid demanded a day off to boot" (Sembène 1997, 46).

The verb "demanded" presupposes that the speaking subject knows her rights, and it can be read as an allusion to the fact that Madame is perfectly aware that only her colonial logic enables her to reinvent Diouana's status as a maid. A few days before leaving for France, she threateningly asks whether Diouana is sure of her decision: "je ne veux pas que tu me dises, au dernier moment, aujourd'hui même, que tu me plaques [I don't want you to tell me at the last minute that you're dumping me]" (Sembène 1962, 165). The "tu me plaques" is at best improper, suggesting as it does that "Madame"'s relationship to Diouana is comparable to a form of romantic involvement that would allow Diouana to "dump" her employer.

The second experiment with a French cleaning lady is even more significant because it allows the author to denounce the hypocrisy of the system but also marks the limits of his own intervention or of his own critical thinking. Madame decides not to meet the "demands" of her first employee and to hire another one. Here is what happens: "Madame had to let her go and hired another. The next one was no different from the first, if not worse. She answered Madame tit for tat. 'Anyone who is capable of having children should take of them. I can't live in. I have my own children to take care of and a husband, too'" (Sembène 1997, 46, translation slightly modified).

The exchange between the two women reveals some of the ideological implications of a system that creates the need for a live-in maid. The second woman thinks that spending the night at the employer's house is an activity and not an identity. For her, the idea of "living with" or even of "residing at" is ruled out. If the maid is perceived as talking back, it is because she puts into words the ambivalence of Madame's thinking: she refuses point-blank to go along with a narrative that establishes a perverse confusion between hospitality and servitude. In that sense, the confrontation between Madame and the second employee formulates the idea that it is not a privilege or even a favor to share the children's room.

The pattern that Sembène Ousmane criticizes has been identified by many feminist postcolonial critics, and perhaps most famously by Gayatri Spivak. In her study of the different variables of the Jane Eyre figure, she points out that the white female subject, caught in an imperialist history, often becomes split between a domestic and a civil scene. In the space of that contradictory intersection, she turns into a "not-quite-not-male" (Spivak 1999, 116), the mirror of Homi Bhabha's "not-quite-not-white" colonized man, who excludes the "native subaltern woman" (ibid., 117).

For there is a strange and relatively problematic shift in Sembène's text at this point, and I am not convinced that the story as a whole is willing to distance itself from the implications of the second employee's speech: when she blames Madame for not taking care of her own children, the woman seems to imply that Madame is somehow naturally expected to do so. Similarly, in *Boudu sauvé des eaux*, M. Lestingois systematically expects his wife and servant to take care of his guest because they are women. In "La noire de . . . ," Diouana's lot is denounced as unfair and dehumanizing because the system replaces one person's labor with another's while disguising the employee as a guest. We are evidently expected to approve of the European servant who is, in a sense, speaking for Diouana when she points out that she and Madame should be equals: as she puts it, she has a husband and children of her own.

But there is a blind spot in the employee's reasoning, and it is relayed by the narrative as a whole: this denunciation of a corruption of the idea of hospitality stops short of going back to its origins. When she blames Madame for not taking care of her children, the second cleaning lady seems to believe in a sort of biological law that expects the mother (and not the father, for example) to be entirely responsible for the domestic care of children. What she implicitly proposes is that each woman should take responsibility for her own workload, and she is implying that Madame should not even hire her for that kind of work. And although her ambiguous use of *on* ("Si *on* est capable de faire des enfants") can refer, in French, to either a man or a woman, she does not seem to realize that what Madame is trying to do is to reproduce a model that tradition has completely authorized as long as the master of the house is a man.

What the colonial system permits, then, is not a simple form of domination hidden under a pretense of hospitality. It legitimizes a redistribution of roles in which Monsieur can afford to disappear (symbolically and physically) while Madame, who must pick up the task of domestic care in his absence (including, as we shall see in a minute, the reception of guests), is allowed to find a substitute. The servile aspects of hospitality can be delegated, because another woman, the colonized woman, will take over. If "La noire de . . ." adequately criticizes the unfairness of such a displacement of labor, where the host can afford to do no work without giving up on the prestige of entertaining guests in his own house, the short story does not seem to realize that its satire opposes the logic of such a dichotomy, as if only Madame, the lazy biological mother, were guilty of adulterating the sacred law of hospitality. Madame, it could be argued, is at a disadvantage, because she can only rely on colonialism to perpetuate a conventional and traditional system that M. Lestingois can count on.

The redefinition of the hostess as a figure who is no longer relegated to a third space on the margins of the pair constituted by the man and his guest is a particularly revealing gesture, especially when the story concentrates on that archetypal rite of bourgeois hospitality, the dinner party. When guests are sitting around a table, either the host consents to become a cook and waiter or a waitress for a while or professional help must be enlisted, introducing the excluded third that Diouana has consistently represented. In Sembène Ousmane's text, the invitation to dinner is completely reinvented by Madame, who turns Diouana into a sort of itinerant pseudohostess, whom she drags from house to house to display her exotic cook's talents and earn vicarious praise.

It seemed the hundredth time that she'd been trailed from villa to villa. To this one's house and then to that one's. . . . Some silly people, who followed her about, hanging on her heels in the kitchen, had been there for dinner. . . . These strange, self-centered, sophisticated beings never stopped asking her idiotic questions about how African women do their cooking. (Sembène 1997, 52)

I find Madame's redefinition of the role of the hostess particularly original and radical, and particularly cruel, too. Not only does she refuse to cook for her guests, but she also manages to skip the reception ritual altogether. She does not have to welcome her guests into her own house. She invites people at their own houses, and she imports her cook. She thus reaps a maximum symbolic profit from an operation that demands no investment and no labor. The fact that Diouana's cuisine is "African" adds a sort of exotic prestige, because the identity of *négresse* that the guests confer upon her becomes a spectacle in itself. When Madame forces Diouana to cook for her (and to adapt her supposedly authentic recipes to the taste of European guests who do not like spicy food), she knows that she is also taking advantage of Diouana's value as a remarkable object of curiosity: it is as if she was offering her guests a postdinner performance or some sort of live entertainment. Diouana, mutatis mutandis, functions as a belly dancer, whose body adds flavor to her dishes. The specter of cannibalism is not too far off.

What Madame achieves, in the end, is an even more successful and cynical reappropriation of the principle of hospitality. She goes further than the "white master" whose model she has adopted and perfected. And it is certainly no coincidence that when Diouana commits suicide she does so with a kitchen knife, which she uses to cut her own throat. Reduced to silence, she treats herself as a sort of sacrificial lamb, in a ritual where she is both the priestess and the offering, the sacrificed object and the sacrificing subject, a redoubling that hands an accusatory mirror to her employers, who were trying to force her to be both the host and the servant, the welcoming master and the humble slave. Here, gender serves as the hinge on which all the ambiguity of the status of the host can support the complex interactions between race and social class. Once again, hospitality, like the gift, becomes impossible the minute the host and the guest identify as such (Derrida 1991, 1992).

In a less absolute model, we may hope that hospitality could draw its ethical value from the fact that it can never be reduced to what is exchanged (economically, politically, or even morally). As Alain Montandon puts it, thinking of hospitality as a high-risk activity does not amount to making a radical difference between unconditional and ordinary. Hospitality, he suggests, is structured like an ordeal.[4] If even the most seemingly altruistic forms of hospitality are tainted with forms of utilitarianism and selfishness, it would probably be a mistake to try to replace them with purer types of hospitality, because pure hospitality may be the absence of hospitality. For the guest's sake (knowing that the guest shares the ambivalent structure of the host), the host can afford to be someone who benefits from his or her hospitality. It may be hoped that a sort of one-upmanship will be put in place, generating potlatches and endless reciprocation. In other words, imbalances are more desirable than undesirable here. And in practice, this type of disparity manifests itself in a constant oscillation between the host as master and the host as slave, the guest as protégé and the guest as usurper. And the more ambiguity exists between rituals of welcoming (gestures that generate prestige) and the taking care of guests (which tends to require humble forms of servitude), the more difficult it will be to distinguish between power and powerlessness, between the expression of mastery and of subservience. Conversely, if the definition of the host becomes less complex, less ambiguous, then forms of violence might creep into the system. Gender is the most obvious variable in this game, where dichotomies and the multiplication of roles shield some actors from the potentially humiliating features of hospitality. But violence will be even more likely to infiltrate relationships between fake hosts and fake guests when the binary pair are troubled by other well-identified categories such as gender and ethnicity in colonial or postcolonial situations.

For servants obviously do not disappear when nations become independent, as we shall see in the next example: just as Diouana's Madame introduces, within the *métropole*, the principles tolerated by colonial mentalities, Europe continues to function as a crucible in which gender tests the category of race while racially marked subjects point to the limits of Western feminism. Long after Diouana's fictional death, another dead character invites us to ask questions about how women are treated when they force men to redefine their positions as powerful hosts: this time, the guest is an undocumented immigrant and the host is the son of an unemployed working-class Belgian, whose exploitative strategies have the same consequences as Madame's cruelty.

Protection or Hospitality: The Young Man and the Illegal Immigrant in La promesse

Before *La promesse* was presented at Cannes, Jean-Pierre and Luc Dardenne, two Belgian directors who had previously primarily specialized in documentaries, had failed to gain the recognition they deserve (Burdeau 1996a, b; Derobert 1996). And yet, when the film was hailed by critics and international audiences in 1996, the two directors were hardly beginners: their fiction films have inherited a sensitivity developed during the first phase of their careers, when they concentrated on a type of social cinema exemplified in their documentaries, and in the work produced by their companies (Les Films du Fleuve and Dérives productions).[5] The quality of their cinematographic studies of blue-collar workers and of the urban underclass (especially around Seraing, a suburb of Liège) was largely ignored by the public, although it was recognized, in 1997, by the European Documentary Award for "the excellence of their work, their social and human concerns, and its research-oriented spirit" (Dorzée 1999). Commenting on the *palme d'or* awarded to their latest film, *Rosetta* (1999), Louis Honorez notes that "many foreign journalists thought that *Rosetta* was only their second film, after *La promesse*" (Honorez 1999; my translation).

If *La promesse* changed the course of the directors' careers, it might be because the story of Igor, a young teenager (Jérémie Rénier) whose father is involved in the trafficking of immigrants, resonated powerfully in a European cultural echo chamber in which the status of the foreigner has become a crucial issue. Francophone films of the past decade have reflected a general European interest and concern for the stranger, whose presence in Europe's cosmopolitan cities often represents the return of the colonial repressed. In France, the emergence of so-called *banlieue* films and *beur* cinema,[6] made both by children of immigrants[7] and European directors,[8] has presented the public with a vision of life in suburbs, where *métissage*, or rather ethnic and cultural cohabitation, is the norm rather than the exception (Sherzer 1996).

With a few exceptions, however,[9] French cinema has focused on the "second generation," and it may take a while before directors choose to reflect on the most recent evolution of migration patterns and to portray undocumented immigrants. That *La promesse* should have been released at the same time as the "Saint-Bernard" crisis might be a good indication that the next generation of immigration films will concentrate on the issues raised by illegality and social precariousness rather than on the delicate and often problematic process of integration.[10] It should also be noted that *La promesse* is exceptional in its decision to confront the issue of the trade in human beings: in the Dardennes' film, the hiring of undocumented laborers is not a vague collective practice that takes place off-camera and that journalists and politicians self-righteously condemn on the national news: Igor's father, Roger, is one of the film's protagonists, and his sordid activity is pictured down to the most gruesome practical details. The spectator, who is used to vague governmental promises about penalizing anonymous people who encourage illegal immigrants by providing them with jobs, gets a completely different picture in *La promesse* because the film refuses to treat the "illegal immigrant" as a separable entity. This story is predicated on the idea that the "illegal immigrant" cannot be treated apart from the figure of the "illegal employer," and it studies the evolution of one such tragic couple, Igor and Assita, who have no choice but to become inseparable. *La promesse* can thus be viewed as the exploration of how the relationship between the host and the guest, the native and the immigrant, must be reinvented if both do not want to see their humanity destroyed by preexisting roles (the exploiter and the exploited, the cynical host and the victimized guest).

At the beginning of the film, we discover that Roger (Oliver Gourmet) employs a few illegal immigrants in building his future house. The episode that explains the title occurs toward the beginning of the film, when the workers are interrupted by the arrival of work inspectors, who are obviously looking for irregularities. Alerted by his father, Igor warns the men who are on the premises that day, and they all run away, well aware that if the law penalizes the illegal employer (who collects unemployment benefits), they themselves risk nothing less than deportation. But as he tries to jump from the scaffolding, one of the African immigrants, Hamidou, falls off the ladder and lies there, severely injured. In the few minutes that it takes Roger to get rid of the inspectors and to come back, Igor tries to help Hamidou, who

makes him promise that he will take care of his wife, Assita (Assita Oue-
draogo), and their baby son, who have just recently arrived in Belgium and
live in one of the squalid rented houses managed by Roger. That promise is
the narrative engine of the movie and the tragic crucible in which hospitality will have to be redefined and reinvented by the characters.

For when Roger discovers how badly injured Hamidou is, he adamantly
refuses to take him to the hospital for fear of legal complications. And in
spite of his obvious reservations and long hesitations, Igor finally obeys his
father when he orders Igor to help him hide the injured man and, later, to
bury his body under freshly mixed cement. It is not absolutely clear to me
whether the African worker is really dead at that stage, and the rest of the
film continues to insist that something, in Hamidou, refuses to die.

There is no doubt that the episode is one of the most spectacular junc-
tures of this uncompromising story, but rather than concentrating on that
specific moment, rather than analyzing the ways in which the directors have
chosen to tell the visual story of a murder, I would like to explore the long-
term consequences of Roger's and Igor's act on the relationship between Assita, the immigrant, and Igor, the native host: after Hamidou's disappearance, Igor keeps his promise and takes care of his wife and son, but, until the
very end of the film, he does not tell her the truth. Assita will continue to
believe that her husband has temporarily disappeared, and that he may have
decided to go away of his own free will (gambling debts are conveniently
suggested by Roger). Her ignorance puts her at a disadvantage and main-
tains an imbalance between her and Igor, who, although doing everything
he can to help her, refuses, until the very last minutes of the film, to share
the guilty secret that links him to his father like a perverse umbilical cord.

Remarkably, the film suggests that this belated revelation cannot constitute a narrative closure, but that it functions like a beginning, an open door:
here, the end, in the form of a confession, is an inaugural gesture that allows both characters to enter the realm of shared hospitality between
equals. The scene during which Igor finally tells the truth to Assita is crucial
from both dramatic and cinematographic perspectives, in that it defies the
visual and narrative conventions that usually govern the topos of revelation
and confession. For example, we could reasonably expect the sequence to be
structured like a *face-à-face*, a confrontation where the two characters symbolize, respectively, the universes of home, legitimacy, and power, and that

of homelessness, illegality, and powerlessness. This could be the moment when the two worlds slowly created by the movie (Africa versus Europe; black versus white; man versus woman; employer versus employee; in a word, same versus other) are finally brought together: the two entities may be irreconcilable, but at least the two characters acknowledge each other's reality.

The directors, however, have opted out of that possibility and chosen an unexpected way of filming this final dialogue. The last scene is not a conclusive discovery that puts an end to a long game of hide-and-seek, but a strange ballet, in which one character is always positioned behind, and not facing, the other. Until that moment, the logic of the film has led us to believe that the secret of Hamidou's death would continue to function as the spring that keeps the plot moving: both characters are set in motion by this structuring absence that keeps them in a perpetual forward movement, a reverse migration away from the murderous father. The destination of this trip is explained as a quest for safety, and the aim, for Assita, is to find a place where she can take care of her son without being threatened by Roger. After a few discussions with Igor and the rare characters willing to help her along the way, it becomes clear that she has some relatives in Italy, which provides her with a new destination, her extended family weaving a tight network of solidarity across hostile national borders that are emotionally and politically irrelevant to her. Inverting a traditional and culturally meaningful axis of migration between Italy and Belgium, Assita, who comes from a third country, would have to cross borders as an invisible pawn on the international chessboard.

Hamidou's disappearance is thus the cause of new migrations. Ever since Igor and Assita have met, their relationship has been based on a shared experience of forced exile. They travel together; they are constantly going somewhere else, sometimes turning in circles around the original place of the murder. At first, they have to run away from the father, Igor practically kidnapping Assita, who does not know that Roger plans to take her to Germany to sell her as a prostitute. After this initial flight, they stay together, hiding in the city except for a few incursions into institutional buildings, where Assita's status has to be negotiated: they both go to a police station, because Assita insists on reporting that her husband has been missing; they must go to a hospital when the baby becomes sick, and they also consult an

African traditional healer before returning to Igor's employer's flat, where they stay until they are discovered by the father, whose threatening presence triggers another flight.

Apparently, the two characters stay together, but the film makes the point that they are not fellow travelers: they are separated by a narrative abyss. Igor knows that Hamidou is dead, whereas Assita wants to know what happened to her husband. The film links their traveling to a metaphorical movement toward or away from the truth: Assita seeks to reach a coherent narrative that would explain Hamidou's absence, whereas Igor is metaphorically running away from the telling. In other words, the film manages to suggest that two characters who seem to be traveling together are, in reality (and until the very last scene of the film), moving in opposite directions or, perhaps, that their frantic and continual movements are compensated for by the stubborn immobility of the plot in another domain: literally and figuratively, these two people are going nowhere, because the only element that would create change remains unsaid, silence accumulating as growing tension between them. Assita wants to know; Igor knows, but she does not know that he knows. And to complicate the issue, Igor's position forces him to reconcile two completely incompatible imperatives: his promise (Assita is under his protection) and the need to lie to her owing to his own role as an accomplice in Hamidou's murder, and a sense of loyalty that prevents him from reporting his own father to the police.

I suggest that this split in Igor's consciousness has thought-provoking consequences for the spectator because it affects the European character rather than the immigrant: traditionally, the type of uncertain allegiance caused by "double consciousness," "creolization," and "hybridity" is expected to be the immigrants' province, because they are supposed to bear the burden of integration (Gilroy 1993; Bhabha 1994; Glissant 1989). Linguistically, culturally, and emotionally, the stranger is perceived as living in an ambiguous space that is described either as a "neither here nor there" or, sometimes, euphorically, as a "both here and there." Here, the impossibility of choosing one side and the effects of double consciousness rest squarely with the European character, who is entirely responsible for the immigrant's situation.

Assita's loyalty to her son and to his absent father is unproblematic, and her relationship to her environment is tactical and practical: it is a matter of survival for herself and her infant. But Igor's contradictory desires are symbolized by his ambiguous attitude toward the truth: he wants both to tell and not to tell. He is terrified that Assita will discover the truth, but at the same time, he would like her to find out. Both characters are tragically lonely, but Igor is even more isolated than Assita because he alone carries the weight of the secret: during the whole film, he is seen carrying Assita's bag. The typical attribute of the immigrant is displaced onto him, as if the film wanted to suggest the impossibility of immunity from the fate of those whom the protagonists treated as "they" before Hamidou's death.

Their wandering through Liège is punctuated by key moments when Assita gets closer to the truth, to Igor's intense fear and dismay. Her desire to know is thwarted, however, not only by Igor's silence but by the fact that her search produces a multiplicity of fragmented and complex narratives that she cannot correctly decipher. The tragically simple and brutal story ("Hamidou is dead") is withheld, its elements being replaced by sometimes accurate but incomplete versions provided by well-meaning friends or foes (Hamidou has disappeared, he may or may not come back, he ran away from gambling debts, he is in Germany). Each time, Igor witnesses the emergence of a story, placing the spectators (who share his knowledge) in the uncomfortable position of having to ask themselves if they would have done the same thing, whom they would have protected, whom they would have sided with. The situation brings home a dilemma that is supposedly reserved for the other, the stranger.

The entrails of a chicken sacrificed in Igor's presence thus reveal that Hamidou "has not gone away and that he is not very far." Technically, the chicken is right: Hamidou never decided to leave, and he is buried on the premises. But only the spectator, now an accomplice of Igor's silence, knows that nondeparture and proximity signify the confirmation of the worst rather than a glimmer of hope. The film does not blame Assita for relying on typically despised methods of truth seeking, but it shows that, like any narrative, the chicken's prediction is interpretable and overdetermined by the context and by the characters' wishes.

Even Assita's will to know is colored by her own situation: in one of the worst episodes of the movie, when two racists urinate on Assita and brutalize her, attacking her when she is at her most vulnerable, because she fears for her sick child's life, the issue of the truth comes up once more: overwhelmed and distraught, Assita now begs Igor to tell her, not the truth, but the truth that she wants to hear. She wants him to say that Hamidou is not dead. At that moment, faced with a desperate plea, Igor deliberately chooses to continue to carry the burden of the secret. Their moment of complicity and solidarity is dependent on Igor's willingness to lie. And yet, when he least needs to speak, when the end of the film seems to promise the possibility of a definitive burial of the truth, he decides against that closure.

It is true that the film as a whole constantly proposes and withdraws the hypothesis that a buried body can be hidden forever. Burial and the disappearance of the corpse are structuring references from the very beginning of the story, even before Hamidou's death. The Chicago-based critic Jonathan Rosenbaum (1997) notes that the very first scene establishes a parallel between crime and burial: when we are first introduced to its young protagonist, the scenario hastens to suggest that Igor is not only a thief but a definitely unglamorous, cowardly, and cynical character. At the gas station where he works, he is asked to check the engine of an old woman's car and takes advantage of a few seconds inside the vehicle to steal her wallet from the passenger's seat. And he not only remains totally unfazed when she discovers its absence but recommends that she quickly go back where she has just come from, because "there are so many unscrupulous people around." Already, the film is making us his accomplices. Only Igor and the spectator can appreciate the irony, because no one else will ever find out. The episode makes us accessories to the crime and also suggests that burying evidence might just work: once the victim has disappeared, Igor empties the wallet and digs a hole to dispose of it.

Similarly, when Hamidou falls off the scaffolding, Roger covers him with a dark tarpaulin, which he pulls over his face, as if to start erasing his identity. And on top of this already shapeless form, he places a door, a door separated from its frame, which opens on nothing anymore but ironically reminds us of other metaphorical doors that could have been opened to let in the immigrant and his wife. Here, the host does not open doors but closes them back on him, or rather transforms the door into the lid of a non-coffin, in which Hamidou lies, half-dead, half-alive, so that the murder can go unpunished. And when the body is finally covered with cement, Hamidou becomes a fragment of the house that Roger is building, as if the immigrant has literally become a piece of cheap raw material imported from the colonies. Invisible, impossible to find, and impossible to forget, his body is removed from normal human communication and finds itself locked in some sort of hellish non-place that Assita's and the seer's fragmented stories half guess at without being able to explain it to themselves. Hamidou cannot be integrated, but he cannot be deported, either. Or, rather, the specific form of "integration" that he undergoes is a monstrous form of absorption.[11] As with the administrative aberrations created in France by the Pasqua laws, he is beyond the opposition between *expulsable* and *régularisable*. Murdered, then buried without proper funeral rites, without even a grave, he becomes the symbol of the repressed, which psychoanalysis has taught us can only lead to future traumas and incomprehensible narrative renditions.

After repeated allusions to the possibility of hiding the corpus delicti, the film has thus been preparing us for a final departure that will seal Hamidou's fate: in the hospital where she must take her sick baby, Assita has met a nurse, a fellow African, who is willing to let her borrow her identification papers so that she can cross over into Italy. In one of the rare vaguely amusing scenes in which Igor makes fun of Europeans' inability to identify African faces, he makes her wear her new friend's multicolored head scarf and shows the latter's identity card to a passerby. Predictably, the man mistakes Assita (or the scarf) for the person whose photograph is affixed to the official paper. Assita's invisibility thus works both ways: it deprives her of her right to be protected by the police (they cannot look for an illegal immigrant who "does not exist") but also allows her to move through barriers controlled by human beings who interpret passports with a biased sense of recognition. Having established that Assita is read as an interchangeable immigrant, the film makes us expect that she will leave Belgium and go to Italy, and that her getting on the train will coincide with the end of their shared adventure.

But this forward movement is suddenly stopped: unexpectedly, Igor reverses the direction of the trip that he has carefully organized. After helping Assita with her fake papers and her new identity, after selling his father's ring to buy her a ticket, after taking her to the train station and accompanying her almost all the way to the platform, he abruptly stops, and the logic of the film turns around. The story as a whole seems to move backward, as if we were in a montage room, or as if an interactive narrative were suddenly offering us the possibility of another direction, of another migration, whose destination will remain untold.

This last scene is shot in a strange, hybrid space that is not conventionally associated with revelations and important conversations: Igor's confession takes place on the stairs leading to the platform. From a filmic point of view, the platform is almost a cliché, or at least an intertextual reference to a number of departure and arrival scenes.[12] It represents the last horizontal space before one character is separated from the other by the train's departure; it is a sort of in-between stage, designed to accommodate last declarations, promises, and good-byes. But if the platform represents a last chance to stage a meaningful conversation, that is not the case with the flight of stairs that sometimes leads to it: stairs connote passage, movement, no one stops there, which makes it all the more remarkable for Igor to choose this interstitial space to shatter the precarious equilibrium that he has managed to maintain around the fiction of Hamidou's willing departure.

Before we can see the two characters on this flight of stairs, for almost a minute, three long silent shots follow Assita and Igor, the camera slowly getting closer and closer to the protagonists. In the first shot, they are walking together, or rather one in front of the other, without saying a word. The camera follows them as they cross the frame from right to left. In the next shot, that direction is reversed: we now see them moving inside the frame from left to right, which gives us the impression that they are retracing their steps, as if to announce that the ultimate destination and meaning of the trip is about to be turned around. When they reach the train station and proceed through a long and dark corridor, the camera lets them move away from its gaze, and we see their backs as they walk together. The last shot catches up with them with a close-up of their faces as they are about to disappear at the end of the hallway. They still have not exchanged a word, but this shot, which begins with their two faces captured at the same level, right next to each other, will be the point of Igor's confession and revelation. And the first word uttered by Igor coincides with the moment the camera separates them: for several long and monotonous seconds, we have been watching the characters' parallel progression, but when Assita climbs the first few steps, the camera moves away from Igor, eliminating him from the frame. From the spectator's point of view, the screen is now completely filled with Assita's back. Her head, covered with a multicolored scarf, and her baby boy's red bonnet add striking touches of color to an otherwise somber image.

When Igor abruptly says, "Hamidou is dead," Assita stops climbing the steps and remains immobile. Around her, everything becomes still, as if the film were paralyzed. Only the camera retains a tiny margin of latitude, panning slowly away from the woman's back to Igor's face and back again. Although we normally understand what happens "behind people's back" as betrayals and unforgivable acts of cowardice, although we could interpret Assita's turned back as a symptom of vulnerability and distress, I would suggest that this scene reinterprets the characters' position as the sign of a fragile return to a form of communication that remains tainted with a pathological silence.

As if all the resources of normal dialogues had been exhausted, Igor's confession resonates in a bleak silence. There is no reply. The camera can do nothing but register the silence and the only other possible form of communication between Igor and the woman, who can no longer function as the ostracized foreigner. Dialogue is now reduced to subtle body language, intense looks, a code that we can decipher or feel comfortable with only because we have become familiar with the two protagonists' backgrounds. When Igor finishes his confession (and the camera does not seem too sure of when the end has come, insisting, as it does, on the teenager's downcast eyes), Assita does not move for a few seconds, and her first gesture is not to turn around but to remove the headscarf that added a bit of color to the picture, that seemed to promise that ordinary racism could be humorously reappropriated against racists. The disguise was supposed to make her resemble the documented immigrant who was willing to let Assita borrow her identity card and give Assita the freedom to travel. By removing the mask that lets her pass for another African woman, she deliberately chooses to claim her own identity. She is now Assita, an illegal immigrant from Burkina Faso, whom the police are bound to stop on the border. But giving up on her ruse is also the first real act of freedom that Assita can perform: she can make her own decision about her identity only because Igor has recognized her, has acknowledged her as a real interlocutor. He not only gives her the freedom to choose, but, as his father's accomplice, he also places his own destiny in her hands.

From that moment on, Assita entirely recaptures her power of decision. And when she finally turns around, the two characters look at each other as equals. Their relationship is almost indescribable but it is also unique. Nothing is said, as if words were ruled out, as if no one trusted them anymore.

And during the same long shot, when Assita turns around without a word and starts walking back in the direction they have come from, Igor does not question her. Neither Igor nor the spectator knows where Assita is going, what she intends to do, or why she refuses to leave for Italy, but Igor does not try to understand or to dissuade her. After a short moment of hesitation, during which the frame separates them one last time, he runs after her, catches up with her, and starts walking alongside her, as if the silent look they have exchanged has established a new protocol: it is not clear that she accepts him, or that she has forgiven him, nor does she express any affection or sympathy, but they walk together in the same direction as if they cannot do anything else, as if his place is now beside her no matter what happens. The camera is happy to let the African woman, her baby, and the young man who carries her bag disappear under the credits at the end of the corridor: it does not seem to know whether the corridor in question opens onto some kind of future for the two immigrants and their companion.

Conclusion

I would like to conclude on the meaningfulness of this new form of complicity that definitively excludes the father. I suggest that Igor's decision radically modifies the relationship between Assita and himself because it inaugurates a new era: now they are equal partners in a game in which each can now be host and guest. Rather than portraying the immigrant as the eternal guest of a powerful native host, *La promesse* reaches a point at which the imbalance is corrected. And, remarkably, the gender of each character adds a powerful comment on the problematic intersection between gender and hospitality. The relationship between Igor and Assita has never been stable, but it has always rested on a hypothesis that Igor's confession renders obsolete: that Assita was under the protection of men, of her husband, of Igor, and even of Roger, who pretends to take her under his wing when Hamidou goes missing. His way of "protecting" Assita is certainly a cynical trick: he stages a fake rape so as to pretend to rescue her from her attacker and then insist that she cannot take care of herself. "What would have happened if I had not arrived?" he asks Assita. She very correctly interprets his show of protection as a disinvitation: answering his rhetorical question with a real one, she replies: "Are you throwing me out?" a formulation that makes it obvious that she understands what Roger's hospitality really means. Igor's efforts to help her, on the other hand, are a genuine attempt not only at defending her interests but also at identifying what such interests might be before presuming that he knows better than she does. But until the moment he finally tells her the truth, Assita functions as an entity that is exchanged rather than as a guest greeted by the host. In her introduction to the special issue of *Communications* devoted to hospitality, Anne Gotman notes that there is a radical difference between welcoming and protecting. When a woman is a potential guest, she is often perceived as unthreatening because she is assumed to be weaker or harmless. As a consequence, she is often offered degraded forms of hospitality (Gotman 1997, 11). I would argue that in *La promesse*, at least until the very last scene, Roger, Igor, and Hamidou share this definition. Igor takes care of Assita because of the promise he made to a dying man: ultimately, his responsibility is to the husband. That husband's goal was to protect his wife, but he does not survive. As for Roger, he is cynically hiding behind the cliché that women need protection to refuse her his hospitality.

The whole film demonstrates that the French characters would be more than happy to treat her as merchandise, to act as if the stories of sacrificed women mentioned in the Introduction still made perfect cultural sense. Throughout the movie, it is as a woman that Assita is rejected by the other characters, who invoke her vulnerability and what they choose to see as her powerlessness. When Roger barges into the room where his foreman is attacking Assita, the camera lets us witness money passing from one man to the other, sealing the pact between them. And when even that attempt fails, because Assita refuses to be intimidated into leaving, he goes further down the same logical road: after pretending to "protect" the woman, he now blatantly tries to sell her. He is seen negotiating her price with her would-be pimp. After killing her legitimate protector, Roger usurps the role, and his cynicism highlights the invisible link between protection and possession.

When Igor takes control of the situation, his role consists, at first, of dealing with the situation on an emergency basis. He steals his father's van to prevent the transaction between Roger and the pimp. But theoretically, at that point, his function is not fundamentally different from his father's: he protects her by displacing her body, by preventing her from being exchanged.

Only when he tells her the truth does he give her back her freedom by treating her like an agent with whom he can share a dangerous story, that is, by offering much more than his protection. If there is a true moment of hospitality in this film, it is probably the moment when Igor shares his story, the way, elsewhere, people share a meal, or bread, or salt. His revelation turns Assita into an etymological companion, who now has as much power over him as he did have over her. Her identity as an illegal immigrant is not negated by this rearrangement of roles, but the implications of her status are profoundly redefined.

CHAPTER SIX

New Definitions of Hospitality and Philosophical Experiments: From Inhospitable States to Cities of Refuge

This last chapter is about closing doors and establishing borders, about recognizing that individuals can both benefit from public experiments and find themselves forced to adapt and theorize their own interpretations of the law (of hospitality). It is about the often-tragic difference between freedom within and freedom between, or rather about the difficulty of reconciling them whenever a general atmosphere of inhospitality prevails. As I have done previously, I shall compare two narratives that ask similar questions about ethics and freedom, although they do so from within almost incompatible domains: the realm of urban policies and that of cinematographic fiction. And I hope that the mutual hospitality required by the comparison will function as a discursive commentary: the examples combine to form a bouquet of practices that we, as individuals, can choose to reinvent in our own lives.

Let me then return to the issue of invisibility: because the "sans-papiers de Saint-Bernard" were deliberately fighting the myth of their clandestinity, because they opted for full visibility, they also gave up on the illusory freedom conferred upon individuals by the anonymity of huge cities: in places like Paris or London, New York, or Chicago, the systematic control of people's identity is not (yet) possible or, at least, systematically feasible on a daily basis (even if films such as Tony Scott's *Enemy of the State* [1998] promise us such a frightening future). The *sans-papiers* refused the precarious refuge of involuntary hospitality. By so doing, they also asked new questions about the relationship between the city and the stranger, between the city and the nation, and raised the issue of the difference between refuge and hospitality. Clearly, as characters such as Mok like to believe, *métissage* is at work in French cities. Many celebrate the new multicultural dimensions of the typical European metropolis. But next-door neighbors, especially in demonized housing estates, continue to be imagined as archetypal enemies who must cohabit but generally hate each other. Powerful politicians have been known to encourage such thinking by pretending to describe a supposedly evident situation of mutual hostility.

If one neighbor (translate, a person of European origin) objects to the smell and noise of the other (probably a non-European immigrant), it is paradoxically seen both as the norm and as an exception to the rule, an undesirable reaction that the powers that be understand but cannot do anything about. When someone like Jacqueline Deltombe proves the model wrong, however, when she opens her doors to the stranger, the limits of her house are suddenly threatened by a national structure that reaches well beyond the limits of the neighborhood, of the city, and that confronts her with laws that she has probably never read. On one side, glib sentences pretend to explain the status quo; on the other, the legislators make sure that no reality contests that constructed inhospitable status quo.

Such episodes remind us that the individual house can always be used as a metaphor for the community at large, for what happens in the city, for what happens at the level of the state. And yet, some latitude exists: mayors of cities and state legislators cannot ignore one another, and mayors cannot forget that their place in the pyramid puts them below national ordinances. But the frontier between governmental prerogatives and regional or urban decision making is clearer in principle than in reality. Thus, the mayors of certain southern French towns (especially those elected on extreme right-wing platforms) have been known to practice forms of inhospitality that the state could not legally condone. Their anti-immigrant policies, often on the verge of being unconstitutional, make their constituencies even less hospitable than the nation as a whole.

When states become inhospitable, then, must we give up on the concept of international right? Must we declare the concepts of political asylum and refugee so dangerously bankrupt that new models have to be invented? After all, the 1951 Geneva Convention does insist that protection is due to anyone persecuted on account of their race, religion, or political opinion. Is it possible to resign ourselves to the fact that the granting of political asylum should depend on the generous reading, by administrators, of what Gérard Noiriel has called "letters of imploration," in which the writer's goal is more to elicit pity and praise the host nation than to claim his or her rights? (Noiriel 1998, 275). Should we accept that the granting of the "right" of asylum is subordinated to a form of examination in which the candidate must produce the narrative that will best correspond to the administration's criteria of what persecution is?[1]

The question may not be whether states or cities are more or less hostile or hospitable entities, whether or not one of them is better structured, better equipped either to welcome or exclude strangers. Instead, we may want to ask under which specific conditions freedom and cities go together or are mutually exclusive. Today, especially in the Western world, cities are normally attached to a state and do not enjoy sovereignty. And in our context, they are attached to a state that often has a clearly defined immigration policy. Consequently, I propose to think about the different possible patterns that would turn the city into a hospitable environment. In each case, I intend to verify whether the host who wishes to welcome strangers deemed undesirable by the state will appeal to the city as a whole as a free unit or to the idea that freedom within the city can be guaranteed by urban hospitality.

The first type of freedom (granted by a city as a whole) is imagined by a recently formed organization called the International Writers' Parliament. Founded in 1993, when the Pasqua laws were still in effect, the Writer's Parliament seeks to defend authors threatened by authoritarian regimes. And one of its first initiatives was to resurrect the concept of "cities of refuge" to help artists persecuted for their work or political opinions.[2] It reached out to city councils in order to create a whole network of urban centers whose authorities accepted the concept of "cities of refuge" where artists could temporarily reside. In an interview granted to *Le Monde* on June 14, 1997, Wole

Soyinka, (the second president of the Parliament after Salman Rushdie) explained that when a state can no longer guarantee safety within its territory, exile becomes mandatory, and that in order to provide material help to artists, the association had persuaded twenty European cities to become cities of refuge.

> Ten cities have already invited an artist, offering him or her a fellowship and a flat for a year. Ten others are in the process of signing up. Strasbourg and Berlin were the first two members of the network. Caen, Venice, Göteborg, and Helsinki followed suit. Four Algerian writers have benefited from this protection, including Rachid Boudjedra. Taslima Nasreen was Berlin's guest in 1996. The Iranian filmmaker Bahram Beyzai, director of *Bashu, the Little Foreigner*, a film that attracted some notice, is currently residing in a French city. In Graz, in Austria, the town hall organized a center of multicultural encounters at the Stadtpark forum, where it employed the Bosnian writer Dzevad Karahasan. (Bedarida, 1997a)

Did the end of the twentieth century thus reinvent the centuries-old concept of cities of refuge? How can this notion be adequately mobilized? Who would benefit from the existence of such spaces, and what would be the practical, theoretical, or political limits of those disputed little oases of freedom in a vast desert of what we imagine is generalized inhospitality? Or, to ask the question in a different way: "Would the City, a right of cities [*un droit des villes*], a new sovereignty of cities open up an original space here that the inter-state-national right [*le droit inter-état-national*] has failed to open?" (Derrida, 1997a, 22).

The issue of asylum already implies that we are starting from a situation of crisis and urgency. No matter to which (un)democratic territory the city is attached, no matter which government, state, city dweller, or individual provides refuge, even if we are only talking about one person who knows of a good hiding place, the very idea of asylum presupposes danger and life-threatening situations. Deconstructive readings would immediately point out that it might be futile to define a hospitality of urgency as opposed to a hospitality of serenity, and I would certainly be willing to heed such warnings. But even if the hospitality of urgency is redefined as the norm rather than the exception, it is worth considering those cases in which a collective body must alleviate the sufferings of individuals who have already been vic-timized by an original act of inhospitality. The definition of the refugee rec-ognizes that the principle of hospitality has already been violated, and that asylum is an exceptional remedy, a moment of excess in the system: an ex-cess of hospitality here responds to a lack of hospitality elsewhere. The body that grants asylum both condemns that lack of hospitality elsewhere while recognizing that, within that space, inhospitality has become the norm, or at least the reality of a law, of a given power. Helping asylum seekers is also an admission of powerlessness, the sign that inhospitality, somewhere, pre-vails unchallenged. The originality of the solution proposed by the Writers' Parliament is that it brackets off any state intervention. It does not request that national authorities take action but, instead, entrusts a city, located within a state, to play the role of exceptional host. A hospitality of crisis is thus created.

Although the Writers' Parliament has tackled a potentially infinite prob-lem, it has been quite careful to narrow the focus of its requests: its cry for help has been formulated in extremely pragmatic and practical terms, but it is more or less implied that the city is expected to function as a response to the general inhospitality of most states: it is because European states are sus-pected of being inhospitable (toward a certain population of immigrants, for example) that a new structure has to be invented as a remedy. Yet, as its name indicates, the Writers' Parliament limits its action to the defense of a very specific group, or even of a few individuals. The network thus consti-tuted will facilitate the free circulation of a tiny intellectual community, whose members are granted limited material support. This type of hospital-ity will remind academics of institutional hospitality, of professional invita-tions, which certainly does not diminish the value of the initiative even if it gives it a very specific character: it may be difficult to extrapolate from there and to adapt that model to a case where more individuals are concerned.

It is no coincidence that the Writers' Parliament decided to create a net-work of cities of refuge at a time when issues of immigration and of private and public hospitality are such sensitive topics for the French and Euro-peans in general. It is also public knowledge that some of the members of the Writers' Parliament were actively involved in the *sans-papiers* move-ment, and that the Parliament as a whole has taken a stance against govern-mental measures intended to reduce the number of Algerian refugees in

1994: "At a time when the lives of so many Algerians are threatened, France should not bolt its doors but open them" (quoted in Rousseau 1994). Yet, if the link between the writers' initiative and European governmental immigration policies is obvious, the reinvention of cities of refuge cannot and does not pretend to be directly applicable to situations in which entire populations are displaced, when huge groups of migrants need help.

How then, is the history of cities of refuge different from that of the right of asylum? What specificity could the members of the Writers' Parliament claim and what is the originality of their model? To what extent did they adapt and modify a preexisting concept? The apparently transparent phrase "city of refuge" has a long history, even if it has disappeared from our cultural memory for long periods at a time. A few journalists wrote that the expression "cities of refuge" had been invented by the Writers' Parliament, and their forgetfulness seems to be less an effect of their ignorance than evidence that the notion has not been culturally active of late.[3] Besides, it would be unwise to assume that the Writers' Parliament intends to resurrect a medieval or biblical concept without modifying it: the context that led to the creation of cities of refuge thousands of years ago will make some characteristics of the ancient "cities of refuge" obsolete or irrelevant. For example, in *Cosmopolites de tous les pays encore un effort!* Derrida writes about the contemporary limits of the right of asylum before exploring the possibilities offered by a redefined city of refuge. He reminds us that medieval cities enjoyed a sovereignty that modern urban centers have lost and "could define their own laws of hospitality, specific, plural, and restrictive articles of law, that served to interpret *The* great law of hospitality" (Derrida 1997a, 46). Today, the sovereignty of European cities is strictly limited by the nation, and no such independence is to be expected. However, no physical frontier around cities will limit the freedom of individuals once they have crossed the official frontier that separates states. Our cities are no longer surrounded with walls, and even if fortifications exist as vestiges, they will most likely be treated as pieces of the national patrimony. What is left of the walls often becomes a promenade for tourists, who are invited to look at the city from another point of view, rather than being expelled and kept out. Short of a full-blown war or a violent conflict, nothing can justify the erection of so-called demarcation lines between and around cities (which, of course, does not mean that undocumented immigrants are not likely to be controlled, or that they can fully enjoy the privileges of urban citizenship). It is, however, quite clear that the Writers' Parliament does not put its hope in the absence of borders between cities and the state: the goal is not to capitalize on the possibility of losing oneself in the urban crowd. The initiative does not count on the freedom of movement authorized by the fact that urban authorities may choose not to intervene, in spite of the clearly ideological bent of repressive national policies. The Writers' Parliament is, on the contrary, quite determined to gamble on ultravisibility: its network of cities of refuges is internationally known, even advertised, and the group of authors is very clear about its political wishes and demands: "We invite these new cities of refuge to modify state policies, to transform and renew the modes of urban belonging, of state belonging, for example, in a Europe in the process of formation or through international legal structures that are still dominated by the rule of state sovereignty, a rule that is or is supposed to be inviolable but is also more and more precarious and problematic" (Derrida 1997a, 14). That type of refuge is not the equivalent of a hiding place, and secrecy or secrets have nothing to do with this decision to appeal to cities. The ambition is that at the end of the process, a change occurring within a part will influence the whole, and that decisions made within the smaller urban unity will modify the general rule.

The Writers' Parliament's definition of a city of refuge is therefore quite specific, and it constitutes a radical modification of earlier models, to which Derrida refers, however, quite consciously when he mentions the Judaic tradition and the analysis that Emmanuel Levinas makes of it (Derrida 1997a, 44–45). In *Beyond the Verse*, Levinas devotes a whole chapter to cities of refuge, and it is interesting to note to what extent his definition differs from that proposed by the Writers' Parliament. Levinas quotes the Bible (Deut. 4:41–42) and underscores the complex and ambiguous status of refugees and of the definition of refuge: for inasmuch as they are designed in response to very specific situations, cities of refuge are both hospitable and inhospitable, they welcome and protect, but they also constantly remind the refugee that he (or more rarely she) is in exile, and that (s)he cannot go back to the scene of the crime (for crime there is in this case). For in Levinas's example, the city of refuge is conceived of as a place where the identity of the refugee remains ambivalent, complex, and contradictory. Here the refugee is neither completely innocent nor the victim of persecution, and certainly not unjustly treated by a sovereign state. A city of refuge is a place of forgiveness and of punishment at the same time. Or, put another way, a form of forgiveness that implies exile is what constitutes punishment.

This (rich) ambiguity, it seems to me, has more or less disappeared from our contemporary discourses, where the refugee is always imagined, or fantasized, as innocent. I would even venture to propose that this need to be a victim is what makes the status of international or political refugees so problematic. Today, the figure of the (ideal) refugee engenders less xenophobia or racist hostility than that of the immigrant in general. The "real" refugee is welcome, but it is often assumed that individuals who invoke the Geneva Convention are not "real" refugees, that they are cheating: they are suspected of self-servingly taking advantage of the treaty. They are implicitly or overtly accused of lying about their lives, of embellishing (so to speak) their autobiographies to include some of the elements of persecution that give them the right to seek asylum in another territory. In other words, even the most simplistic anti-immigrant discourses are quite able to make a distinction: they are willing to protect the victims of state persecution while suspecting every asylum seeker of deceiving the authorities, by, for example, transforming a supposedly voluntary economic departure into a narrative of political persecution. The bad refugee stretches the definition: the real refugee must be innocent, powerless, a victim.

In that case, the state, rather than the city, bureaucratically grants a right. And that principle has two consequences on the practical and theoretical planes: strangely, the status of refugee grants an individual the right to become the anonymous inhabitant of a city whose authorities are not supposed even to know that he or she is a refugee. The state thus grants a right that city dwellers, in order to respect it, must paradoxically ignore. The new neighbor who moves into the next-door apartment must be able to blend into the anonymous crowd, into the national melting pot. His race, her religion, their political opinions (in other words, what motivated persecution in the first place) must no longer count one way or another: they cannot harm them, but they cannot be celebrated; they cannot be of any use. The city will not change to accommodate the refugee's difference. And if the process of integration fails, if the refugee suffers from being treated as an undesirable foreigner, the national authorities that granted him the status of refugee may not be able to guarantee that this right is adequately respected within the city. And the second consequence is that if a state reneges on its duty to offer hospitality to individuals whom other states (or other nonsovereign powers) persecute, cities or towns will be utterly powerless: they will not be able to offer any kind of assistance, because they have no intrinsic sovereignty.

Levinas's writings propose a very different scenario: going "beyond the verse" as he puts it, he takes up this notion of "punishment," which may seem very problematic to the modern reader because it forces us to redefine the identity of the innocent refugee. For at least one of the characteristics of the inhabitants of ancient cities of refuge makes them radically different from the contemporary asylum seekers, and we need to go back to Levinas's biblical illustrations to understand this crucial distinction. How does the philosopher define the potential inhabitant of a city of refuge? The example he borrows from the Bible is that of a man who has accidentally killed another: we are not talking about persecution but about an act of violence committed by the subject who asks for asylum. The refugee is a perpetrator, not a victim. Yet, and the distinction is naturally crucial, the violence in question was not only unpremeditated but also accidental: "When a murder is committed as an unwitting act of homicide, when, for example—a biblical example—an axe-head comes away from its handle during the work of the woodcutter and deals a mortal blow to a passer-by, this murder cannot be pursued before the court of judgement. This 'objective' murder is committed without intent to harm" (Levinas 1994, 39).

So far, the case outlined by Levinas corresponds to the distinction established by modern legal systems between premeditated murder and manslaughter. But the consequences of the act as explained in the rest of the passage are foreign to our modern understanding of justice and refer to practices long fallen into disuse: "However, a close relation of the victim, called an 'avenger of blood'—or, more exactly, a *go'el hadam*, a 'redeemer of spilt blood,' whose 'heart is heated' by the murder committed (*ki yicham levavo*)—has the right to carry out an act of vengeance" (ibid).

Whereas our contemporary justice categorically forbids individuals to engage in acts of vendetta, here the legal system apparently admits that it cannot completely control the passionate feelings of those who have lost a close relative. The notion of guilt is, however, legally eliminated by the accidental and involuntary nature of the fatal act. The system acknowledges that no judgment can make sure that a final and absolute distinction will ever exist between guilt and innocence: there is a radical difference between the a murderer and someone responsible for an accident (what Levinas rather strangely calls an "objective" murder), but the opposition cannot simply erase the way in which the person who killed will be perceived by those for whom the death constitutes a personal loss. The ancient city of refuge distinguishes between guilt and responsibility but recognizes the impossibility of eliminating a certain desire for vengeance, and treats the feelings experienced by those who have lost a relative as legitimate. Such human desires coexist with the right of the legal system to exonerate a person who has committed manslaughter rather than murder. The law admits that the grief of a relative may take the form of a thirst for personal justice and admits that it is impossible to deprive the "avengers of blood" of the right to act.

In the rhetoric adopted by the Writers' Parliament, that ambiguity disappears altogether, or, at least, is carefully buried in the historical intertext of the phrase "cities of refuge," which will grant asylum to artists and intellectuals who are persecuted because they have expressed their opinions. And the assumption underpinning this is the principle of freedom of speech, which makes the term "crime of opinion" an oxymoron. Cities of refuge are created because nations persecute innocents. The internationally recognized authors who will be given access to the network of foreign cities are, without any possible ambiguity, the victims of injustice done to them by the very powers supposed to guarantee their freedom. The refugee is a victim. The refugee is innocent. And that definition of the refugee turns the city of refuge into a place where some universal moral order is triumphantly reestablished, in its transparence, in its clarity. The innocent writer who has been the victim of violence is granted a right that he or she should always have enjoyed at home: the right to live in peace while expressing one's opinions.

Clearly, the definition that Levinas gives of his "innocent culprit" seems very anachronistic in a system that outlaws personal vendettas, but it seems to me that his vision may nonetheless be a precious intertext in the case of artists: for the will to defend everyone's right to express political opinions only makes sense if we believe that words, writings, plays, and works of art in general can indeed be interpreted as forms of political resistance that have the power to jeopardize a regime. If that is the case, then artists are participating in guerrilla warfare, in an undeclared war in which the right to name and to narrativize (precisely the domain where authors excel) is one of the highest stakes and the subject of heated dispute. In that model, treating writers as harmless, powerless intellectuals is disparaging and almost tantamount to claiming that their acts are worthless.

And yet, in order to save individuals from governments that persecute them, that imprison or torture them, spokespersons and mediators will have to make them fit into the category of the refugee and insist on their status as helpless and innocent victims. One may therefore ask what happens to the principle of resistance when a state grants asylum: should the militants immediately cease to engage in the struggle that led them to that point to begin with? How long does one remain the leader of an opposition in exile? When does one become a simple immigrant? In that particular scenario, cities of refuge may well be more liberal than states: although dependent on a national territory, they could grant a type of refuge distinct from international asylum. Perhaps a hybrid status would enable the individual who has found refuge in a city to keep his or her double status as both (active) opponent of a regime and victim of persecution.

History confirms that states have often added conditions to the granting of asylum: refugees have been asked to cease all political activity, their struggle being deemed harmful and capable of endangering the security of the host nation. For those whose exile is precisely motivated by their commitment to their ideals, inactivity is presumably one of the most painful and exorbitant prices to pay. In *Les camps de la honte*, Anne Grynberg notes that in 1938 the minister of the interior of the Daladier government sent a memo to his prefects asking them to

> demand that immigrants "refrain, on our territory, from any action related to the conflict of opinion in which they may have engaged in their country of origin." Like all other foreigners, refugees had to promise to remain absolutely neutral. That decision was especially resented by anti-fascist militants and by many Jewish immigrants—in the second half of the 1930s, more and more joined various communist, Bundist, or Zionist political groups.[4]

The demand for neutrality turns the refugee into someone who has successfully established him- or herself in free territory, but who is not free within that territory.[5] For a writer forced into exile by a political regime, a similar type of contract would be a contradiction in terms, and cities of refuge obviously expect their writers to write, their painters to paint, their poets to compose. Therefore, they recognize that their political action will continue. But then, a new question arises: what would be the relationship between the city of refuge that accepts that type of presence within its limits and the state in which it is located? Can a city grant asylum according to laws that differ fundamentally from the rules that the nation adopts when it consents to consider someone a refugee? And how can the demands made on the foreigner be different within the city and within the state as long as we think of the city as being within the state? If cities of refuge wish to preserve the right for refugees to act politically, what freedom of movement will the state and the city guarantee them: is being free within the city of refuge the same as living in a free city that has become more independent of the state than other cities? I presume that the local authorities who make the decision to adhere to the network of cities of refuge and who agree to take care of persecuted foreigners and support them for a year will privilege freedom of movement within the city. They cannot take responsibility for freedom of movement beyond it, in states or larger international entities: even if those very same individuals are willing to help the newcomer at the national level and provide administrative assistance, I don't suppose that the guest of a city of refuge such as Berlin will necessarily have the right to cross German borders or European frontiers.

But what happens to a city that wishes to grant its refugees privileges that the state won't allow? Will the city have to free itself from the tutelage of the state to be able to grant its guests the type of freedom that the nation cannot afford or will not give? In that case, doesn't the city reconstitute itself as a microstate, which means that its borders will start functioning like the administrative borders of a nation? Will a city of refuge start having tense relationships with the state within which it is located, and can the refugee become a sort of supplicant who might become the object of negotiations between the city and the state? In the model invented by the Writers' Parliament, the issue of freedom of movement remains an intriguingly problematic issue: for the city of refuge may be able to guarantee the safety of one or two persons within its own frontiers but the refugee would lose that protection if he or she traveled away from the city of refuge.[6]

If the city of refuge can only offer freedom within its own borders, if the guests know that they are at risk if they leave, if they are aware that they cannot leave the city without losing their rights or perhaps endangering their lives, will the city of refuge start resembling a prison rather than providing freedom? Can a city of refuge avoid the ambiguity and deal with the issue of confinement, can it avoid becoming a metaphorical fortress under siege, a gilded cage?

Of course, I want to anticipate an objection and emphasize that the question of confinement is relative: personal trajectories force people to redefine the idea of chains once they have experienced their literal meaning. Cities of refuge may not be a theoretical solution to the issue of freedom of movement, but theoretical limits have to be seen in context when a writer has just spent several years in a cell, if he or she has been tortured. Even in that case, however, changing circumstances and time will eventually foreground questions that go beyond immediate safety. Although the fear of persecution may be alleviated by a relatively serene daily routine, belonging and participating in the life of the city may become a frustrating impossibility for the refugee who remains a protected outsider.

At that point, the city of refuge starts resembling the prison that the refugee seeks to escape. This paradox, where the place of refuge ends up standing for the same constraints that motivated the original departure, is examined by Julien Duvivier's classic film *Pépé le Moko* (1937), the story of a gangster who has fled to the Casbah in colonial Algiers, which he can now no longer leave. Here, the viewer does not need to wonder how the guest experiences his ambiguous refuge-exile: his voice is plainly audible, expressing the feeling of confinement that haunts him. *Pépé le Moko* is the story of a glamorous criminal and of the metropolitan policemen who try to arrest him. But it is also an almost documentary exploration of the status of cities, of their limits, and of the idea of freedom within their walls. The film forces us to think about what the ideal characteristics would be of a city within which the freedom of a stranger would be protected in spite of the efforts of a central government that thinks of that city as part of its territory.

If Pépé is free within the Casbah, it is because his own freedom of movement is increased, whereas that of the policemen looking for him is greatly limited. And their failure is clearly explained by the first scenes of the film, in which the characters who have just arrived from Paris are confronted with a description of the Casbah presenting it as the ideal place of refuge. Making

fun of his colleagues who imagine that physically going to the Casbah is going to add clarity to the muddy picture ("Pour y voir clair? C'est amusant!
[To get a clear picture? That's funny!]"), Inspector Meunier explains that the
Casbah will always be opaque to them, for not only is it plural ("Il n'y a pas
une Casbah, il y en a cent, il y en a mille [There isn't one Casbah, there are
a hundred, thousands]"), but it is also structured like a labyrinth: it is "un dé-
dale . . . des ruelles qui se croisent, se chevauchent, s'enlacent, se désenlacent
. . . dans un fouillis de labyrinthe [a maze . . . winding little streets that cross
and overlap, interlock and disentangle in a chaotic labyrinth]."

Why would a labyrinth mean safe haven for the refugee who dwells in it?
At first sight, it is not clear why the ancient image of the labyrinth could signify refuge for its inhabitant. Why is the maze the equivalent of freedom
here? Originally, the labyrinth was designed as a space of confinement, a
prison for the dangerous Minotaur. The Minotaur is in no way a refugee but
a prisoner. The labyrinth was built to contain the monster. The Casbah is
different: Pépé uses the complexity of the maze as a margin of maneuver, a
space of internal freedom that only he can read. It is a labyrinth only for
those who wish to arrest him. Pépé knows exactly who is where, when, and
when we see him fleeing from the police, who complain that all the terraces
are linked and look alike, he knows exactly where he is and where he is
going. In other words, the idea of the Casbah as a labyrinth is only the point
of view of the baffled officers. The frustrated policemen's vision is the translation of their impression that they are lost, that they need an Ariadne's
thread.[7] Their lack of imagination matches their inability to arrest Pépé.[8] In
other words, the multiplication of their attempts at imaging the city (their
geography, their maps, their bird's-eye-view readings) is a symptom of their
desire to control a place that they hope not only to contain but to make
transparent.[9]

Rendered powerless by the complex geography of a place that excludes
them, the policemen see the Casbah as a chaotic shambles, "oozing with
vermin and damp." Its physical characteristics are displaced onto the inhabitants of the labyrinth, in which one finds "women from all countries, of all
forms and shapes, tall and short, ageless and shapeless, abysses of fat where
no one would dare venture." The misogynistic description hardly hides a
generalized fear of shapelessness: what is inside is linked with disorder. Usually, when the outside is perceived as the cause of anxiety, it is described as

an uncivilized place, as a jungle, as a desert. Often, if the fear of foreigners triggers the desire to close doors, discourses will insist that order reigns inside the walls of the house, of the city, of the state. Chaos is then relegated to the outside. But in *Pépé le Moko*, the only comprehensible structures are the walls (or rather the stairs) that surround the Casbah and contain its dangerous monsters.

What is striking, however, is that Pépé himself is not immune to that vision. The winding streets, the network of terraces, and each house's multiple entrances do guarantee his safety, but he still perceives the city of refuge as a prison: the Casbah offers him a kind of ambiguous hospitality, where the host does not tolerate the guest's desire to leave. Constantly turned toward the past, or toward Paris, Pépé has not completely lost his earlier professional identity: he remains a successful and highly respected thief (i.e., a dissident within the system). But the city of refuge will never be seen as a second motherland, and integration is out of the question. The Casbah remains a prison, the symbol of exile, a form of punishment: "Deux ans de Casbah [two years inside]," he bitterly complains when his nostalgic desire to see Paris tortures him. During a fight with his native lover, whom he clearly identifies with the city itself, he cruelly calls her a "Casbah portative [portable Casbah]," adding that he will, under no circumstances, take her back with him to France. To which she maliciously explains that Paris no longer exists for him, and that he will never be able to leave the Casbah. She even wonders why the police are going to so much trouble to arrest him, observing: "They don't realize that they have already succeeded."[10]

For Frantz Fanon, the Casbah is the emblem of all colonial cities: it is split from the inside, separated from itself by the colonial system (Fanon 1961, 28; 1963, 39). But this symbolic divide is here redoubled by the fact that the Casbah is both an inside and an outside: anticipating our postcolonial condition, where the inhabitant of previously colonized countries will emigrate to the ex-*métropole* and haunt the ex-colonizer, *Pépé le Moko* scrutinizes and exposes the system of perverse cohabitation between colonized city and colonial city. Although the presence of Arabs is paradoxically erased in the film (Vincendeau 1998, 59), the incomprehensible labyrinth symbolizes the supposedly impossible presence of the other at the very core of the city of Algiers. The multiple and unreadable non-place that everyone seeks to clarify, on which Europeans want to shed light, is at the center of a dou-

ble dilemma: it stands for the impossibility of either completely fusing or totally separating the Casbah and the European part of the city. The constantly policed and porous border between the two marks the space of an infinite ambiguity between the dweller and the stranger, a reminder of the
dream of assimilation that is always both imposed and denied.

The invention of a city of refuge within an inhospitable state could thus
be the very symbol of dissident hospitality and provide us with the picture
of the limitations of such transgressive practices: between the city and its
surroundings (I am assuming that the city is within a state), a border exists
where the sovereignty of any asylum-granting authority is constantly renegotiated. Inside the Casbah, Pépé is always already arrested (since completely cornered by a law that has already condemned him) and forever free
(since the Casbah symbolizes the margin of latitude within a repressive system, the room for maneuver that even the most totalitarian regimes fail to
completely eliminate).

In the end, the beautiful concept of "cities of refuge" is marred by two
difficulties that can be expected to emerge whenever one tries to create a
small territory of freedom in the middle of a xenophobic state. On the one
hand, a city may well emulate the model proposed by the state that surrounds it. If that is the case, the foundation of (imaginary, future or present)
cities of refuge might be matched by the development of a corresponding
network of cities of non-refuge, cities of inhospitality. Such places would
probably advertise themselves differently, invoking national preference or
other symbolically loaded identity. And they could try to manipulate the
ambiguity of the relationship between cities and states to better exclude,
rather than to better include, those considered undesirable guests (be they
foreign books or foreign children). On the other hand, a city of refuge always runs the risk of becoming a microcosm in which confinement and
refuge will always coexist, the ambiguity deconstructing the very notion of
refuge introduced by the new urban entity meant to remedy the dangers of
national xenophobia. The city then becomes dangerously close to the models that we have seen in *Salut cousin!* and *La promesse*, in which the notions of
protection and freedom are insidiously presented as if the guest has to
choose between them. The city of refuge is always in danger of becoming a
kind of prison, a place of a social exile that erases the rest of the world rather
than improving it.

Pépé dreams about a Paris that Algiers has eradicated for him. For him, Paris is not only off-limits, it simply no longer exists. Hospitality coincides with the borders of the Casbah. Of course, it would be a form of silly idealism not to remember that there are prisons and there are prisons: if *Pépé le Moko* makes the point that the price of freedom within the Casbah is a total absence of freedom to move between the Casbah and Paris, the very last scenes remind the viewer that Pépé's margin of latitude could have been even more severely restricted. At the end of the film, his hands wrapped around the bars of the gate that forever separates him from the woman he loves, Pépé can hope to escape only by dying.

Pépé le Moko and the artists adopted by a city of refuge have one point in common: they are offered a sort of marginal hospitality, a hospitality that both individually corrects and collectively exposes the fact that there is a crisis of hospitality, that some individuals are expected to be set aside, excluded, banned from the community. They are not total outsiders, but their mode of belonging makes them eternally fragile guests. Alain Milon calls this status *relegation* and observes: "A relegated individual is neither banned nor imprisoned, s[h]e is in a unique situation, because s[h]e is inside without being able to belong fully" (Milon 1999, 22). Such situations are not necessarily short-lived, and when the length of such stays increases, the hospitality of urgency is no longer a gift or an invitation: it becomes a form of exchange that might become extremely onerous for the refugee. For the postcolonial guest, the price of hospitality is sometimes a form of imprisonment and exile whose realities the city of refuge will have to imagine and anticipate if it is to become less painful.

Conclusion: Imperfections and Hospitality

Many authors dread concluding, and I am no exception. Many authors feel that their chosen topic makes it particularly arbitrary to select one form of closure; again, I recognize the symptom. On one hand, symbolically I would like to leave doors open, to invite continuation and further exchanges. How dare I close a book on hospitality? On the other hand, the host who prevents the guest from leaving is just as rude (and insidiously violent) as the guest who overstays his or her welcome.[1] If the readers of a book are like guests, I must remember not to test their patience, and one might think of the ideas developed here as the equivalent of the limited number of beds, or rooms, or resources in a house: excess or lack can be reconstructed or deconstructed by generosity, but on the infinitely stretchable border of gifts, there is a place for happy endings and harmonious separations.

The conclusion of a book on hospitality might be equated to several highly ritualized rites of passage. It might be like the end of a dinner among friends, when the guests who have arrived together start exchanging discreet glances to see whether they are both ready to go, when one of them risks a "I hate to break up the party but . . . ," or some equivalent formula. Of course, the hosts are not boring, one would love to stay forever, but an evening's hospitality should now be rewarded by a return to privacy, by the guests' departure. A more or less implicit promise of reciprocation is also made. Sometimes, the leaving stage lasts very long, several ritualized announcements that "we should really go" rhythmically marking the passage of time, as guests and hosts try arbitrarily to put an end to their conversation in the hall, on the porch, in front of the garage. It is to be hoped that two sides share a sense of satiation, completion, and the anticipation of new encounters. A chain of hospitality has been strengthened, lengthened, started for some, and its true value can only be (approximately) measured in time. And like guests who reciprocally invite their host, each new book on hospitality might be seen as enlarging a community of scholars whose growing circle is both imagined and real. Affinities form, disagreements also develop, new guests and new hosts are included, others are excluded, but the chain of hospitality does not break, creating a general continuum and perpetual fluidity between the role of the guest and that of the host, a flexibility that compensates for the specific imbalances of power that each invitation risks creating.

What the writing of this book has taught me is that if the guest is always the guest, if the host is always the host, something has probably gone very wrong: hospitality has somehow been replaced by parasitism or charity. Hospitality may be incompatible with a meticulous keeping of scores that forecloses future generosities and replaces them with precise debts. Yet, if the roles of guests and hosts are set in stone, if immigrants are treated as if they always have to behave as guests, if hosts are always generous to their poor relations, if the fox of the fable constantly takes off with the cheese that the host was not yet offering, the continuum between guest and host disappears. Ironically, guests who are forced into the systematic position of the guest are often accused of parasitism, the host refusing to take responsibility for the historical position that deprives others of the pleasure and pride of taking their place.

And like the economy of a given country, the guest-host continuum will always be a precarious equilibrium that several factors can upset: hospitable inflation can develop if the guests feel that they must always surpass the host's performance, either because the first invitation overwhelmed them with gratitude or because the need to impress becomes part of the contract. We may need more "hospitalists," who, like economists, would theorize the ideal ratio and pace of hospitable inflation, or it may be even more desirable to conclude that it is impossible to determine whether hospitable inflation is good or bad in an absolute sense. The multiplication of reciprocal invitations functions in and of itself as a form of inflation, and we have seen that there is more to this one-upmanship than generosity or a desire to give something in return. Ostentation and the desire to impress one's neighbors are also components of the hospitable contract. As Jean Starobinski puts it, "Gifts can circulate on the basis of equality, but also on the basis of disparity, in which case they involve rich and poor, sovereign dispenser and humble beneficiary" (Starobinski 1997, 2). This is one of the imperfections of even perfect hospitality. Another way of making this point would be to remember the lessons of Didier van Cauwelaert's Old Vasile: we should neither idealize hospitality in general nor seek to embrace each and every type of hospitable practice.

In some cases, entertaining is a form of flaunting one's social success, one's house, one's spouse, one's servants. Nineteenth-century novels ridicule bourgeois etiquette and its implicit aping of the aristocracy. Here, the assumption is that hospitable inflation is slowly corrupting the chain, turning each host into a more and more servile worshipper of conformist materialism. But, at times, the principle of hospitable inflation is more ambiguous, because a whole culture revolves around the idea of outdoing one's host, because the law of hospitality itself prescribes this form of exponential expenditure.

Taken to extremes, ostentatious hospitality could start looking like a form of addiction. But any judge of just how undesirable ostentation is will be confronted with the difficult task of quantifying the unquantifiable: pride, generosity, but also humiliation and shame. If a man ruins himself to better receive his guests, is he guilty of bad hospitality, of poor management? What if he also ruins his family, his community, his nation? Seen from the outside, isn't such generosity interpretable as a form of madness? And isn't that type of interpretation a form of violence done to the idea of (the other's) hospitality?

Christopher Bracken's *The Potlatch Papers* is an analysis of precisely such a moment in history, when one stranger chooses to intervene to change the other community's supposedly wasteful law. The issue is a very specific form of hospitality: the so-called potlatch, a ceremony during which a host gives away as much as he can to establish or increase his social status. Thanks to the work of anthropologists and cultural critics, the system of the potlatch is relatively well known. Many are aware that potlatches involve a systematic principle of excess and expenditure, where prestige and glory are obtained by the extravagant giving away of as much wealth as possible in public ceremonies. Since the ritualized distribution of property increases the giver's social status, any attempt at acquiring property is seen as leading to and culminating in the moment when it will be given up, given away. There have been many studies of the logic of the potlatch and of equivalent manifestations in the Western world (Mauss 1990; Certeau 1980, 1984), but Bracken's book is a fascinating account of how and why, in 1884, Canada's Parliament passed a law banning potlatches among the First Nations of British Columbia. And at one level, one can certainly understand why potlatches would have been perceived as an aberration by settlers who valorized growth, savings, the slow and steady accumulation of land, capital, and resources. Potlatches may appear as an irrational excess of generosity, a futile display of one-upmanship, but why would a government feel so threatened as to go to the trouble of banning them? When is the other's hospitality considered so dangerous that the (powerful) other would want to step in and change it radically? Is too much hospitality a disease of hospitality?

In essence, this is exactly what the colonial regime argued when Canadian legislators tried to ban the practice altogether. They viewed what they perceived as an excess of generosity, as a form of addiction. Potlatch went against their very idea of limits; it was a law that undermined the very principle of the law by mandating excess, that is, potentially, transgression. Not surprisingly, observers equated potlatches with other forms of supposedly antisocial behavior, including gambling: in 1874, George Blenkinsop, "a former Hudson's Bay Company trader" (Bracken 1997, 37), was sent to the West Coast to gather information about the controversial practice of potlatch. Until the Indians were "*cured* of their propensity for gambling and accumulating property, solely for the purpose of giving [it] away to other Indians, there can be little hope of elevating them from their present state of degradation and bettering the condition and appearance of their wives and families," Blenkinsop concluded (Bracken 1997, 37; my emphasis).

We may regard the outsider's intrusion here into the other's laws of hospitality as insufferable arrogance and unethical replacement of a form of expenditure with cruder forms of commercial reasoning. But even if the government had not tried to intervene to suppress the custom, there is no guarantee that neighboring communities would have found a way to compare their definition of generosity and come to an agreement about which aspects of which law they would abide by during cross-cultural encounters. For the trouble is that subjects who belong to a given community always implicitly refer to *their* laws of hospitality, and their laws may be radically different from those of the stranger, who either has or does not have the power to impose his. In the introduction to his book *French Hospitality*, Tahar Ben Jelloun remembers:

> In an unpublished novella called "The invitation" I tell the true story of a television crew who went to Algeria to produce a program about an immigrant who had gone home. The shooting lasted a week, and throughout the whole time the villagers entertained the crew. The immigrant's father went into debt to provide presents and sumptuous meals all around. The director, touched by such warmth and generosity, gave the old man his business card. "If ever you're in Paris," he said in typical Parisian style, "be sure to come and see me!" But when one evening six months later the old man rang at his doorbell, it took the director some time to realize who he was. Very embarrassing for all concerned. (Ben Jelloun 1999, 3)

Ben Jelloun is technically right to conclude here that "Hospitality doesn't always imply reciprocity" (ibid.), but the story makes other points as well. First of all, while the potlatch is a practice judged from the outside by someone who objects to the rule as rule, this situation involves two communities who do not even share the same laws of hospitality and who do not even know that they are mobilizing two sets of laws. Interestingly, however, Ben Jelloun's narrative is not too concerned with issues of cultural ignorance.

One alternative lesson of this fable might be that it is dangerous to overinvest in a bad guest who will not even know how to reciprocate. The story does not really address the relationship between the old man's attitude, his own rules, and the notion of excess: was "borrowing" to serve "grandiose" meals a cultural norm, a form of potlatch, an exceptional gesture? Was the director genuinely "touched" or intrigued by what he read as someone else's definition of hospitality? Was there too much of a difference between "grandiose" in his book and "grandiose" in the old man's universe? The story does not provide answers to such questions because Ben Jelloun obviously privileges other points: the short story invites us to admire the generous host. The old man, the story implies, was in the right; the trouble is not that he spent too much but that the Westerner was dense and selfish, incapable of reciprocating. And in this episode, the Parisian does embody scandalous ingratitude. However, the summary of the story also alludes to the types of difficulties that arise when hospitable practices cross borders without being translated: knocking on someone's door at night in Paris six months after even a long encounter may not be the right code, even if the host is willing to honor his earlier invitation. Perhaps the "embarrassment" was caused more by the obvious gap between expectations and behavior. Perhaps another short story might have made that moment of discomfort the prelude to better-understood hospitality. This could have been a beginning rather than an end, it could have been a tale of imperfect hospitality renegotiated between agents who realize that they do not have the same assumptions about how to invite and how to accept invitations. In other words, reciprocity may not be the same thing as perfect symmetry but asymmetry may not be the opposite of hospitality. Perhaps, rather than focusing on the laws of hospitality in each culture, we should think about what types of laws would be necessary to guarantee that different sets of laws become aware of each other's existence. Creolized and/or globalized hospitality would thus be a mechanism whereby laws of hospitality could start interacting with one another.

Hospitable exchanges often create situations in which one party must second-guess the other's desire or needs. And not knowing what the other expects, or wants, will create moments of malaise and discomfort, as well as moments of pleasure and joy. Hospitality is also about resigning oneself to friction, approximations, gradually altered protocols. At least, when the host and the guest have the impression that they share the same assumptions about what it means to be hospitable, they both have agency: they can share the responsibility for formulating an objection to a given rule, their strong dislike of another, their attachment to a different principle. If they share a certain cultural patrimony, if they speak the same language, if the guest or the host is not intent, like Merzak Allouache's character, on imposing his own references at all cost, then they may eventually discuss their understanding of the law of hospitality, they may agree on which part of the code needs to be redefined and made individual.

Systematically cooking for one's guest or for one's host may be a privilege and a burden for both parties. And the most delicate aspect of hospitality is not deciding whose desire is going to be respected (even at the expense of the other's will), but how the host and the guest tactfully point out their discomfort with the current practice. The host may be convinced that s/he is feeding the guest to make sure that s/he is not hungry, but the guest may accept the food simply to avoid offending the host, regardless of whether s/he is hungry. Formulating the distinctions between need, desire, politeness, the respect of the rule, and the customizing of the rules is perhaps much more difficult than abiding by what one assumes is the rule. Guests and hosts usually keep in mind that they may both blunder because certain intricacies of the rules escape them: is it appropriate to refuse three times before accepting something to eat? What if the host takes your second refusal at face value and stops offering?

The host and the guest are often locked in a complicated ballet of proposals, expectations, careful interpretations of seemingly infinite offers. It is an art to know how to decline subtly: as a Moroccan proverb puts it: "Noble is he who spreads his rug; foolish is he who sits on it" ("Noble est celui qui étale son tapis / fou celui qui s'assied dessus" [quoted in Depaule 1997, 26]).

But at some point, someone must take the risk of sitting down and accepting the consequences. Risk, as we have seen throughout the book, is one of the keys to all hospitable encounters. Hostility is part and parcel of the contract between the host and the guest, and accepting the possibility of violence endangers both the guest and the host. "To welcome is to accept excess, to accept that the other rules over my house. He leaves a trace. In that sense, hospitality is threatening. I unconditionally accept the other, without setting out criteria, and the other might be the worst, because that threat is at the core of the *pure principle of hospitality*" (David 1999, 21).

Pascal David's point of view is even more pessimistic than that of Derrida, whose notion of desirable "risk" is discussed in the Introduction, but he raises similar questions: hospitality also puts the host in a situation that requires delicate decisions. The abstract notion of hospitality as a "pure" principle must constantly be renegotiated as a series of moments when the "worst" and the "pure" are interpreted, weighed, and put into practice.

Hospitality does not always have such radical consequences, but hospitable inflation and its inherent discomforts remain two of its almost necessary features. We could imagine this imbalance as a force, rather than as a specific law, as an infinite differing of equilibrium, and the sense of expectation thus created within the community is a perfect metaphor for the existence of hospitality as law: by accepting the risk of inflation, and its potentially harmful consequences for the subjects that fill all the possible roles on the guest-host continuum, a group keeps hospitality alive. The perfect reception, the unmatchable dinner party would be the equivalent of a flat line on the social monitor of hospitality. Consequently, a completely harmonious and pacified level of interaction may not be the best test of successful hospitable gestures: a total absence of friction might signify that other inhospitalities (such as the usurpation of the land by colonizers, for example) have instituted a *Pax Romana* in which hosts are always hosts, where guests are always guests.

Unconditional hospitality is a risk, but hospitality without risk usually hides more serious violence. A perfectly gracious and generous host may be capitalizing on dark shadows, on ghosts that haunt his land, his house, his social position: closing the door on supposedly undesirable strangers is clearly inhospitable, but an open-door policy may be the different side of the same coin if the host forgets about the condition that constructed him or her as a potential host. The repressed may be that the land was here before the host, that recent wars and spoliation may have legitimized current forms of ownership. It is not that a colonizer cannot be a host, and a generous host at such, *au contraire*. The colonizer will practically be structured as the obvious host: if recent settlers are empowered (by the granting of land, a cultivated sense of being the first to till the soil despite obvious signs to the contrary), they may have a strong desire to welcome other even more recent settlers, people of their own class, origin, nationality. But increased hospitality to "their own" kind is based on the fundamental exclusion of how the land came to be owned. We could say that the powerful and secure host tends to forget that what he gives was taken from somebody else. Less dramatically, when political borders have been stable for so long that no living expropriated subject can resent the host's occupation of the land, we could describe the host's graciousness and generosity as part of a cultural legacy that includes a whole series of practices taught by well-bred mothers, well-educated fathers, hospitable relatives, and extended families or neighbors.

Naturally, if perfectly peaceful moments of shared hospitality sometimes hide ugly structures of larger inhospitality, they also coexist with other forms of dissident hospitality. Hospitality then goes underground, becomes a form of resistance where a subject deliberately chooses to occupy the position of host that the system denies him or her. From the point of the view of the authorities, that type of host is often dismissed and accused of being a parasite, like the Town Rat who chooses to invite his cousin even though the meal he has to offer consists of leftovers.

Each context requires a careful rethinking of who is free to give, to receive, and of who has enough power to define freedom. At times, different subjects will have different expectations about what is more or less acceptable. Marius Alliod notes that in the eighteenth century, enlightened thinkers were outraged by the fact that, when they were destitute, ill, or old, the poor were often forced to choose between survival and liberty, and that in having to "ask the rector of the Hôtel-Dieu to grant them unconditional hospitality," they were obliged to "trade their freedom for a few crumbs." Becoming a guest of the Hôtel-Dieu amounted to accepting a life sentence, because "'unconditional' meant that those whose request had been granted would never be expelled from the Hôtel-Dieu. The regulations required that they stay there until their deaths, and they took a written oath to do so upon their admission" (Alliod 1999, 56).

No wonder eighteenth-century philosophers found the principle questionable: it is easy to interpret this type of contract as a betrayal of the law of hospitality. Pretending that the poor were guests was a cruel irony. Alliod, however, feels the need to point out that it may be hasty to conclude that the guests themselves viewed this scenario as a form of abusive hospitality, "For we know nothing of their experience, and we don't know whether they thought of themselves as prisoners when they were in the rector's care, after signing their wills" (ibid., 57). If historians admit that they will never know, it might be up to writers of fiction to stage this dilemma and to try to bring home to the modern reader the type of hesitation that such issues generate. Fiction can also introduce the possibility of dissident narratives and invite us to conceptualize oppositional practices of hospitality.

When the host reigns supreme over the land, illegal and rival hosts may surface, and they double the risk involved in hospitality. Like any host, they have to accept that the guest may be dangerous to them, but they are also challenging the powerful supra host that keeps them in the shadow. The supra host can be the nation or a representative of the nation's authority, a father, or the prince's palace, where servants and masters cohabit, harmoniously, the master would say, tragically, from the servants' point of view. In Moufida Tlatli's 1994 film *Samt al-qusur* (*The Silences of the Palace*), the female domestics are quasi-owned by the residents of the palace. Occasionally treated as if they were guests when they are too young to be perceived as sexual temptations, the women live in a space that they occupy without having any rights to it. They are toys rather than guests. But this does not stop them from allowing a stranger to stay with them in their quarters. The guest they (reluctantly) invite will put them in terrible danger if discovered: he is involved in the struggle against colonialism, against the French presence in Tunisia, and also against the duplicitous attitude of the Tunisian authorities. His secret presence within the palace symbolizes what had to be excluded from this self-contained universe in which one grand reception follows another. The servants manage, in spite of everything, to institute some disruption of the host-guest encoding, to introduce some exteriority into the system, the possibility of future exchanges. Here, the refugee is the materialization of the ghost that haunts any place where the roles of hosts and guests are rigidly assigned by power differentials.

Of course, the assignment of rigid roles to social actors is not the only way of introducing violence into the equation of hospitality. We have seen that even if the guest and the host can exchange places, their mutual encounter must always situate itself on the course of a pendulum that swings wildly between generosity and cannibalism: the continuum between generosity and cannibalism always threatens to turn hospitable practices into potentially harmful encounters. Two dark scenarios always lurk between the provisional definition of two subjects as guest and host: the host can always devour the guest, the guest can always devour the host. As we have seen, devouring can be a metaphor for assimilation, for exploitation, or for sexual abuse. Hospitality is always precariously poised between those two evils.

At the same time, if the guest and the host are not willing to take that risk and do not welcome the possibility of being challenged, shaken, changed by the encounter, then there is no hospitality either. The very precondition of hospitality may require that, in some ways, both the host and the guest accept, in different ways, the uncomfortable and sometimes painful possibility of being changed by the other. Some degree of mutual metamorphosis, brought about by the presence of the other, of his or her different values or points of view, will undoubtedly constitute the by-product and the visible evidence of hospitable gestures. Perhaps, then, it is the paradoxical nature of conditional and unconditional hospitality alike to be a practice that cannot tolerate perfection, that is inherently perverse, always and eminently corruptible. It constantly tests the host's and the guest's thresholds of fear, and their willingness to live with that fear, and with their malaise.

Reference Matter

Notes

Unless a translated source is specifically cited, translations are by the author.

1. Conventionally named after Charles Pasqua, the right-wing minister of the interior who defended them, the controversial series of texts constituted one of the most repressive versions of the regularly revisited set of ordinances that defines immigrant status. For a violently critical analysis of all the elements of the new texts, see Naïr 1997.

2. For more information about the *sans-papiers* movement, including a historical account of how the group formed and developed, see its web site (http://bok.net/pajol), and Diop 1997, Sané 1996, and Cissé 1999, the autobiographies of three undocumented immigrants.

3. See "Comment vous fabriquez des clandestins" in Naïr 1997, 25–27, for an explanation of how some immigrants were both authorized to stay in France (because one element of their situation made it illegal to deport them) and denied documents (because of another factor): they became known as the *inexpulsables irrégularisables* (unexpellable-unregularizable).

4. The members of the committee of mediators were Lucie Aubrac, Raymond Aubrac, Jean-Michel Belorgey, Jean-François Berjonneau, André Berroir, Paul Bouchet, Bernard Brunhes, Noël Copin, Monique Chemillier-Gendreau, Jacqueline Costa-Lascoux, André Costes, Mireille Delmas-Marty, Stéphane Hessel, Paul Kessler, Camille Lacoste-Dujardin, Pierre Lyon-Caen, Henri Madelin, Edgar Morin, Paul Ricoeur, Antoine Sanguinetti, Laurent Schwartz, Louis Schweitzer, Yves Sultan, Germaine Tillion, Jean-Pierre Vernant, and Pierre Vidal-Naquet.

5. Such linguistic changes can be treated as symptoms, as signals that certain horizons have changed, and that some tactics are now preferable to others: the fact that the term *sans-papiers* has unofficially replaced *clandestins* is a means, rather than an end. And yet, I tend to agree more with Didier Fassin, who insists that the word *clandestins* implicitly justified repressive measures (Fassin 1996, 77; Rosello 1998b),

than with Jacques Derrida, who worries that "the terrifying phrase" *sans-papiers* adds new, perverse implications to their plight: "Those we call, in a word, 'undocumented,' supposedly lack something. He is un——. She is un——. What is missing exactly?" (Derrida 1997b, 4).

6. Saint-Just, articles 1, 2, 3 of chapter 9 in the second part of *Essai de constitution*, in id., *Oeuvres complètes*, ed. Michèle Duval (Paris: Gérard Lebovici, 1984), 441–42, quoted in Wahnich 1997b, 109.

7. *Archives parlementaires*, 70: 107, fifth decree adopted August 1, 1793, quoted in Wahnich 1997b, 23.

8. The slogan "Touche pas à mon pote!" (Hands off my buddy!) highlights personal friendship and to downplay ethnic differences, although S.O.S. Racisme as a whole was criticized for promoting culturalist tendencies. Some critiques came from the relatively traditional French left, which continues to fear communitarism and identity politics, while others pointed out that "difference" was already politically coopted by the far right (Kristeva 1988, 1990; Taguieff 1988, 1990). The (rather illusory) "closing of borders" can be said to have taken place in 1974, when work immigration was officially stopped by President Valéry Giscard d'Estaing.

9. Compare, for example, the titles of recent books on hospitality with the previous generation of essays, whose authors tend to privilege different key words: see, e.g., Mohand Khellil's 1991 *L'intégration des maghrébins en France*, Alain Bockel's 1991 *L'immigration au pays des Droits de l'homme*, Dominique Schnapper's 1991 *La France de l'intégration: Sociologie de la nation en 1990*, and Catherine Wihtol de Wenden's 1988 *Les immigrés et la politique*.

10. In 1997, Anne Gotman edited a special issue of the journal *Communications* entirely devoted to hospitality: the volume is particularly interested in the relationship between the stranger and the city but also raises interesting issues of gender and ethnicity. In *L'hospitalité*, Anne Dufourmantelle debates Jacques Derrida in a dual text that explores some of the issues raised in a seminar taught by the philosopher at the Ecole des hautes études en sciences sociales (Derrida and Dufourmantelle 1997). Mohammed Seffahi published the proceedings of a colloquium organized around Jacques Derrida under the title *Manifeste pour l'hospitalité, aux Minguettes: Autour de Jacques Derrida* (Manifesto in Favor of Hospitality, at the Minguettes: Around Jacques Derrida [Seffahi 1999]). The book features one article by Jacques Derrida and the transcription of a dialogue between the philosopher and Michel Wieviorka.

11. This is even more obvious in German, where the arguably oxymoronic phrase "guest worker" has become one word: *Gastarbeiter*.

12. I suspect that the same masculinist sense of wonder is at work in Diderot's *Supplement to Bougainville's Voyage*, even if the form of the dialogue between different commentators introduces a suitably critical analytical gaze into the pastiche, comment, or rewriting of the original (Diderot [1796] 1951; see also the English translation in Feher 1997, 76–113).

13. According to structuralist anthropologists who have looked at primitive soci-

eties as if they represented an earlier version of Western cultures, this model of exchange may even have been the most widespread of norms.

CHAPTER I

Earlier versions of this chapter were presented at a conference on "Europe, the New Melting Pot" (Old Dominion University), at the University of Notre Dame, and at Stanford University. I thank Cynthia Marker, Fredrick Lubisch, Elizabeth Mudimbe, and Seth Lerer for giving me the opportunity to present the work in progress, and especially Dominic Thomas for his invitation and his reading of this chapter. A short version of the chapter appeared under the title "Interpreting Immigration Laws: 'Crimes of Hospitality' or 'Crimes Against Hospitality,'" in *Diaspora* 8.3 (winter 1999): 209–24, which I thank for permission to reprint.

1. After being expelled from the first church they occupied (Saint Ambroise), the 300 undocumented African immigrants, who had been relatively ignored by the media, found refuge in the Théâtre du Soleil at the Cartoucherie, and after leaving the Church of Saint Bernard, they returned there. In 1997, the guiding spirit of the Théâtre du Soleil, Ariane Mnouchkine, put on a "collective creation," the play *Et soudain, des nuits d'éveil*, which retells the *sans-papiers*'s story as a tragic adventure of Tibetans, in collaboration with Hélène Cixous and Jean-Jacques Lemêtre.

2. I am borrowing the title of Shmuel Yosef Agnon's *Oreakh natah la-lun*, published in 1968 in Tel-Aviv. In *A Guest for the Night*, a "guest" who comes to Galicia to honor his ancestors' memories is entrusted with the key to the study room where books and thoughts are preserved, while most of the inhabitants must desert the town to make a living elsewhere.

3. The cover of the new edition is a picture of the interior of the Saint-Bernard Church showing a group of African women. The photographer has deliberately allowed the human beings to remain blurred, while the church and their sleeping bags are in sharp focus.

4. Ben Jelloun 1999, 14. I suspect that it is both very difficult and indispensable to show that there is a connection between supposedly "administrative" decisions and a general level of xenophobia and racism in popular discourses. Administrators, like lawmakers, are (but should probably not be) expected to leave their own opinions and fears at the doors of their offices: laws may be more or less generous and hospitable, but they are texts to be interpreted with more or less generosity by human beings who have been placed in the position of the "excluded third" between the potential host (the abstract nation) and the potential guest (the very concrete human being who wishes to migrate). See Rosello 1999, 53–64.

5. I am borrowing from the title of Ghosh 1998, *Huddled Masses and Uncertain Shores*.

6. For example, Lemoine 1989 tells the story of North African immigrants caught

between their desire to stay in the neighborhood where they have lived for more than ten years and the administration's determination to "rehabilitate" the area. The author points out that the reason why the city was able to expel the immigrants was that their housing situation was juridically described in terms of services and not in terms of dwelling: "Legally, a furnished flat is not a lodging but a [form of] commerce. In other words, whoever lives in a furnished apartment is not a tenant but a customer, a fundamental distinction, since tenants benefit from certain protections" (ibid., 136–37).

7. It is fair to note that national borders do not correspond to linguistic borders, and that the language obstacle is less daunting for some than for others: when immigrants move to what used to be the colonial *métropole* in Europe, they will not experience the language barrier in the same manner as people who have traveled from neighboring states because of wars, for example. The fact remains that cultural competence is indistinguishable from language and may even be defined as a type of language.

8. For parliamentary debates on the *certificat d'hébergement*, see Montvalon 1997; Bernard and Herzberg 1997a (both at http://archives.lemonde.fr/lemonde).

9. For another testimony on the practical consequences of the *certificat*, see a text signed "Une Malgache": "La grandeur de la France à l'aune d'un consulat," *Politique africaine* 67, *La France et les migrants africains* (Oct. 1997): 63–65

10. In December 1997, the *certificats d'hébergement* were replaced by an *attestation d'accueil* that was not subject to the same verification procedures. See Montvalon 1997.

11. For a historical account of the evolution of the *certificat d'hébergement*, see Bernard and Herzberg 1997a.

12. See also Derrida 1997b.

13. "Cinquante-neuf réalisateurs appellent à 'désobéir,'" *Le Monde*, Feb. 12, 1997, reprinted in *Saga* 1 (Jan. 1998): 80. The manifesto circulated in the form of printed and electronic petitions. It was reprinted in the first issue of *Saga*, a new journal that devoted its inaugural volume to the republication of famous manifestos. The text thus finds itself associated with other famous interventions such as "Le manifeste des 121" during the Algerian war, surrealist tracts, and women's pleas for reproductive rights.

14. "It took the Lille affair, highlighted by the media, and a traumatic political event in Vitrolles for an initiative spawned by the cultural world to start a wave of protest whose spontaneity and issues made it similar to the social movement of December 1995" (Viledier 1997, 17).

15. See "Poètes, vos papiers!" *Saga* 1 (1998): 78–79.

16. Timera 1997, 43. The other paths mentioned by Timera are the military, work-related migrations, and family reunions.

CHAPTER 2

The second part of this chapter was first presented at a workshop organized by Fran-çoise Lionnet at Northwestern University in 1998. That earlier version is reprinted here with kind permission of *Studies in Twentieth Century Literature* (forthcoming).

1. http://europa.eu.int/en/record/mt/top.html. See especially titles V and VI of the Maastricht treaty.

2. For a detailed explanation of the Schengen agreement, see http://gov.austria-info.at/ForeignAffairs/intern/s4scheng_e.html. See especially the agreements about a common visa policy and a common policy on illegal migration. See also, in French, http://www.ib.be/euroj/cee/francais/mieux/droit/schengen.html. For an angry and perceptive account of what Schengen means to non-Europeans, especially when they come from Africa, see Raafat 1995. Attempts were made to anticipate objections or to reassure the public in brochures that explain the Système d'information Schengen: "Le S.I.S. n'est pas une menace pour notre vie privée" (http://www.ib.be/euroj/cee/francais/mieux/droit/schengen.html: Dépliant Un vent de liberté souffle sur l'Europe - L'Europe ça me touche - Le Ministère des Affaires Etrangères [Service Accords de Schengen] - E. Goffin - Rue des Quatre Bras 2 - 1000, Bruxelles).

3. http://www.bz.minbuza.nl/english/Policy/amstfact.html. It is to be noted that the general atmosphere of the treaty reflects and perpetuates fears that the new fortress has already been under siege and threatened by outsiders. As Ali Behdad demonstrates in a perceptive article entitled "Nationalism and Immigration to the United States," this mentality is not specifically European; rather, it is almost the very definition of the border between states: "The so-called 'crisis of immigration' is neither a historical exception nor a series of cyclical eruptions of a unique disorder. Rather, the state of siege is the rule in the narrative of nationalism: it is what legitimates national authority and state power" (Behdad 1997, 165).

4. On the evolution of the tradition and its various manifestations from ancient Greece to the seventeenth-century French monarchy, see Jean Starobinski's *Largesse* (Starobinski 1997).

5. Cauwelaert 1994, 6. All translations from the novel are mine.

6. Etienne Balibar calls them the "false nationals" (Balibar 1990, 284).

7. Tony Gatlif's trilogy consists of *Latcho Drom*, a 1993 documentary on Gypsy music; *Mondo*, a 1996 adaptation of a short story by Jean-Marie Le Clézio; and *Gadjo Dilo*, or *L'étranger fou*, 1997, an interesting reversal of the immigrant trope: here the French Gypsy emigrates. See also Chuz Gutiérrez's 1996 *Alma Gitana* (Spain) and Andrej Mlakar's 1995 *Halgato* (Slovenia).

8. In "Ethnicity on the French Frontier," Winifred Woodhull suggests that "minority literature and scholarship in France have devoted considerable attention to the divisions *within* ethnic groups and have thus called into question essentialist

notions of ethnic identity. So far, however, they have not explored the relations *between* ethnic groups in a critical, productive way" (Woodhull 1997, 48).

9. "The obligation to give is intrinsically paradoxical, because it is nothing less than that of being spontaneous. A purely obligatory gift isn't one" (Caillé 1991, 109).

10. This a quotation from the Niceno-Constantinopolitan Creed proclaimed in Catholic churches as part of every holy liturgy.

CHAPTER 3

An edited version of this chapter originally appeared in *Women, Immigration and Identities*, ed. Jane Freedman and Carrie Tarr (Oxford: Berg, 2000), 135–51. I thank the publisher for permission to reprint it here.

1. I thank Jean Mainil for bringing this scene to my attention.

2. The separation between communities continues to function as a meaningful social reality even if many actors are aware that it is artificial: as Abdelhafid Hammouche puts it, "The Arab is no longer one of the opposing poles of our identity, [s]he is 'within us,' if we may say so, and no longer 'in front of' us, not to speak of 'against' us" (Hammouche 1999, 40).

3. I am referring to the model of hospitality inherited from the revolutionary ideal, which, according to Fassin, Morice, and Quiminal, is in danger of deteriorating into principles of inhospitality (Fassin et al. 1997).

4. For a fascinating analysis of different forms of hospitality in the Arab world, see Depaule 1997, which carefully distinguishes between different types of guest and host, showing how the words used to refer to the host and hospitality (*dayf* and *diyâfa*) are both related to and separated from the notions of neighbor, protection, pilgrim, and travel companion. Depaule examines the role played by gender (female/male relationship or the issue of single men, who often complicate the traditional repertoire of laws). Exploring proverbs and spatial configurations in Maghrebian houses, including their polysemy and hybrid architecture, he shows to what extent hospitality means "making room for the other but also putting the other in his/her place" (ibid., 26).

5. "Imagine a French worker who lives with his wife in a housing estate, and who sees that the neighbors packed into the next-door apartment are a family with a father, three or four wives, and twenty children, who get Fr 50,000 in benefits, without working, naturally. Add the smell and the noise. Well, the French worker goes crazy. And to say that is not to be a racist." Statement made at a dinner in Orléans (June 19, 1991). See also *Le Monde*, June 21, 1991. For an analysis of the reactions triggered by this xenophobic explanation of xenophobia, and especially of the legal action taken by the MRAP (Mouvement contre le racisme et pour l'amitié entre les peuples), see *Le Monde*, Feb. 28, 1992.

6. The figure of the female colonizer whose power over her maids is just as

tyrannical as that of the settler over his slaves is well documented. For a literary example, see André Schwarz-Bart's *La mulâtresse Solitude*, in which the settlers' little girls copy their parents' violence when given slaves as toys.

7. In chapter 5, I look at Sembène Ousmane's "La noire de . . .", where a Senegalese woman who has been "invited" to spend a summer in France ends up committing suicide. Her death can be read as the result of a form of perverse hospitality, where the guest is slowly but surely turned into a poor relation, a servant, a slave. See also Michèle Maillet's *L'étoile noire*, where the Martinican main character leaves her island because she believes that a rich family is inviting her as a guest to further her education. As it turns out, she is used exclusively as the children's nanny and then deported because the German soldiers who raid the house cannot decide whether she is Jewish or not.

8. For particularly problematic examples of such predatory photography, see Michel Tournier's novels, especially *Le roi des Aulnes* and *La goutte d'or*.

9. For sociological approaches to the link between social and architectural issues in the French *banlieues* built in the 1960s (and studies of what has been seen as the quintessential inhospitality of high-rises), see Jazouli 1992; Bachmann and Basier 1989; Lepoutre 1997.

10. For an analysis of the different possible roles of the much-maligned *foulard* in the Maghreb, see Woodhull 1993; Yeğenoğlu 1998; Gaspard and Khosrokhavar 1999.

11. Note that the English translation cannot specify that the man was not present. The "all" even implies otherwise.

12. For a good analysis of what happens when superior knowledge and powerlessness coexist, see the beginning of Sedgwick 1993.

13. Western cultures stereotypically think of the recipient of a gift as the obliged party, but Mauss's analysis of the Maori legal system reveals more complex forms of debts that resemble what occurs between the little girl and the neighbor. Mauss notices that the ritualizing of the gift-giving practices has consequences over who has or loses power: if the gift is correctly given, "Coming from one person, made or appropriated by him, it gives him power over the other who accepts it. In the case where the prestation provided is not rendered in the prescribed juridical, economical, or ritual form, the giver obtains power over the person who has participated in the feast and has taken in its substances, the one who has married the girl or has bound himself by blood relations, the beneficiary who uses an object enchanted with the whole authority of the giver" (Mauss 1990, 29–30).

CHAPTER 4

A version of this chapter was presented at the Society for Cinema Studies Convention in 1999. I thank Peter Bloom for his invitation. A shorter version of the chapter appeared in *Cinéma engagé: Activist Filmmaking in French and Francophone Contexts*, a special issue of *South Central Review*, ed. Van Kelly and Rosemarie Scullion, 17.3 (fall 2000): 104–18, under the title "Merzak Allouache's *Salut cousin!*: Immigrants, Hosts, and Parasites." I thank *South Central Review* for permision to reprint it here.

1. Bensmaïa writes: "[O]n the one hand, the Agricultural Revolution and the So-cialist Management of Businesses [Gestion Socialiste des Entreprises] were firmly in place, and a debate had started about the National Chart [charte Nationale] and about the issue of cultural minorities and popular languages. On the other hand, new social groups had emerged and developed. Slowly, but surely, we left the idyllic realm of Manichean oppositions that characterized the first era of Algerian cinema. I suggest that certain films belong to that moment of critical self-awareness: every-body (including the Algerian public) agrees that they represent a moment of discon-tinuity. Naturally, Allouache's films are such critical turning points, deconstructing the conditions that used to limit filmic national production to a unique genre and therefore to a specific public. We should also mention films such as Assia Djebar's *La Nouba des femmes du Mont Chenoua*, Afrouk Beloufa's *Nah'la*, and Mohamed Bouam-rarii's *Premier*" (Bensmaïa 1981, 59). For Djelfaoui, Allouache is the exception to rule because he produces "works close to our sense of touch, of the certain imaginary real, of funny everyday life, risqué and not as clear-cut as slogans or the necessary marching orders of political struggles" (Djelfaoui 1981, 54).

2. The Chevènement legislation "makes official the procedure of 'territorial asy-lum' that allows the minister of the interior to grant a permit to any foreigner whose life is threatened. The representatives demanded that the individual should establish that 'his/her life or freedom is threatened in his/her country' or that he/she is sub-jected to torture or to 'inhuman or degrading treatments or punishments,'" accord-ing to Bernard and Herzberg 1997b, which summarizes the main points of Weil 1997. See also the "dossier" entitled "La République et ses immigrés," published in *Le Monde*, Dec. 19, 1997.

3. P. J-C. 1996 explains that in spite of the "Prix de la Critique Arabe" and sev-eral *prix du public* at film festivals, *Salut cousin!* had trouble finding a distributor until Christian Caillo decided to involve his own production company, Les Films du Roseau.

4. The unfamiliar word *trabendo* confuses Mok, who cannot decide, at first, whether his cousin is in Paris on vacation or on "business," which makes his status as a guest problematic: although Alilo has obviously come to France on a tourist visa, his purpose is to trade, even if the transaction in question belongs to an economy that remains marginal and illegal. The consequences of *trabendo* are some of Merzak Allouache's recurring concerns. *Trabendo* is depicted in *Bab el-Oued City* as one of the practices that the FIS wants to eradicate, it reappears in *Salut cousin!* as the main rea-son for Alilo's trip, and the word *trabendo* is one of forty phrases or expressions glossed by Allouache and Colonna 1992, which gives the following definition:

It is the sale of products that have been illegally imported from abroad or removed from normal commercial circuits. When "hittistes" [literally, those who push the walls, who hang out outside doing nothing] are not standing against a wall, they practice "trabendo," offering everything from underwear to fridges. It is estimated that this parallel economy generates a turnover of 60 billion dinars. With underground circuits masterminded by discreet, wealthy, and powerful individuals, it affects both Algerian and imported goods. The advantage of this parallel economy is that it enables many young people to work and make ends meet. The disadvantage of the system is that the country is literally fleeced by predators, often occupying high-ranking administrative positions, who have no interest in the implementation of economic reforms. (Allouache and Colonna 1992, 23)

5. Some writers, however, do use the term *seconde génération* to refer to other minorities. "The second generation [of the Armenian refugees who arrived in France in 1922–23] was literally torn between two cultures, juggling between languages and moving between two universes," says Amselle 1996, 161.

6. *Beur* or *rebeu*, formed by inverting the syllables of the French word *Arabes*, are typical examples of *verlan*, a type of back slang that has come to be identified with *banlieue* youth. Like *meufs* (*femmes*) and *keufs* (*flics*), *beur* has crossed over into standard French.

7. Local dialects and accents (e.g., Lyonnais dialect) are naturalized to the extent that in following a character's story, readers will tend to pick up on the exoticism of references to the home country or the parents' language but may be unconscious of regionalisms. See for example the little glossary placed at the end of Azouz Begag's *Le gone du Chaâba* (1986).

8. See Duneton 1976 and Duneton and Pagès 1984, which criticize French national education for ignoring regional and immigrant culture.

9. At one level, the children of Algerian immigrants are not more different from the children of "autochthonous" Parisians than, say, the children of Bretons who immigrated to the capital. Except that such statements usually trigger a whole list of "yes, buts" from people who wish to justify the impression that the differences continue to make a difference. For counterexamples, see Malik Chibane's *Hexagone*, a film that explores the subtle relationships between regional and national stereotypes, in which a young Breton woman dates an Algerian, taking him for an Italian, in a scene full of tragicomic misunderstandings. See also Michel de Certeau's comments in *The Capture of Speech and Other Political Writings*:

[A]n Upper Voltan and a Vietnamese are no closer to each other than they are to a Parisian, and the welcome they receive in Paris separates them even more: to pigeonhole the former two into the category of "foreigners" means effacing their heterogeneity; conversely, to assign them naturalization as the only means of access to political rights (and, above all, the right to vote) means granting them political legitimacy at the cost of a procedure that usually signifies an erasure of their specificity.

Preferable to the policy of fetishizing foreigners by isolating them, or fetishizing citizenship by positing it as the only solution, would seem to be an alliance between collectivities that have in common the demand for rights recognized in the very name of their belonging to an ethnic group and of the role that it already plays in political life. We would thus have a slogan such as "Algerians and Bretons, the same struggle!"—a slogan that rejects, for the former, enclosure into the ghetto of a "foreign" label, and for the latter, the domination of national ideology. (Certeau 1997, 166)

10. In Azouz Begag's *Le gone du Chaâba*, the little boy is asked to translate for the policemen who have come to the *bidonville* to investigate an illegal meat market and slaughterhouse. Azouz derives a rather flattering feeling of being accepted from the encounter, but there is price to pay: he does not realize that he is betraying his community by revealing where the butcher's shop is located. Without even knowing that he is taking sides, he is forced to do so.

11. See Sherzer 1996, 1–19.

12. *Le Film français*, 2636 (Oct. 25, 1996): vii.

13. *La Marseillaise*, June 12, 1996, quoted in *Avant-scène*, 457 (Dec. 1996): 66.

14. In the French version, there is no mention of who the intruder is. Michel Serres's analysis suggests that the noise is caused by the return of the owner, the ultimate host.

15. See the introduction to Chevrier 1998, which argues that rather than seeing without being seen, as Sartre suggests in his famous "Black Orpheus," Western colonizers were able to ignore the gaze of the colonized.

16. See Fielder 1999 on the way slang, and particularly *verlan*, is sometimes perceived as the parasitic vernacular of uninvited guests infiltrating the body of the nation.

17. In Dadié 1955, a student who spoke his native language at school had to wear a special "symbol," which he could only get rid of if he caught someone else not speaking French.

18. Roudajia 1992, 111. The author gives the following example: "Arriving late for their class, two college students explain: 'Jaïna à bieu [à pied] barce que Al-Cous kan rotard' (We walked because the bus was late). In that sentence, one finds two Arabic words out of six; *jaïna* (come) and *kán* (be); the rest is made up of badly distorted French words." Fouad Laroui, a francophone Moroccan writer who claims that he does not have a mother tongue, derogatively refers to his non-native Moroccan as a "magma," a "ratatouille" (stew) of Arabic, French, and Spanish words (Laroui 1999, 91).

19. Allouache's *Omar Gatlato*, raï music, the cartoonist Slim, played by Slimane

Benaïssa (*Boualem zid el gouddam! Babor ghrak*, *Anta khouya ouana chkoum*), and the television series *Inspector Tahar* are cited as successful uses of *algérien*.

20. The miserable failure of Mok's potentially creative performance here raises an interesting issue: Mok is not recognized by the youth of the *banlieue*, but his rapping will be appreciated by the supposedly lowbrow audience of a karaoke bar in Paris. Commenting on an earlier version of this chapter, Alec Hargreaves made the following point: "Mok isn't really young. Compared with the teenagers who boo him off the stage, he looks (and in some ways thinks) old enough to be one of their parents. By casting Mok in this way, Allouache seemed to me to be implicitly making the point that it is now anachronistic to think of the 'second generation' as young people to whom one might arguably deny the full rights and respect accorded to adults. Au contraire, Mok is obviously much older than he tries to behave, which implicitly shows just how *enraciné* he is in France."

21. Like some of La Fontaine's fables, the first scene of Racine's comedy *Les plaideurs* belongs to the relatively limited number of canonical texts that have been memorized by French pupils and students for generations. "Qui veut voyager loin . . ." is as well known as some of the lessons drawn by the animals in the fabulist's tales. It may well be the case that people remember the lines but forget the origin of the quotation: when I first watched the film, I wondered whether this often-quoted proverblike statement was not here mistakenly attributed to La Fontaine. It comes from Petit Jean's tirade in act 1, sc. 1

> Je lui disais parfois : "Monsieur Perrin Dandin,
> Tout franc, vous vous levez tous les jours trop matin.
> Qui veut voyager loin ménage sa monture."

> [Sometimes I would tell him: "Sir Perrin Dandin
> Honestly, you get up too early every day.
> He who wants to travel far looks after his mount."]

22. See the first chapter of Emile Copfermann's *Dès les premiers jours de l'automne*: forced to leave their home and to hide on a farm, two young Jewish brothers realize how important their suitcase has become: it contains an indescribable smell, the smell of home (the only thing that the children were able to save), and it is a sort of insurance policy: "The suitcase was pushed under the bed where my brother and I were going to sleep. It came to signify return. We knew that pulling it out from under the bed would mean going back to Paris. Which was imminent: weren't we here for a few weeks only until life became normal again?" (Copfermann 1997, 14).

23. The film may also be reactivating one connotation of the word *valise* that is probably lying dormant in the French political unconscious (except for historians or those who actively remember the war in Algeria): I am thinking of the terms *porteurs* or *porteuses de valise*, which referred to those who helped the Algerian FLN by carry-

ing weapons or bombs (see Gillo Pontecorvo's film *The Battle of Algiers* for a representation of the fear of "false bottoms" in suitcases).

24. "Walter Benjamin's melancholy metaphors of exile, taken over by Raymond Williams and Edward Said, become leitmotifs for the twentieth century, markers for the modern consciousness," Geeta Kapur observes. "Infused with their own generational anguish of the diaspora, we can track through them modernity's émigré soul and the political opponent's exile. We can also extrapolate therefrom the postcolonial condition of refugee labor developing into a new kind of peripheral identity" (Kapur 1998, 198).

CHAPTER 5

An earlier version of this chapter appears in French as "Le maître et les gens de maison: Accueil et servitude dans 'La noire de' et *Boudu sauvé des eaux*," in *Espaces domestiques et privés de l'hospitalité*, ed. Alain Montandon (Clermont-Ferrand: Presses universitaires Blaise-Pascal, 2000). An earlier version of the study of *La promesse* was first presented at a conference on Gender in French Cinema organized by Lynn Higgins, Dalton Krauss, and Steve Ungar at the Château de la Bretesche in Brittany in 1999; it was subsequently published as "Protection and Hospitality: The Young Man and the Illegal Immigrant in *La Promesse*," in *Media and Migrations*, ed. Russell King and Nancy Wood (New York: Routledge, 2001) 71–82. I thank the editors and publishers for permission to reprint these materials here.

1. See also Heal 1990.

2. Anne-Marie is not given a last name, exemplifying the lack of identity that goes with the impossibility of becoming a full-blown hostess. In Sembène Ousmane's text, the loss of identity goes even further: "Les voisins disaient: c'est la Noire de . . ." (Sembène 1962, 180); "The neighbors would say, "It's the Pouchet's black girl . . ." (Sembène 1997, 52). As for "Mademoiselle" (whose identity is reduced to her familial title), she systematically butchers Diouana's name by abbreviating it: "'Douna,' l'appelait Mademoiselle. Impossible qu'elle dise: Diouana. (Sembène 1972, 183); "'Douna'—it was Mademoiselle calling her. Why was it impossible for her to say Di-ou-a-na" (Sembène 1997, 54).

3. Remarkably, the film that Sembène adapted from his own text makes a different decision: this time, Diouana's suicide occurs after the independence of Senegal, and "Monsieur" is now a *coopérant* (i.e., an emissary of the French government). For an analysis of the difference between the film and the short story, see McCallum 1998, 161–62.

4. Montandon suggests that Derrida "is probably wrong to assume that absolute or unconditional hospitality 'involves a radical departure from ordinary hospitality, from conditional hospitality, with the rights or pact of hospitality'" (Montandon 1999, 21). Instead, he proposes the concept of the "ordeal," which has the advantage

of accounting for situations in which the notion of risk is precisely indistinguishable from the ethical dimension of the host's decisions. *The Odyssey*, he says, "constantly rewrites the story of the ordeal of hospitality and of hospitality as an ordeal: it is an ordeal for the *xenos* who does not know how s/he will be received and how to interpret the host's signs, it is also an ordeal for the host shaken by the threatening presence of the stranger whose status is unknown, and who could just as easily be a divine being as a pirate" (ibid., 11–12).

5. Documentaries by Jean-Pierre and Luc Dardenne include *Le chant du rossignol, Lorsque le bateau de Monsieur Léon descendit la Meuse pour la première fois, Pour que la guerre s'achève, les murs devraient s'écrouler,* and *Jean Jouvet*. See also their 1992 *Je pense à vous,* a portrait of steelworkers in Seraing.

6. See Tarr 1993, 320–42; Wilson 1999, 120–36; Rosello 1998a, 65–82.

7. Malik Chibane's *Hexagone* and *Douce France,* or Karim Dridi's *Bye-bye*.

8. Mathieu Kassovitz's *La haine*; Jean-François Richet's *Etats des lieux* and *Ma 6-T va crack-er*.

9. Merzak Allouache's *Salut cousin!* would be one.

10. See, e.g., Philippe Galland's *Merci mon chien* and Milka Assaf's *Les migrations de Vladimir* (I thank Alec Hargreaves for drawing my attention to these films).

11. Just as Diouana is almost fused with her employers' house, the undocumented immigrant is absorbed into the undifferentiation of a cannibalizing whole.

12. *Salut cousin!* is framed by two sequences filmed on a plaftform: the first scene shows us the two cousins' feet. At the end of the film, Alilo and Fatoumata are also waiting on a platform with the suitcase. As in *La promesse,* the movement of the migration is about to be inverted, but the decision is made precisely on the platform, where the characters have plenty of time, while waiting for the train, to make a last-minute decision. Unlike Assita's bag, Alilo's suitcase will stay on the platform, abandoned by its owner.

CHAPTER 6

A version of this chapter originally appeared in French in *Nottingham French Studies,* special issue, *Errances urbaines,* ed. Jean-Xavier Ridon, 39.1 (fall 2000): 52–63. I thank the editor for permission to reprint it here.

1. See also the climbing of "Mount Prefecture," an administrative ordeal comically narrated in Bessora 1999, 125. In this farcical representation of the trials and tribulations of an undocumented immigrant who needs to get her *cat' de séjour* (residence permit) renewed, the issuance of an administrative document is presented as if it were the result of a form of examination. Foucaldian in tone but closer to surrealist humor, the novel makes a point of confusing the female characters' medical and university examinations with administrative procedures that require that she "pass" identity tests.

2. And just as the International Writers' Parliament was meant to function as the ideological counter to the anti-immigration policies that restricted foreigners' freedom, some of the events organized by the association have become symbolic moments of resistance against the rise of inhospitable far-right ideas. In March 1997, when the second colloquium on cities of refuge coincided with the congress of the still powerful National Front party, Edouard Glissant declared: "The scheduling of a public debate entitled 'Cosmopolites de tous les pays encore un effort!' one day before the opening of the National Front's Congress is a timely coincidence" (quoted in *Le Monde*, Mar. 29, 1997; see also Bedarida 1997b).

3. In an article published in the newspaper *L'écho* in 1998, Sophie Creuz describes the original mandate of the Writers' Parliament: "In 1993, sixty writers took an initiative that appeared to them as their democratic duty in the face of the murder of one thousand of their peers over the past six months. Creating an international structure capable of organizing concrete forms of solidarity, inventing the concept of cities of refuge meant to form an 'imaginary archipelago,' they sought to break with the trivialization of censorship by opening up oases of creation free from any influence" (Creuz 1998, 17).

4. Grynberg 1991, 33. A footnote indicates that the quotation comes from the archives of the Paris prefecture (file 64; see Badia 1979). I thank Jean Mainil for bringing this text to my attention.

5. Gérard Noiriel points out that the same type of situation prevailed in the 1830s in France: by careful management of aid and surveillance, refugees were effectively controlled, potential allies being dispatched to different regions to prevent political activity and the formation of groups (Noiriel 1998, 55).

6. During a roundtable on "Unconditional Hospitality," Derrida was asked what would constitute the novelty of cities of refuge and what their relationship would be to the state as a whole. The philosopher's answer reveals that he is conscious of the limitations of the concept. He replied: "I think that a politics of 'cities of refuge' can only be a temporary strategy, a symbol in the fight against intolerable state legislations, comparable to what is known as 'civil disobedience' but always in the name of an implicitly superior law written in the country's constitution" (Derrida 1999b, 135–37). A city of refuge is therefore challenging the state to apply its own law, a paradox that will be worth keeping in mind when we discuss the place of the Casbah in Algiers during the colonial period.

7. J. Hillis Miller muses that the word "labyrinth" in its original sense "properly means 'rope-walk,' or 'coil-of-rope-walk'" (Miller 1992, 1). The image is interesting because it proposes the labyrinth not so much as a place, but as a way of dwelling, or better, as a way of moving through a place that requires dexterity and know-how. As we are about to see, labyrinth dwellers like Pépé le Moko are always in danger of a fatal faux pas if they fail to remain on an almost impossibly narrow borderline between refuge and prison.

8. Very early in *Pépé le Moko*, it becomes clear that point of view is the key to control or absence thereof: when the policemen penetrate the Casbah in an attempt to arrest Pépé, their efforts at hiding behind walls are ridiculed by the fact that both the eye of the camera and Pépé's friends observe them from above, from a terrace. The spectator who shares the privileged vantage point becomes Pépé's accessory but also occupies the position of the refugee-prisoner: it becomes obvious that reading the Casbah is a function of the positioning of the gaze and of the subject's location.

9. For an analysis of how the camera superimposes the language of documentaries (a whole series of rapid shots fail to add up as a coherent picture) and Inspector's Meunier's narrative, see Vincendeau 1998, 12–14; O'Brien 1997.

10. For a study of who was "at home" in Algeria and/or France (as constructed by the colonial regime), see Ross 1995, 123–24.

CONCLUSION

1. I can't help thinking of Rob Reiner's 1990 film *Misery* (an adaptation of Stephen King's novel), in which an injured writer at first thinks that he has been rescued and is being nursed by one of his readers. It does not take long before he realizes that he is, in fact, being held prisoner, kept in a state of abject dependency, and forced to rewrite a book whose ending the host does not like.

Bibliography

Agnon, Shmuel Yosef. 1968. *A Guest for the Night.* Translated by Misha Louvish. New York: Schocken Books.

Ajar, Emile [Romain Gary]. 1975. *La vie devant soi.* Paris: Mercure de France.

Alliod, Marius. 1999. "Petites digressions sur l'hospitalité." In *Manifeste pour l'hospitalité, aux Minguettes: Autour de Jacques Derrida*, edited by Mohammed Seffahi, 55–65. Grigny: Paroles d'aube.

Allouache, Merzak. 1996. *Salut cousin!* [film]. JBA-Productions La-Sept-Cinema [S.l.]. Videorecording, Leo Films, 1997.

Allouache, Merzak, and Vincent Colonna. 1992. "Les mots pour capter l'Algérie nouvelle." In *Algérie, trente ans: Les enfants de l'indépendance*, ed. id., 17–23. Série Monde H.-S. 60. Paris: Autrement.

Amselle, Jean-Louis. 1996. *Vers un multiculturalisme français.* Paris: Aubier.

Bachmann, Christian, and Luc Basier. 1989. *Mise en images d'une banlieue ordinaire.* Paris: Syros.

Backmann, René, with Farid Aïchoune, Véronique Blamont, Emmanuelle Bosc, Anne Crignon, Lawrence Lesache, and Isabelle Monnin. 1997. "Ce que ni la gauche ni la droite n'ont voulu dire. Immigration: La grande hypocrisie." *Nouvel Observateur*, 1685, Feb. 20, p. 44.

Badia, Gilbert. 1979. *Les barbelés de l'exil.* Grenoble: Presses universitaires de Grenoble.

Bailey, Derrick Sherwin. 1955. *Homosexuality and the Western Christian Tradition.* London: Longman.

Balibar, Etienne. 1990. "Paradoxes of Universality." In *Anatomy of Racism*, edited by David Theo Goldberg, 283–94. Minneapolis: University of Minnesota Press.

Baudrillard, Jean. 1993. *The Transparency of Evil: Essays on Extreme Phenomena.* Translated by James Benedict. New York: Verso. Originally published as *La transparence du mal: Essai sur les phénomènes extrêmes* (Paris: Galilée, 1990).

Beauvoir, Simone de. 1943. *L'invitée.* Paris: Gallimard.

Bedarida, Catherine. 1997a. "Le Parlement des écrivains se mobilise contre de nouvelles formes de censure." *Le Monde*, June 14 (http://archives.lemonde.fr/lemonde).

———. 1997b. "Salman Rushdie se joint aux écrivains qui défendent le cosmopolitisme." *Le Monde*, Mar. 29 (http://web.lexis-nexis.com/univers or http://archives.lemonde.fr/lemonde).

Begag, Azouz. 1986. *Le gone du Chaâba*. Paris: Seuil.

Behdad, Ali. 1997. "Nationalism and Immigration in the US." *Diaspora* 6.2 (1997): 155–78.

Benaïcha, Brahim. 1992. *Vivre au paradis: D'une oasis à un bidonville*. Paris: Desclée de Brouwer.

Benguigui, Yamina. 1997. *Mémoires d'immigrés*. Paris: Canal + Editions.

Ben Jelloun, Tahar. 1998. *Le racisme expliqué à ma fille*. Paris: Seuil.

———. 1999. *French Hospitality: Racism and North African Immigrants*. Translated by Barbara Bray. New York : Columbia University Press. Originally published as *Hospitalité française: Racisme et immigration maghrébine* (Paris: Seuil, 1984; rev. ed., 1998).

Bensmaïa, Reda. 1981. "Une rhétorique trop souvent codée." *Cinémas du Maghreb*, *CinémAction* 14: 55–61.

Bernabé, Jean, Raphaël Confiant, and Patrick Chamoiseau. 1989. *Eloge de la créolité*. Paris: Gallimard.

Bernard, Philippe, and Nathaniel Herzberg. 1997a. "La disparition du pouvoir de contrôle des maires sur l'immigration." *Le Monde*, Dec. 13 (http://archives.lemonde.fr/lemonde).

———. 1997b. "Une législation assouplie par le gouvernement et les députés." *Le Monde*, Dec. 19 (http://archives.lemonde.fr/lemonde).

Bessora. 1999. *53 cm: Roman*. Paris: Serpent à plumes.

Bhabha, Homi. 1994. "The Other Question: Stereotype, Discrimination and the Discourse of Colonialism." In *The Location of Culture*, 66–84. New York: Routledge.

———. 1997. "The World and the Home." In *Dangerous Liaisons: Gender, Nation and Postcolonialism*, edited by Anne McClintock, Aamir Mufti, and Ella Shohat, 445–55. Minneapolis: University of Minnesota Press.

Bockel, Alain. 1991. *L'immigration au pays des Droits de l'homme*. Paris: Publisud.

Boswell, John. 1980. *Christianity, Social Tolerance, and Homosexuality*. Chicago: University of Chicago Press.

Boudjedra, Rachid. 1997. *La vie à l'endroit*. Paris: Grasset.

Bougainville, Louis-Antoine de. 1772. *A Voyage Around the World*. Translated by John Reinhold Forster. London: Nourse.

Bracken, Christopher. 1997. *The Potlatch Papers: A Colonial Case History*. Chicago: University of Chicago Press.

Burdeau, Emmanuel. 1996a. "L'offensive des Dardenne." *Cahiers du cinéma*, no. 506 (Oct.): 40–47.

———. 1996b. *"La promesse." Cahiers du cinéma*, no. 503 (June): 17.

Caillé, Alain. 1991. "Une soirée à 'l'Ambroisie': Rudiments d'une analyse structurale du don." *Revue du M.A.U.S.S.*, 11 (First Semester): 106–12.

Cauwelaert, Didier van. 1994. *Un aller simple*. Paris: Albin Michel.

Certeau, Michel de. 1984. *The Practice of Everyday Life*. Translated by Berkeley Randall. Berkeley and Los Angeles: University of California Press. Originally published as *L'invention du quotidien* (Paris: UGE, 1980).

———. 1997. *The Capture of Speech and Other Political Writings*. Introduction by Luce Giard. Translated by Tom Conley. Minneapolis: University of Minnesota Press. Originally published as *La prise de parole et autres écrits politiques* (Paris: Seuil, 1994).

Césaire, Aimé. 1972. *Discourse on Colonialism*. Translated by Joan Pinkham. New York: Monthly Review Press. Originally published as *Discours sur le colonialisme* (Paris: Réclame, 1950).

Chemillier-Gendreau, Monique. 1998. *L'injustifiable: Les politiques françaises de l'immigration*. Paris: Bayart.

Chevrier, Jacques. 1998. *Les blancs vus par les Africains*. Paris: Favre.

Cissé, Madiguène. 1999. *Parole de sans-papiers*. Paris: La dispute.

Cixous, Hélène. 1975. *La jeune née*. Paris: UGE.

———. 1998. "My Algeriance, in Other Words: To Depart Not to Arrive from Algeria." Translated by Eric Prenowitz. In *Stigmata: Escaping Texts*, 153–72. New York: Routledge. Originally published in *Les Inrockuptibles* 115 (Aug. 20–Sept. 2, 1997): 71–74 (under the title "Mon Algériance") and in *Triquarterly* 100 (1997): 259–79.

Copfermann, Emile. 1997. *Dès les premiers jours de l'automne*. Paris: Gallimard.

Courade, George. 1997. "Des papiers et des hommes: L'épreuve des politiques d'endiguement." *Politique africaine* 67, *La France et les migrants africains* (Oct.): 3–20.

Crépeau, François. 1995. *Droit d'asile: De l'hospitalité aux contrôles migratoires*. Brussels: Bruylant.

Creuz, Sophie. 1998. "Bruxelles, ville des Lumières." *L'écho*, June 23, 17.

Dadié, Bernard. 1955. *Climbié*. Paris: Seghers.

David, Pascal. 1999. "Ses visages." In *Manifeste pour l'hospitalité, aux Minguettes: Autour de Jacques Derrida*, edited by Mohammed Seffahi, 19–22. Grigny: Paroles d'aube.

Davis, Colin. 1996. *Levinas*. Cambridge: Polity Press.

Depaule, Jean-Charles. 1997. "Seigneur, prisonnier et poète." *Communications*, special issue, *Hospitalité*, edited by Anne Gotman, 65: 21–34.

Derobert, Eric. 1996. "La Promesse: La flèche Wallonne," *Positif*, 428 (Oct.) 37–38.

Derrida, Jacques. 1992. *Given Time. I, Counterfeit Money*. Translated by Peggy Kamuf. Chicago: University of Chicago Press. Originally published as *Donner le temps: 1, Fausse monnaie* (Paris: Galilée, 1991).

————. 1997a. *Cosmopolites de tous les pays encore un effort!* Paris: Galilée.

————. 1997b. "Quand j'ai entendu l'expression 'délit d'hospitalité.'" *Plein droit* 34 (Apr.): 3–8.

————. 1998. *Monolingualism of the Other, or, The Prosthesis of Origin.* Translated by Patrick Mensah. Stanford: Stanford University Press. Originally published as *Le monolinguisme de l'autre, ou, La prothèse d'origine* (Paris: Galilée, 1996).

————. 1999a. *Adieu to Emmanuel Levinas.* Translated by Pascale-Anne Brault and Michael Naas. Stanford: Stanford University Press. Originally published as *Adieu à Emmanuel Lévinas* (Paris: Galilée, 1997).

————. 1999b. "Débat: Une hospitalité sans condition." In *Manifeste pour l'hospitalité, aux Minguettes: Autour de Jacques Derrida*, edited by Mohammed Seffahi, 133–42. Grigny: Paroles d'aube.

————. 1999c. "Une hospitalité à l'infini." In *Manifeste pour l'hospitalité, aux Minguettes: Autour de Jacques Derrida*, edited by Mohammed Seffahi, 97–106. Grigny: Paroles d'aube.

Derrida, Jacques, and Anne Dufourmantelle. 1997. *De l'hospitalité: Anne Dufourmantelle invite Jacques Derrida à répondre.* Paris: Calmann-Lévy. Translated by Rachel Bowlby as *Of Hospitality* (Stanford: Stanford University Press, 2000).

Diderot, Denis. [1796] 1951. *Supplément au voyage de Bougainville ou dialogue entre A et B.* In id., *Oeuvres*, edited by André Billy, 963–1002. Paris: Gallimard, Pléiade.

————. 1997. *Supplement to Bougainville's Voyage.* Translated by Jacques Barzun and Ralph Bowen. In *The Libertine Reader: Eroticism and Enlightenment in Eighteenth-Century France*, edited by Michel Feher, 60–112. New York: Zone Books.

Diop, Ababacar. 1997. *Dans la peau d'un sans-papiers.* Paris: Seuil.

Djebar, Assia. 1995. *Le blanc de l'Algérie.* Paris: Albin Michel.

Djelfaoui, Abderrahmane. 1981. "Un cinéma limité par le conformisme." *Cinémas du Maghreb, CinémAction* 14: 50–55.

Dorzée, Hugues. 1999. "Cinéma du réel et les frères du fleuve." *Le soir*, May 16, p. 12.

Dridi, Karim. 1997. *Bye-bye* [film]. Alain Rozanès / ADR Productions. Videorecording, Fox Lorber Home Video.

Duneton, Claude. 1976. *Je suis comme une truie qui doute.* Paris: Seuil.

Duneton, Claude, and Claude Pagès. 1984. *À hurler le soir au fond des collèges.* Paris: Seuil.

Durmelat, Sylvie. 2000. "Transmission and Mourning in *Mémoires d'immigrés: L'héritage maghrébin*: Yamina Benguigui as 'Memory Entrepeneuse.'" Translated by John Ryan Poynter. In *Women, Immigration and Identities in France*, 171–88, edited by Jane Freedman and Carrie Tarr. New York: Berg.

Fanon, Frantz. 1963. *The Wretched of the Earth.* Translated by Constance Farrington. New York: Grove Press. Originally published as *Les damnés de la terre* (Paris: Maspéro, 1961.)

Fassin, Didier. 1996. "«Clandestins» ou «exclus»? Quand les mots font de la politique." *Politix* 34: 77–86.

———. 1997. "Pour une politique de l'hospitalité." In *Les lois de l'inhospitalité: Les politiques de l'immigration à l'épreuve des sans-papiers*, edited by id., Alain Morice, and Catherine Quiminal, 263–79. Paris: La Découverte.

Fassin, Didier, Alain Morice, and Catherine Quiminal, eds. 1997. *Les lois de l'inhospitalité: Les politiques de l'immigration à l'épreuve des sans-papiers*. Paris: La Découverte.

Feher, Michel, ed. 1997. *The Libertine Reader: Eroticism and Enlightenment in Eighteenth-Century France*. New York: Zone Books.

Ferenczi, Aurélien. 1996. "Algérie si je t'oublie!" *Télérama* 2406 (21 February): 32–33.

Fielder, Adrian. 1999. "The Tactical Poetics of Urban Nomadism." *Die Kinder der Immigration—Les enfants de l'immigration. Studien zur Literatur und Geschichte des Maghreb*, special issue, edited by Ernspeter Ruhe, 4: 95–114.

Fonseca, Isabel. 1995. *Bury Me Standing: The Gypsies and Their Journeys*. New York: Vintage Books.

Foucault, Michel. 1975. *Surveiller et punir: Naissance de la prison*. Paris: Gallimard. Translated by Alan Sheridan under the title *Discipline and Punish: The Birth of the Prison* (New York: Pantheon Books, 1977).

Freedman, Anne, and Carrie Tarr, eds. 2000. *Women, Immigration and Identities in France*. New York: Berg.

Gaspard, Françoise, and Farhad Khosrokhavar. 1995. *Le foulard et la République*. Paris: La Découverte.

Genet, Jean. 1954. *Les bonnes: Pièce en un acte*. Sceaux: Jean-Jacques Pauvert.

Ghosh, Bimal. 1998. *Huddled Masses and Uncertain Shores: Insights into Irregular Migration*. Boston: Martinus Nijhoff.

Gilroy, Paul. 1993. *The Black Atlantic: Modernity and Double Consciousness*. London: Verso.

Glissant, Edouard. 1989. *Caribbean Discourse: Selected Essays*. Translated by Michael Dash. Charlottesville: University Press of Virginia.

Gotman, Anne. 1997. "La question de l'hospitalité aujourd'hui." *Communications*, special issue, *Hospitalité*, 65: 5–19.

Gremelek, Bronislaw. 1978. *La potence ou la pitié: L'Europe et les pauvres du Moyen-Age à nos jours*. Paris: Gallimard.

Grynberg, Anne. 1991. *Les camps de la honte: Les internés juifs des camps français, 1939–1944*. Paris: La Découverte.

Ha, Marie-Paule. 1995. Review of *Culture and Imperialism*, by Edward W. Said. *Research in African Literatures* 26.1 (spring): 154–57.

Hammouche, Abdelhafid. 1999. "Altérité et état nation." In *Manifeste pour l'hospitalité, aux Minguettes: autour de Jacques Derrida*, edited by Mohammed Seffahi, 37–47. Grigny: Paroles d'aube.

Hargreaves, Alec. 1995. *Immigration, "Race" and Ethnicity in Contemporary France*. New York: Routledge.

Heal, Felicity. 1990. *Hospitality in Early Modern England*. New York: Oxford University Press.

Hénaff, Marcel. 1997. "Supplement to Diderot's Dream." In *The Libertine Reader: Eroticism and Enlightenment in Eighteenth-Century France*, edited by Michel Feher, 52–112. New York: Zone Books.

Hervo, Monique, and Marie-Ange Charras. 1971. *Bidonvilles*. Paris: Maspero.

Higgins, Lynne. 1996. "Looks That Kill: Louis Malle's Portraits of Collaboration." In *New Novel, New Wave, New Politics: Fiction and the Representation of History in Postwar France*, 186–206. Lincoln: University of Nebraska Press.

Hoffman, Eva. 1989. *Lost in Translation: A Life in a New Language*. New York: E. P. Dutton.

Honorez, Luc. 1999. "Ces disciples de Stork et de la fleur maigre." *Le Soir*, May 15, 11.

Irigaray, Luce. 1977. *Ce sexe qui n'en est pas un*. Paris: Minuit.

Jabès, Edmond. 1991. *Le livre de l'hospitalité*. Paris: Gallimard.

Jazouli, Adil. 1992. *Les années banlieues*. Collection l'histoire immédiate. Paris: Seuil.

Jordan, Mark. 1997. *The Invention of Sodomy in Christian Theology*. Chicago: University of Chicago Press.

Kapur, Geeta. 1998. "Globalization and Culture: Navigating the Void." In *The Cultures of Globalization*, edited by Fredric Jameson and Masao Miyoshi, 191–217. Durham, N.C.: Duke University Press.

Kemedjio, Cilas. 1999. "La femme antillaise face au faubourg et à la durcification dans *Texaco* de Patrick Chamoiseau et *Mélody des faubourgs* de Lucie Julia." *LittéRéalité* 11.2 (fall–winter): 31–47.

Khatibi, Abdelkebir. 1983. *Amour bilingue*. Paris: Fata Morgana. Translated by Richard Howard as *Love in Two Languages* (Minneapolis: University of Minnesota Press, 1990).

Khellil, Mohand. 1991. *L'intégration des maghrébins en France*. Paris: Presses universitaires de France.

Kincaid, Jamaica. 1988. *A Small Place*. New York: Penguin Books.

Klossowski, Pierre. 1965. *Les lois de l'hospitalité*. Paris: Gallimard.

Kortenaar, Ken. 1995. "Beyond Authenticity and Creolization: Reading Achebe Writing Culture." *PMLA* 110.1: 30–42.

Kristeva, Julia. 1988. *Etrangers à nous-mêmes*. Paris: Fayard. Translated by Leon S. Roudiez under the title *Strangers to Ourselves* (New York: Columbia University Press, 1991).

———. 1990. *Lettre ouverte à Harlem Désir*. Paris: Rivages. Translated by Leon S. Roudiez under the title *Nations Without Nationalism* (New York: Columbia University Press, 1993).

La Fontaine, Jean de. [1668] 1979. *Selected Fables*. London: Penguin Books.

Lallaoui, Mehdi. 1993. *Du bidonville au HLM*. Paris: Syros.

Laronde, Michel. 1993. *Autour du roman beur*. Paris: L'Harmattan.

Laroui, Fouad. 1999. *Méfiez-vous des parachutistes*. Paris: Julliard.

Lefort, François. 1980. *Du bidonville à l'expulsion*. Paris: C.I.E.M.

Lemoine, Maurice. 1989. "Le centre, le souk et l'hypermarché." *Autrement*, special issue, *Marseille, histoire de famille*, 36 (Feb.): 126–39.

Lepoutre, David. 1997. *Coeur de banlieue: Codes, rites et langages*. Paris: Odile Jacob.

Levinas, Emmanuel. 1961. *Totalité et infini: Essai sur l'extériorité*. The Hague: Martinus Nijhoff. Translated by Alphonso Lingis under the title *Totality and Infinity: An Essay on Exteriority* (Pittsburgh: Duquesne University Press, 1969).

———. 1994. *Beyond the Verse*. Translated by Gary Mole. London: Athlone Press. Originally published as *L'au delà du verset: Lectures et discours talmudiques* (Paris: Minuit, 1982).

McCallum, Pamela. 1998. "Irony, Colonialism and Representation: The Case of Sembène Ousmane's *La noire de*." *Mattoid*, special issue, edited by Jonathan Hart, *Crossing Cultures*, 52–53: 158–65.

McClintock, Anne. 1995. *Imperial Leather: Race, Gender and Sexuality in the Colonial Contest*. New York: Routledge.

Maillet, Michèle. 1990. *L'étoile noire*. Paris: François Bourin.

Manzi, Joachim. 1999. "Comment accueillir, aimer, nommer la femme étrangère." In *Mythes et représentations de l'hospitalité*, edited by Alain Montandon, 325–39. Clermont-Ferrand: Presses universitaires Blaise-Pascal.

Marchi, Marie-Paule. 1996. "Si loin, si proche: *Salut cousin!* de Merzak Allouache." *Film français*, 2612.17 (May): 21.

Maspero, François. 1994. *Roissy Express: A Journey Through the Paris Suburbs*. With photographs by Anaïk Frantz. Translated by Paul Jones. New York: Verso. Originally published as *Les passagers du Roissy-Express* (Paris: Seuil, 1990).

Mauss, Marcel. "Gift, gift." 1997. Translated by Koen Decoster. In *The Logic of the Gift: Toward an Ethic of Generosity*, edited by Alan D. Schrift, 28–32. New York: Routledge. Originally published in *Mélanges offerts à M. Charles Andler par ses amis et ses élèves* (Strasbourg: Istra, 1924).

———. 1990. *The Gift: The Form and Reason for Exchange in Archaic Societies*. Translated by W. D. Hall. London: Routledge. Originally published as "Essai sur le don," in Marcel Mauss, *Sociologie et anthropologie*, 143–279 (Paris: Presses universitaires de France, 1950).

Miller, J. Hillis. 1992. *Ariadne's Thread*. New Haven: Yale University Press.

Milon, Alain. 1999. *L'étranger dans la ville*. Paris: Presses universitaires de France.

Montandon, Alain. 1999. *Mythes et représentations de l'hospitalité*. Clermont-Ferrand: Presses universitaires Blaise-Pascal.

Montvalon, Jean-Baptiste de. 1997. "La République et ses immigrés: La majorité obtient la suppression des certificats d'hébergement." *Le Monde*, Dec. 13 (http://archives.lemonde.fr/lemonde).

Mouffok, Ghania, and Luc Chaulet. 1992. "Petite chronique de nos déceptions médiatiques." *Autrement*, special issue, *Algérie, trente ans: Les enfants de l'indépendance*, edited by Merzak Allouache and Vincent Colonna, 45–56. Série Monde H.-S. 60. Paris: Autrement, 1992.

Naïr, Sami. 1997. *Contre les lois Pasqua*. Paris: Arléa.

Noiriel, Gérard. 1988. *Le creuset français: Histoire de l'immigration, XIXe–XXe siècle*. Paris: Seuil.

——. 1998. *Réfugiés et sans-papiers: La République face au droit d'asile, XIXe–XXe siècle*. Paris: Hachette. Originally published as *La tyrannie du national: Le droit d'asile en Europe, 1783–1993* (Paris: Calmann-Lévy, 1991).

O'Brien, Charles. 1997. "The *cinéma colonial* of 1930s France: Film Narration as Spatial Practice." In *Visions of the East: Orientalism in Film*, edited by Matthew Bernstein and Gaylyn Studlar, 207–31. New Brunswick, N.J.: Rutgers University Press.

Pineau, Gisèle. 1996. *L'exil selon Julia*. Paris: Stock.

P. J-C. 1996. "*Salut cousin!* ou la naissance d'un distributeur." *Film français*, 2637 (Nov. 15): 22.

Pratt, Mary Louise. 1992. *Imperial Eyes: Travel Writing and Transculturation*. New York: Routledge.

R. A. 1996. "*Salut cousin!* Film franco-algérien de Merzak Allouache." *Nouvel Observateur* 1672 (Nov. 21): 140.

Raafat, Samir. 1995. "The Darker Side of Schengen." *Egyptian Mail*, June 3 (reproduced http://www.privacytools.com/schengi.html).

Ridon, Jean-Xavier. 2000. "Un barbare en banlieue." *Nottingham French Studies* 39.1 (spring): 25–38.

Rosello, Mireille. 1997. "Bidonvilles, Urbanism and Individual Freedom." *Renaissance and Modern Studies*, special issue, *Reading the City*, edited by Mark Millington and Neil Leach, 40: 97–110.

——. 1998a. *Declining the Stereotype: Ethnicity and Representation in French Cultures*. Hanover, N.H.: University Press of New England.

——. 1998b. "Representating Illegal Immigrants in France: From *clandestins* to *l'affaire des sans-papiers de Saint-Bernard.*" *Journal of European Studies* 38: 137–51.

——. 1999. "La loi et les métaphores qui la hantent: Esprit d'ouverture, invasion, angélisme et flux migratoire." *Studien zur Literatur und Geschichte des Maghreb*, special issue, *Die Kinder der Immigration—Les enfants de l'immigration*, edited by Ernspeter Ruhe, 4: 53–64.

Rosenbaum, Jonathan. 1997. "Buried Blues: *La promesse.*" *Chicago Reader*, Aug. 22, 7.

Ross, Kristin. 1995. *Fast Cars, Clean Bodies: Decolonizing and the Reordering of French Culture*. Cambridge, Mass.: MIT Press.

Roudajia, Ahmed. 1992. "La mosquée confisquée." In *Algérie, trente ans: Les enfants de l'indépendance*, edited by Merzak Allouache and Vincent Colonna, 106–19.

Série Monde H.-S. 60. Paris: Autrement, 1992.

Rousseau, Denis. 1994. "Le Parlement des écrivains poursuit son idée de 'villes refuges.'" *Agence France Presse*, Nov. 6 (http://web.lexis-nexis.com/univers).

Said, Edward W. *Culture and Imperialism*. New York: Knopf, 1993.

Sané, Mamady. 1996. *Sorti de l'ombre: Journal d'un sans-papiers*. Paris: Le temps des cerises.

Sartre, Jean-Paul. 1985. "Orphée noir." In *Anthologie de la nouvelle poésie nègre et malgache*. 5th ed. Paris: Quadrige/Presses universitaires de France.

Sayad, Abdelmalek. 1991. *L'immigration, ou, Les paradoxes de l'altérité*. Brussels: Editions universitaires De Boeck.

Schérer, René. 1993. *Zeus hospitalier: Eloge de l'hospitalité*. Paris: Armand Colin.

Schnapper, Dominique. 1991. *La France de l'intégration: Sociologie de la nation en 1990*. Paris: Gallimard.

Schwarz-Bart, André. 1972. *La mulâtresse Solitude*. Paris: Seuil.

Sedgwick, Eve Kosofsky. 1993. *Tendencies*. Durham, N.C.: Duke University Press.

Seffahi, Mohammed, ed. 1999. *Manifeste pour l'hospitalité, aux Minguettes: Autour de Jacques Derrida*. With the participation of Michel Wieviorka. Grigny: Paroles d'aube.

Sembène Ousmane. 1962. *Voltaïque, La noire de . . . : Nouvelles*. Paris: Présence africaine.

———. 1997. "Black Girl." Translated by Ellen Conroy Kennedy. In *Under African Skies: Modern African Stories*, edited by Charles Larson, 43–54. New York: Farrar, Straus and Giroux.

Serres, Michel. 1982. *The Parasite*. Translated by Larry Schehr. Baltimore: Johns Hopkins University Press. Originally published as *Le parasite* (Paris: Grasset, 1980)

Sherzer, Dina, ed. 1996. *Cinema, Colonialism, Postcolonialism: Perspectives from the French and Francophone World*. Austin: University of Texas Press.

Silverman, Maxim. 1992. *Deconstructing the Nation: Immigration, Racism and Citizenship in Modern France*. New York: Routledge.

Spivak, Gayatri. 1999. *A Critique of Postcolonial Reason: Toward a History of the Vanishing Present*. Cambridge, Mass.: Harvard University Press.

Starobinski, Jean. 1997. *Largesse*. Translated by Jane Marie Todd. Chicago: University of Chicago Press. Originally published as *Largesse* (Paris: Edition de la réunion des musées nationaux, 1994).

Taguieff, Pierre-André. 1988. *La force du préjugé: Essai sur le racisme et ses doubles*. Paris: La Découverte.

———. 1991. *Face au racisme*. 2 vols. Paris: La Découverte.

Tarr, Carrie. 1993. "Questions of Identity in Beur Cinema: From *Tea in the Harem* to *Cheb*." *Screen* 34: 320–42.

Thoreau, Henry David. 1993. *Civil Disobedience and Other Essays*. New York: Dover Publications.

Timera, Mahamet. 1997. "L'immigration africaine en France: Regards des autres et repli sur soi." *Politique africaine: La France et les migrants africains* 67 (Oct.): 41–47.

Tlatli, Moufida. 1994. *Samt al-qusur* [*The Silences of the Palace* = *Les silences du palais*] [film]. A Mat Films, Cinétéléfims, Magfilm coproduction. Videorecording, Capitol Home Video, 1996.

Tournier, Michel. 1970. *Le roi des Aulnes*. Paris: Gallimard. Translated by Barbara Wright as *The Ogre* (New York: Doubleday, 1972).

——. 1985. *La goutte d'or*. Paris: Gallimard. Translated by Barbara Wright as *The Golden Droplet* (New York: Doubleday, 1987).

Viledier, Philippe. 1997. "L'honneur de désobéir: Immigration et conscience citoyenne." *Le Monde diplomatique*, May, 17.

Vincendeau, Ginette. 1998. *Pépé le Moko*. London: BFI.

Wahnich, Sophie. 1997a. "L'hospitalité et la Révolution française." In *Les lois de l'inhospitalité: Les politiques de l'immigration à l'épreuve des sans-papiers*, edited by Didier Fassin, Alain Morice, and Catherine Quiminal, 11–26. Paris: La Découverte.

——. 1997b. *L'impossible citoyen: L'étranger dans le discours de la révolution française*. Paris: Albin Michel.

Weil, Patrick. 1991. *La France et ses étrangers: L'aventure d'une politique de l'immigration de 1938 à nos jours*. Paris: Gallimard.

——. 1997. *Mission d'étude des législations de la nationalité et l'immigration*. Report submitted to Prime Minister Lionel Jospin, July 1997. Paris: La documentation française (http://www.ladocfrancaise.gouv.fr/).

Wihtol de Wenden, Catherine. 1988. *Les immigrés et la politique: Cent cinquante ans d'évolution*. Paris: Presses de la Fondation nationale des sciences politiques.

——. 1999a. *L'immigration en Europe*. Paris: La documentation française.

——.1999b. "Immigrés." *Encyclopedia Universalis* (CD-ROM).

Wilson, Emma. 1999. *French Cinema Since 1950*. London: Duckworth.

Woodhull, Winifred. 1993. *Transfigurations of the Maghreb*. Minneapolis: University of Minnesota Press.

——. 1997. "Ethnicity on the French Frontier." In *Writing New Identities: Gender, Nation and Immigration in Contemporary Europe*, edited by Gisela Brinker-Gabler and Sidonie Smith, 31–61. Minneapolis: University of Minnesota Press.

Yeğenoğlu, Meyda. 1998. *Colonial Fantasies: Towards a Feminist Reading of Orientalism*. New York: Cambridge University Press.

Index